DESIGNING MEDIA

Mainstream media, often known simply as MSM, have not yet disappeared in a digital takeover of the media landscape. But the long-dominant MSM—television, radio, newspapers, magazines, and books—have had to respond to emergent digital media. Newspapers have interactive Web sites; television broadcasts over the Internet; books are published in both electronic and print editions. In *Designing Media*, design guru Bill Moggridge examines connections and conflicts between old and new media, describing how the MSM have changed and how new patterns of media consumption are emerging. The book features interviews with thirty-seven significant figures in both traditional and new forms of mass communication; interviewees range from the publisher of the *New York Times* to the founder of Twitter.

We learn about innovations in media that rely on contributions from a crowd (or a community), as told by Wikipedia's Jimmy Wales and Craigslist's Craig Newmark; how the band OK Go built a following using YouTube; how real-time connections between dispatchers and couriers inspired Twitter; how a *BusinessWeek* blog became a quarterly printed supplement to the magazine; and how e-readers have evolved from Rocket eBook to QUE. Ira Glass compares the intimacy of radio to that of the Internet; the producer of PBS's *Frontline* supports the program's investigative journalism by putting documentation of its findings online; and the developers of Google's Trendalyzer software describe its beginnings as animations that accompanied lectures about social and economic development in rural Africa. At the end of each chapter, Moggridge comments on the implications for designing media. *Designing Media* is illustrated with hundreds of images, with color throughout. A DVD accompanying the book includes excerpts from all of the interviews, and the material can be browsed at **www.designing-media.com**.

Bill Moggridge, Director of the Cooper-Hewitt National Design Museum in New York City, is a founder of IDEO, the famous innovation and design firm. He has a global reputation as an award-winning designer, having pioneered interaction design and integrated human factors disciplines into design practice.

DESIGNING MEDIA

DESIGNING MEDIA

Bill Moggridge

The MIT Press
Cambridge, Massachusetts
London, England

For information about special quantity discounts, please email
special_sales@mitpress.mit.edu

This book was set in Trade Gothic and Minion Pro by Katie Clark.
Printed and bound in the United States of America.

Library of Congress Cataloging-in-Publication Data

Moggridge, Bill.
Designing media / Bill Moggridge.
    p. cm.
Includes bibliographical references and index.
ISBN 978-0-262-01485-4 (hardcover : alk. paper)
1. Multimedia systems—Interviews.
2. Digital media—Design—Interviews. I. Title.
QA76.575.M645 2010
006.7—dc22

                                                            2010014419

CONTENTS

INTRODUCTION

What's happening to books, magazines, newspapers, television, and radio? The information revolution is in full swing, with digital versions of mainstream media taking hold and changing everything! Um … but are they really changing everything, or are some traditional media here to stay? How are the new Internet entrepreneurs designing their offerings? Is it possible to thrive in both worlds, working happily in traditional and virtual media? Does content need to be designed differently for each medium, or can it be easily transferred without changes? I embarked on this book because I wanted to know the answers to these questions, and I thought, "What better way to discover the answers than to ask thirty or forty experts?"

My fascination with media has intensified in the past few years: I want to master the use of media to tell people more about design. My career has had three phases. From graduation as an industrial designer in 1965 until the formation of IDEO in 1991, I thought of myself as a designer. I helped others design as I grew the practice and added disciplines, but I continued to think of some designs as my own and others as belonging to the designers working with me. In the 1990s I thought of myself as a leader of interdisciplinary teams, where team members shared the authorship of design solutions and innovative concepts, with the "shared mind" more powerful than the individual contributions. Since Tim Brown took over the leadership of IDEO in 2000, I have thought of myself as a storyteller and have focused more on writing, conference presentations, teaching, and making videos. My desire to become a better storyteller makes me want to understand media and to try to answer those questions about how media are changing in these turbulent times. In my new role as director of the Cooper-Hewitt National Design Museum, I hope to become a spokesperson for design, to help explain the value and processes that design can offer. Learning more about media can help me navigate the flow of narrative.

First, I want to help you navigate the material in this book and accompanying media. In my first book, *Designing Interactions* (MIT Press, 2007),

←···· Author, Bill Moggridge
photo by Alexander Tibbets

I combined text with lots of full-color images, including a DVD to show interactive examples in action and a Web site, Designinginteractions.com, to allow browsing videos and interview materials, with an option to download the "Chapter of the Week" for free. This time I have used a similar format, but I have expanded the scope of the media to match the subject matter. There are thirty-one interview segments recorded on HDV (high-definition video, to improve the quality from last time), with the transcripts used to form the foundation of the text. I have edited the videos into shortened versions of highlights and examples, to fit on the accompanying DVD. The material on the DVD and PDFs of the six chapters are available to download for free from Designing-media.com, where you will also find a blog.

Each of the chapters in the book opens with a discussion of the topic and is followed by the interviews. Each person is introduced with a photograph and a resume. The interviews are mixtures of stories and ideas and include direct quotes. I have tried to reflect the perspectives of those interviewed, writing the text to help the flow of the ideas and using the quotes to reveal the personality of each individual.

Some of the text is set in blue. The color indicates that I have written that section in my own voice, expressing my personal opinions rather than those of the people interviewed. The blue sections include a commentary at the end of each chapter, and a short introduction before each interview segment recounting an anecdote about the interview process. My goal for the commentary sections is to extract the ideas about designing media that I find most interesting in each chapter and to express them as a summary with some comments and explanations.

ACKNOWLEDGMENTS

You can put together this combination of words, graphics, video, Web site, and blog almost single-handed, using a portable kit of laptop, camera, and lights, with much of the material residing in the digital cloud. The resources needed for a traditional film crew and book development team are expensive, so topics for the traditional media are limited to high-profile subjects who can command television broadcasting contracts and best-seller lists rather than an individual author tackling a new topic. I have enjoyed taking advantage of the digital tools to interview, write, and edit video, but I have also had a lot of help from friends and colleagues.

First I want to thank all of the people who were willing to talk to me in front of my cameras and microphones, giving of their wisdom and helping me with my follow-up questions and requests. These are the people I interviewed, in the order that they appear in the book: Paul Saffo, James Truman, Chris Anderson, Neil Stevenson, DJ Spooky, Jimmy Wales, Craig Newmark, Tim Westergren, Blixa Bargeld, Erin Zhu, Fred Deakin, Nat Hunter, Alex Maclean, Roger McNamee, Jorge Just, Chad Hurley, Alexandra Juhasz, Bob Mason, Jeremy Merle, Ev Williams, Mark Zuckerberg, Joel Hyatt, Bruce Nussbaum, Jessie Scanlon, Jane Friedman, Martin Eberhard, Rich Archuleta, Arthur Sulzberger Jr., Alice Rawsthorn, Ira Glass, Colin Callender, David Fanning, Mark Gerzon, Shinichi Takemura, Hans Rosling, Ola Rosling, and Anna Rosling Rönnlund. Thank you all for contributing your ideas and stories.

Many of my colleagues at IDEO have helped me enormously. Special thanks to Katie Clark for working with me on the book design, Nicolas Zurcher for his lovely photographs, Gene Celso for recording many of the video interviews with me and for assembling the final video for the DVD and Web site, Georgia Jurickovich for transcribing the videos, Rebecca Smith Hurd and Laura Moorhead for their editorial skills, Lynn Winter and Alana Zawojski for their sources of images, and Angella Enders and Erin Cornell for their guidance as we developed the Web site. Many thanks also to Whitney Mortimer for her guidance about publishing and to Tim Brown for helping me make time for the book. The MIT Press has been wonderfully supportive and generous throughout the process, particularly my acquisitions editor Doug Sery and his assistant, Katie Helke. This would not have happened without endless encouragement from my wife, Karin.

1 HERE TO STAY

Interviews with Paul Saffo, James Truman, Chris Anderson,
Neil Stevenson, and DJ Spooky

On leaf of palm, on sedge-wrought roll;
on plastic clay and leather scroll, man wrote his thoughts;
the ages passed, and lo! the Press was found at last!

John Greenleaf Whittier, 1807–1892, American poet, reformer, and author

WE WANT TO TELL STORIES, send messages, record music, communicate with one another and to posterity: these desires make us human, and we are not going to stop doing them any time soon. The media that we use are in constant flux, so it is surprising that each individual medium seems to be around longer than expected. You may not have written much recently on "leaf of palm" or "sedge-wrought roll," but if you are marooned on a desert island and want to put a message in a bottle, you may be quite happy to pick up a long neglected medium and scratch out the words on the nearest frond.

The notion of the "paperless office" dates back to the 1960s and seemed plausible for decades.

As computers began to spread and display technology improved, it seemed obvious that more and more documents would be written, distributed and read in electronic form, rather than on paper. Filing cabinets would give way to hard disks, memos and reports would be distributed electronically and paper invoices and purchase orders would be replaced by electronic messages whizzing between accounts departments. What actually happened was that global consumption of office paper more than doubled in the last two decades of the twentieth century, as digital technology made printing cheaper and easier than ever before. Not even the rise of the Internet stemmed the tide. The web's billions of pages provided a vast new source of fodder for the world's humming printers.[1]

Paper is here to stay. Indeed, paper is hard to compete with precisely because it has so many wonderful qualities: It looks beautiful, with

← **Paper**
photos by Nicolas Zurcher

1 "Technological Comebacks: Not Dead, Just Resting," *The Economist,* October 9, 2008. *http://www.economist.com/opinion/displaystory.cfm?story_id=12381449.*

many choices of smoothness, brilliance of white, depth of black, and richness of color. It feels luxurious as you turn a page or sense the bite of the granularity as you scribe or sketch. It's amazingly light and portable and an excellent storage medium. It even smells good— don't you enjoy the smell of new paper and fresh ink as you browse the bookstore?

Bookstores are here to stay because they offer a rich multisensory experience of looking at images, text, the environment around us and other people; feeling the heft of the book and the suppleness of the paper; listening to ambient sounds and the murmur of conversation; and smelling coffee brewing with the hint of cinnamon from a Danish pastry. By comparison the online convenience of Amazon seems efficient but dull.

For this book I have selected people to interview who have contributed new ideas and designs, both in the traditional media and in the emerging new media, as the relationship between the two categories is so fraught with uncertainty and fuel for innovation. In this first chapter we meet people who believe that the traditional media are here to stay to a surprising extent—that books, magazines, film, television, and radio will never go away. They also see profound changes taking place as the new media shake up financial models and offer alternative sources for many attributes that formerly belonged with the traditional media.

In the first interview that follows, with Paul Saffo, you will discover that even this techno-savvy forecaster living in California's Silicon Valley still captures his thoughts and observations about new technologies on the paper pages of old-fashioned bound journals. The new media of the digital revolution might add new possibilities for us and broaden alternatives for communication, record keeping, and creativity, but those traditional media seem surprisingly persistent, even if transmogrified. Paul points out that old media forms never die out entirely—they get repurposed for other uses and stay with us. He gives us an overview of the state of media in the past, present, and future, explaining that what we called mass media was all we had, but we are now creating a whole new world of personal media. He also reveals his S-curve method for forecasting and describes the attributes of the "creator economy."

In the second interview we meet James Truman, one of the most influential voices in the Condé Nast magazine portfolio for more than a decade. James, like Paul Saffo, expects traditional media to survive in repurposed forms.

James was instrumental in introducing Chris Anderson to his role as editor in chief of *Wired* magazine. Chris is featured in the next interview. He explains his conviction that while the acts of journalism, editing, and distribution are here to stay, the forms that contain the content will vary to fit the vehicle. Lavishly produced magazines will be published, but people will choose online versions of content when they are seeking factual information or communal connectivity.

Neil Stevenson contrasts the way in which we consume media, either sitting back to luxuriate in the material that is offered, as in a beautifully produced magazine or a movie, or leaning forward to steer or click, as in a Web search or a message dialog. He also recounts his experiment with user-generated content.

Paul Miller, aka DJ Spooky: That Subliminal Kid, is a New York–based artist, writer, music composer and producer, DJ, political commentator, and impresario. In the final interview of this chapter, he talks about the new order of creative commons and shareware, which, he argues, is here to stay, and he points to the repurposing of the vinyl record as a control device for digital manipulation.

PAUL SAFFO

Interviewed July 31, 2008

PAUL SAFFO

Paul is a forecaster and essayist with more than twenty years of experience exploring long-term technological change and its practical impact on business and society. He teaches at Stanford University and is a visiting scholar in the Stanford Media X research network, studying the design and use of interactive technologies. He was the founding chairman of the Samsung Science Board and serves on a variety of other boards, including the Long Now Foundation, the Singapore National Research Foundation Science Advisory Board, and the Pax Group. Paul has also been as an advisor and forum fellow of the World Economic Forum since 1997. He is a columnist for ABCNews.com, and his essays have appeared in numerous publications, including the *Harvard Business Review*, *Fortune*, *Wired*, the *Los Angeles Times*, *Newsweek*, the *New York Times*, and the *Washington Post*. He is a fellow of the Royal Swedish Academy of Engineering Sciences and holds degrees from Harvard College, Cambridge University, and Stanford University.

Paul Saffo
photos by author

Paul and I have been friends for many years. In 2005 professor Fritz Prinz, the chairman of Stanford's Mechanical Engineering Department, asked him to advise the faculty about the future of engineering design. Instead of proposing a consulting project, Paul suggested that he teach a course on the subject to allow him to harness the collective wisdom of the students. He asked me to help him teach the class, so I had an excellent opportunity to learn more about his way of thinking and the tools that he employs to forecast the future. I enjoy and admire his intellectual prowess and curiosity, his deep knowledge of history, and his ability to tell stories that fascinate his audiences.

When we were preparing material for the course, Paul sent me an email titled "Nerd Fun," with a photo attached of him staring through an esoteric surveying instrument—his baseball cap was on backward as he peered toward the future through the lens. The course ran from January to March 2006. We interviewed experts, developed timelines and maps, and asked the students to prepare papers to support their ideas about the future of engineering. The output was presented to the full faculty of the Mechanical Engineering Department as a workshop. It helped them generate strategic policy for the future. My understanding of Paul's point of view and his contributions as a featured lecturer to the Stanford Publishing Courses for Professionals made me sure that he would be a good person to interview about what is happening in media.

Paul is an outdoorsman who lives in the hills between the San Francisco Bay and the Pacific Ocean. He leads emergency rescue teams in the precipitous woods, and I interviewed him in front of a redwood. He gives us an overview of past and present media and looks to the future as well.

THE COLOR OF
LIGHT DEPENDS
ON HOW YOU TURN
THE PRISM

GINKO LEAVES
FROM ZEM'S
YARD

IT WAS A COLD,
BLUSTERY DAY.
RAIN IN EVENING
AND THUNDER!

DEC. 14.05

MASS MEDIA AND PERSONAL MEDIA

Paul fights a losing battle to define himself as a forecaster rather than a futurist. He characterizes forecasters as objective bystanders who focus on what they think will happen; futurists, in his estimation, tend to be advocates, telling you what they think should happen. As a forecaster, he gravitates toward things that don't fit—a surprising offhand comment by an expert, an event that seems out of the norm, or an artifact that grabs his attention. Because such items by definition don't fit into a category, he captures them in an old-fashioned bound journal along with ideas, essay fragments, and the odd observation. Given the nature of his work, it may seem surprising that his journal isn't electronic, but he uses paper because he still finds it superior to digital media. It is faster to open and far easier to jot down a note in his leather-bound journal than it would be on his laptop or a PDA. It is more flexible: he can easily mix sketches and text and even paste in other objects, and he expects to still be able to read his notes on paper long after his digital files have rotted away into a cloud of random electrons. He demonstrates that the value of paper as a medium is timeless, insisting that paper is here to stay.

Paul points out that we are becoming "paperless" the way we once became "horseless." There are nearly as many horses in the United States today as there were in 1900, but they no longer serve as the dominant engines of transportation. Old media forms never die out entirely; they get repurposed. The role of paper has changed over the past twenty years from being a storage medium to an interface medium, used for review. People used to store things on paper and put them in file cabinets or on shelves, but electronics now provide the place for safekeeping. A Bible in the hands of the most devout

Christian still spends more time on a shelf gathering dust than actually being read. With the advent of the laser printer in the late 1980s, we started using paper as interface—printing on demand, enjoying the high resolution and contrast ratio to read the content, and then throwing it away. Paper is here to stay, but Paul explains that the way we are electing to use it is changing.

I've paid a lot of attention to media just because it's some of the fastest moving water in the current technology revolution. We're right in the middle of a massive shift from an information world to a media world. The difference is that we think of it as information when there isn't very much of it and it isn't very important, but when information becomes much greater in volume and much greater in importance it becomes media. Media is information gone deep into our lives.

We have had media revolutions before, and we have lived in [Marshall] McLuhan's mass media age for the past half-century, but this is a different kind of media revolution. We called it "mass media" when it was the only media we had, but now we are creating a new world of "personal media." We are seeing a whole new personal media order intruding and shoving the old mass media titans aside.

Twentieth-century mass media was a revolution because it delivered the world to our living rooms, but, in fact, all we could do is press our nose against the glass and watch—we couldn't participate. To the extent that you participated with mass media, you participated by consuming things. You watched the ads and you went out and bought stuff, or you sent a letter to the editor. The editor would get hundreds of letters; they would print three and edit several paragraphs out of the ones they deigned to publish. That was interactivity in the mass media world.

The personal media world, in contrast, is a world where answering back is not an option—it's required. Otherwise, you don't have the personal media experience. Take Google. You don't watch Google. Watching Google would be like watching the test pattern on a TV (before test patterns went away).

Encyclopædia Britannica

From Wikipedia, the free encyclopedia
(Redirected from Encyclopedia Britannica)

The **Encyclopædia Britannica** (Latin for "the British Encyclopaedia") is a general English-language encyclopaedia published by Encyclopædia Britannica, Inc., a privately held company. The articles in the *Britannica* are aimed at educated adult readers, and written by a staff of about 100 full-time editors and more than 4,000 expert contributors. It is widely regarded as the most scholarly of encyclopaedias.[1][2]

The *Britannica* is the oldest English-language encyclopaedia still in print.[3] It was first published between 1768 and 1771 in Edinburgh, Scotland and quickly grew in popularity and size, with its third edition in 1801 reaching over 21 volumes.[4][5] Its rising stature helped in recruiting eminent contributors, and the 9th edition (1875–1889) and the 11th edition (1911) are regarded as landmark encyclopaedias for scholarship and literary style.[4] Beginning with the 11th edition, the *Britannica* gradually shortened and simplified its articles in order to broaden its North American market.[4] In 1933, the *Britannica* became the first encyclopaedia to adopt a "continuous revision" policy, in which the encyclopaedia is continually reprinted and every article is updated on a regular schedule.[5]

The current 15th edition has a unique three-part structure: a 12-volume *Micropædia* of short articles (generally having fewer than 750 words), a 17-volume *Macropædia* of long articles (having from two to 310 pages) and a single *Propædia* volume intended to give a hierarchical outline of human knowledge. The *Micropædia* is meant for quick fact-checking and as a guide to the *Macropædia*; readers are advised to study the *Propædia* outline to understand a subject's context and to find other, more detailed articles.[6] The size of the *Britannica* has remained roughly constant over the past 70 years, with about 40 million words on half a million topics.[7] Although publication

Wikipedia
screen capture

If you don't put something into Google first, you don't get something out. That's the world of personal media, where there are no bystanders; you have to participate to have the experience. That is profoundly new territory for people designing systems.

Consider the difference between Wikipedia and *Encyclopædia Britannica*. The only person writing for the *Encyclopædia Britannica* was either an employee or a certified "real smart" person, perhaps a professor. In the personal media world we have Wikipedia, where anybody who cares to go to the trouble of writing gets to create an entry, but it's a very small percentage of the people who consult Wikipedia who actually put in entries. Even though the door says "all are welcome," most people just read.

Thanks to the small percentage of people who actually write pieces for Wikipedia, the site looks like a mass medium to the average person who benefits from the result. Someone who wants to know about something looks it up just as he or she would in *Encyclopædia Britannica*, but more conveniently. The small proportion of users who also contribute indicates that most people will not participate unless it is quick and easy. Writing an entry is too large a task, so the personal media world is evolving minimal formats, such as Twitter. Paul provides this example:

So, we're friends, and I walk up to you and say, "Would you write something for me?" and you say, "Sure."

I say, "Well, you know, I need a 900-page volume on competitiveness, something like what Michael Porter does." You would clear your throat and find an excuse, and duck the assignment.

I say, "Okay, well—no, what I really want is a 250-page best seller like what Geoff Moore does, pithy and practical. You know, it's not too hard." And you would still back away.

And I say, "Okay, I take it back, 20 pages." And you say, "Well … maybe in a couple of months."

But if I say, "Actually, I only need a page—no, I don't need a page, not even a paragraph. I need Haiku. Seventeen syllables, it doesn't even have to rhyme. Just give me a search string to put into Google." And you'll say, "Sure!"

The secret design principle—what I'll call Saffo's law—that encourages participation in a personal media world is this: the smaller the quantum of creative act you ask of participants, the more they participate. Ask for a message of not over 140 characters, a search string, or just a click, and you can create successful personal media. Paul points to Rin, a twenty-one-year-old Japanese woman who wrote the best-selling novel *If You*. It was being dished out one screen at a time to cell phones but became so popular that it was published as a hardcover book in 2008, selling more than 400,000 copies.

Bringing us back to the relationship between mass and personal media, Paul explains three characteristic differences:

1. *The nature of the experience.* With mass media, you watch, but with personal media, you participate.

2. *The location.* Mass media came into our living rooms, but you carry personal media with you everywhere you go.

3. *The nature of the dominant players.* Mass media was the world of the few and the large—the big Hollywood producers, the big TV networks, and the widely circulated newspapers and magazines—but the personal media world is dominated by the many and the small. Paul expands on this:

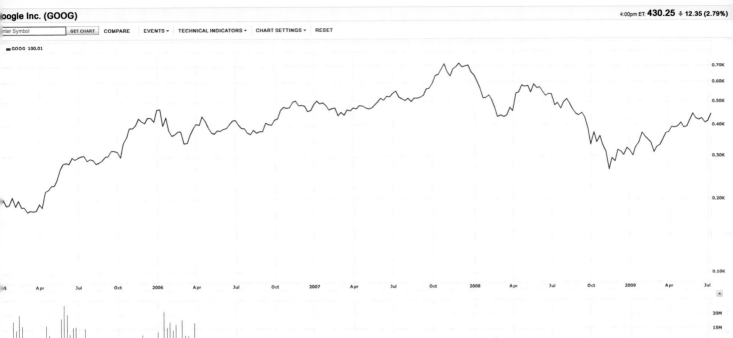

Google's performance history
screen capture

There are vastly more players in this current revolution.
However, what I most emphatically do not mean is that
the big players are dinosaurs and the age of the big player
is over. In fact, we are going to see media players in the
personal media world that will dwarf the largest of today's
mass media giants, but they are going to get big only by
engaging the many and the small. Google is a good indicator.
The Google founders are richer than God because they have
monetized our search strings.

Google also benefitted by being the first search engine to go big, causing
a sweeping momentum that is very hard for competitors to follow.
Just the fact that the votes come from the many and the small means
that the designs that capture the volume of use gain an advantage that
can easily dominate.

THE S-CURVE

A simple rule of thumb that one can apply to the uncertain realm of forecasting is this: look for something that's been failing for about twenty years. Mention it to your friends or your coworkers. They'll say, "Oh yeah, we tried that almost twenty years ago. It'll never happen." That may well be an indicator that the end of the flat part of the S-curve is near and takeoff is approaching. The wise gambler may take this as a sign and immediately look at the topic with a renewed interest, probably seizing the opportunity to sign up, invest, or get involved. Most of us suffer a psychological barrier when it comes to accepting this potential gift because we tend to be linear thinkers; S-curves are nonlinear phenomena. Paul uses this insight to see more clearly through the oncoming haze, and he applies it directly to media.

> Any entrepreneurs who try to do anything with media today, whether they realize it or not, are embarking on a journey along the S-curve of innovation that is riskier than [Mr.] Toad's Wild Ride. In Silicon Valley, we don't draw it as an S-shaped curve; we draw it as a hockey stick because it never ends. We focus on the inflection point—the place where it takes off. In general, people try doing things for about twenty years, and just when they give up and say, "No, that will never happen," that's when the revolution arrives.

> The interesting thing about this phenomenon is that we've seen it before. The pattern of change, the general shape of change, is not unlike earlier innovations. And the best part of this personal media revolution is that, even though the media are profoundly different, they very closely follow the pattern of innovation seen during the birth of mass media in the early 1950s. As a forecaster, I spend a lot of time looking at history because, as Mark Twain was alleged to have said (he didn't

← Lotus pond at the
Robinson House, California
photo courtesy of Phaedra.biz

actually say it, but we don't know who did), "History doesn't repeat itself, but sometimes it rhymes."

History rhymes quite a lot when it comes to innovation. So if you want to have a sense of how things are going to unfold over the next ten or twenty years, it doesn't hurt to look back at previous decades.

Even though we live in the middle of this nonlinear change, it's hard for us to understand it. Paul refers to a metaphor presented by Donella Meadows, a pioneering American environmental scientist, in her 1972 book *Limits to Growth*.

Imagine you are a very lazy gardener with a pond in your backyard, and there is a single lotus in the pond. You think, "I've got to do something about that because the lotus will take over the pond, but I'll wait. I'll wait until the pond's half full and clean it out then, because I like the lotus." Let's assume at day one that there's one lotus, and at the end of day thirty the pond is completely full of lotus, with no space left. So you ask yourself: On what day is the pond half full? Well, a linear thinker would say, around day fifteen, but in fact, it isn't half-full until the twenty-ninth day because of the exponential nature of the growth. Until then, the lazy gardener would think that not much was happening, and wake up to quite a surprise on the thirtieth day.

That's what's going to happen with media. You're going to hear the steady, sonic boom of one inflection point after another tunneling through the zeitgeist in this media revolution; one big company after another coming out of nowhere, like Google; one surprise after another; one opportunity after another. The secret to success is to think in a nonlinear way and to stay entrepreneurial.

Ordinary people get surprised when that inflection point arrives after a twenty-year lag and suddenly changes the world. Like, "Oh my god, where did the PC come from?" or, "Where did the World Wide Web come from?" The problem for you all as professionals is, as visionaries, you now get to be wrong twice, because you're going to stand at the start of that S-curve and think that the inflection point is going to arrive a lot more quickly than it actually does, but by the time it does arrive, you will have dismissed it and say it's not happening at all. So, remember the rule: if you want a short-term success, look for something that's been failing for twenty years!

Another piece of advice is to remember Leo Baekeland. In 1907 Baekeland invented Bakelite plastic, a thermosetting resin. What did they do with this marvelous, new material? They spent their whole time making it look like old stuff. They made it look like wood and tortoise shell because they weren't comfortable with Bakelite just looking like plastic. Then after about ten or fifteen years everybody realized that Bakelite was a poor substitute for wood and tortoise shell but a marvelous material in it's own right. So society collectively concluded, "Let's let plastic be plastic." And then things got interesting. You can see "Bakelite thinking" all over new media today, where people are trying to use a new thing to imitate an old thing.

As you observe our fast-changing revolution, look for the underlying constants. Look for what's permanent. Look for the deep behaviors. New terms like *blog* and *tweet* are intellectual ablative shields (the heat shield on a spacecraft that keeps the astronauts from burning up); they keep us from going crazy while we're entering the atmosphere of new media. Be careful how you use them and don't use them in a place that is going to be preserved for a long time, because you'll find yourself twenty years from now looking at that media term with the equivalent sense of, "Oh God, I can't believe I wore those glasses with the really big frames or that jacket made out of polyester."

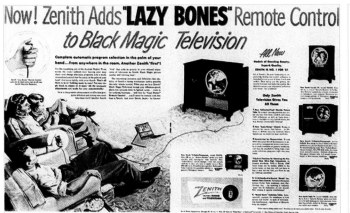

Ads for Zenith Lazy Bones

THE CREATOR ECONOMY

The first television remote controller was developed by the Zenith Radio Corporation in 1950. It was connected to the television by a wire and marketed under the name "Lazy Bones." Unfortunately, the bulky wire often got in the way and people kept tripping over it. Zenith tried again with a cord-free design invented by Eugene Polley, and in 1955 launched the Flash-Matic. This looked like a cross between a pistol and a flashlight. It had a single button that controlled the volume, without anything to change the channel or turn the TV on and off. Eugene McDonald, the CEO of Zenith, was an idealist who believed that television would change the world for the better but that advertisers would stand in the way of the medium's ability to revolutionize education and enlighten us all. The remote was his secret weapon to empower consumers to conquer the advertisers; the moment a nasty ad came on, you'd aim the thing at the screen and pull the trigger. The light would flash at a photo diode on the television, turning off the sound during the ads. Unfortunately, the photo diode could be confused by other light sources, so if your TV faced a window, the headlights from a passing car could kill the sound right in the middle of your show of shows. A deeper problem was that consumers did not want to turn the ads off, as advertisers were clever enough to amuse people, so in short order, the Flash-Matic failed.

A year later Robert Adler, an engineer from Vienna who also worked at Zenith, created the Space Command remote control, using ultrasound

⟵ Zenith Flash-Matic and
   Space Commander 200
   photos by Nicolas Zurcher

Dr. Horrible's Sing-Along Blog
screen capture from DrHorrible.com

instead of light, with buttons to change the channel as well as to adjust the volume. When a button on the remote control was pushed, it clicked and struck a bar, hence the term *clicker*. Each bar emitted a different frequency and circuits in the television detected the noise. The design succeeded, in spite of the fact that some people, especially young women, could hear the piercing ultrasonic signals. Paul points out that we are experiencing that sort of experimentation with new media today.

> Inventors and entrepreneurs are engaged in a conversation with the consumer, trying to figure out what this stuff should be and how it should be used. That's why every week we have a new interactive media experience. One week it's Twitter, and the next week it's something new like Dr. Horrible's Sing-Along Blog on the Web, which two weeks from now will be ancient history. It's this period of mad, wild experimentation. The lesson to take away is to be like Zenith. If you have a failure, ask yourself why it failed. This is a period of interesting failures, which when pursued can lead to real success.

> The feedback loop is tightly linked today between producer and participant. It's not producer and consumer, because there aren't consumers anymore. It's producer and participant. It's fast and tight. You'd better listen to the participant or you're going to be in big trouble! This loop has created a huge headache for the mass media incumbents that are like battleships on the ocean, cruising along and telling us where we should go. It's great news for people who respond very quickly, but it's also a challenge. The revolution is picking up speed. We're building the railroad we're riding on. The image to

think about is that you've got a train going at seventy miles an hour down the tracks, and you're trying to lay tracks six inches in front of the engine.

Meanwhile, remember that revolutions always beget revolutions. In 1517 Martin Luther tacked a memo to a church door and suddenly the pope lost half of his market share because of the printing press. Today, there is an economic shift afoot. You have to go back a hundred years to see what's happening. A hundred years ago we had an emerging industrial economy. It was about manufacturing. And the symbol of that economy was the time clock, with the central actor being the worker. It was all about making things, and the preoccupation of the time was how could we make enough stuff, cheaply enough, to satisfy the desires of an emergent middle class. By 1950 the manufacturers were really good at that. They had gradually overcome scarcity.

By the end of World War II, when the manufacturers stopped making bombs and airplanes and tanks and went back to making consumer goods, to their horror they discovered that they were now so good at making stuff that they were making more stuff than people wanted. And that was the moment at which the manufacturing economy ended and was replaced by the consumer economy. The central actor was no longer the worker, the person who made things, but the consumer, the person who purchased things. The symbol of that economy was no longer the time clock, the relentless robot of worker efficiency, but the credit card, the charge card that allowed people to purchase more than they could afford. Well, we've had that for the last fifty years and it's coming to an end.

We're on the third turning. The new central actor in this economy is neither the worker, the person who makes things, nor the consumer, the person who purchases, but a new economic actor who does both activities at the very same moment. Call them "creators" (not "creatives," who are the elites who make beautiful things that the rest of us want to buy). Creators are ordinary, anonymous individuals with a new role in this new economy. A creator is an economic actor who in one and the same act both creates and consumes. They may not even realize that they are creating, and they sometimes don't even know they are consuming. Wikipedia allows anybody to create an entry, as do MySpace and YouTube.

The best example is Google, because you have to create in order to get results. If you don't put a search string in, that act of creation, you don't get the results out. It changes the basic economic proposition. Think about what your Google subscription [cost] last month—that would be zero. Google is bigger than YouTube because more people put in search strings than produce videos. Somewhere out there in a garage, some entrepreneurs are discovering how to make people create with a single click. Or, better yet, with no click at all, just by living their lives. The company that discovers that will dwarf Google in size.

I think this creator economy is going to last a couple of decades, just like the last couple of economies did. I have no idea what's after it. Ask me in thirty years.

THE NEXT INTERVIEW IS WITH JAMES TRUMAN, who earned the nickname "Prince of Condé Nast" after his meteoric rise to editorial director of the company's entire portfolio of magazines. In the following interview, James asks whether media may be displaced by technology, as the word *media* implies something that intermediates, coming between an organization and an audience, while the Internet allows a direct conversation between creators and consumers, sometimes as members of communities, but also within the actions of single individuals as suggested by Paul Saffo's concept of the "creator economy."

James gives an overview of the changes in magazine design during his tenure at Condé Nast and describes his more recent search for meaning in direct communal experiences. He expects traditional media to reemerge, after a period of decline, in forms that are more luxurious, with magazines reveling in the highest quality imagery and books moving from text to colorful works of art with exquisite bindings and accessories.

JAMES TRUMAN

Interviewed December 20, 2008

JAMES TRUMAN

James grew up in Nottingham, in the middle of England, but left as soon as he could. His father wanted him to be an accountant and sent him to study accounting, but he left after just one day. His real desire was to be in the music world in some way, but because he didn't have the right musical talents for either composing or performing, he started writing reviews for weekly music papers. He eventually got a staff job at one of them, *Melody Maker* in London, and after a short stint there he moved to New York and found himself feeling at home. He wrote a monthly column about music and life in the city that never sleeps for the London based *The Face* magazine. Condé Nast, America's biggest magazine publisher, bought a controlling interest in *The Face* and admired the contribution that James was making. He was soon appointed features editor at *Vogue*. After just eighteen months he was placed in charge of his own magazine, *Details*, and made such a success of it that in 1994, at the age of thirty-four, James was appointed to oversee all of Condé Nast's magazines, including *Vogue, The New Yorker, Vanity Fair, GQ*, and *Wired*. Eleven years later, he walked away from his role as the "Prince of Condé Nast" to experiment with interactive workshops and happenings.

←⋯⋯ **James Truman**
photos by author

I was lucky to be able to interview James in Napa Valley, not so far away from my home base, where he was spending Christmas with friends on the Francis Ford Coppola estate. Gene Celso, the video guru at IDEO who helped me record many of these interviews, and I arrived in the late morning of one of those sunny winter days in California that flood the landscape with gentle light and warmth. We connected with James at a local restaurant and he guided us into the heart of the estate, where he was staying in a visitor's cottage. He sat in the window with the sun dappling through the trees outside, with Roman Coppola sitting in to listen to his story.

At first James seems a little diffident, perhaps because he still speaks in the manner of his English origin, but one soon warms to his intellect and lively wit, which are enhanced by his engaging and impish grin.

FROM DECLINE TO LUXURY

James is interested in what happens to media whose value has expired. What happens to old media that is outmoded or obsolete—the paper telephone directory, the magazine listing current events, or the silent movie? He refers to the ideas penned by Marshall McLuhan in the 1970s, which resonate with the fate of today's newspapers and magazines. McLuhan used the analogy of what happened to the horse after the invention of the automobile. It was no longer the most functional, efficient, or utilitarian technology; the car displaced it. But the horse didn't disappear. The horse *business* went into a decline but much more slowly than predicted. The number of horses went down incrementally each year and then started rebounding after World War II, as they became thought of as a luxury item. James predicts that media will change in a very similar way:

> For the things I grew up with, particularly magazines, that is the most likely fate. I don't think that they'll go away, but I think they need to become more expensive. They're not going to have that mainstream, news-breaking or news-gathering function that they had. They're going to be luxury objects comparable to coffee-table books.

> I have a friend who runs a publishing company and they do incredibly well by making books that have lots of pouches and cutouts and little add-ons, so the book goes from being a very predictable item to a format that's almost like a kit. It's like a box of goodies. I think that's one way books will go, becoming coffee-table books, like what Taschen is doing; these huge, extravagant projects. That's more likely to be the future of the book than the paperback for two dollars.

> The early nineties was the beginning of what became the luxury industrial complex, where the idea of luxury just

←---- **Girl and horse**
photo by Comstock Images

infiltrated everything. Every marketing idea, every product, had to have had some thought about, "What is luxury? What is a luxury good? What is a luxury brand?" I think we'll look back on this as one of the most uninteresting phases in cultural history. Louis XIV became Louis Vuitton!

During this period luxury brands used fashion advertisements with exaggerated images of outrageously expensive items and didn't worry about selling many of them because designers made their money from selling less-expensive products like underwear or purses. They needed to be noticed in the ad in *Vogue*, so that mall customers would spend $35 for underwear rather than $12.

WHISPERS AND SECRETS

In 2005 James decided to search for a new adventure that would offer *direct* rather than *mediated* experience. He wanted to explore and better understand the notion of what a real community is and feels like in the time of virtual community—what it means to create knowledge as entertainment. He has developed a traveling show called *Big Night in Tent*, which harnesses both the people who travel with the show and those in the communities that they visit. They offer a one- or two-week happening that introduces new ideas one-on-one, viscerally, through a kind of display or fair. In one event, they took over an estate on the Hudson River and invited local families from every walk of life to participate. They put kids in cottages, so that they could live with circus performers, and they created a show in the barn on Saturday night. The adults had their own program of learning and discussion, but the kids were running the show. They invited everyone in the "village" to the performance.

Vogue magazine
photo by Nicolas Zurcher

We were just playing with a lot of ideas. The last one really worked. It had some sort of transformational quality about it, which was what interested me about it in the beginning— of letting knowledge and connection and surprise create magic.

I'm interested in whispers and secrets. I'm not interested in announcements and marketing campaigns. I'm averse to brand at this point. I think it's an ugly, discredited philosophy that

Varekai **by Cirque du Soleil**
photo courtesy of Creative Commons

has been part of why the last fifteen years have been so boring, as much as the rise of hedge funds and money culture has. I think brands are poison, so I don't want to become a brand.

The people who were there all exchanged addresses, and there's been email communication. We've even put up a page on Flickr—just people who came and the snapshots they took. It's an open page. I am not too fascistic about this. In the age of information proliferation, the idea of the secret becomes quite exciting, and I'm excited by the idea of secret much more than I am by another piece of marketed media.

When asked if this shared experienced can be designed, James shies away from the idea, as that would imply that one is thinking of it as a brand. He wants to develop a sentiment rather than a form, but design and brand are defined as forms. He would be interested in continuously changing the form to prevent it from becoming a repeatable event. It should be a movement rather than a show, like Cirque du Soleil, which revolutionized the concept of circus but spent two years and $60 million finding a form that could be repeated. Cirque du Soleil is beautifully designed and very successful, and people like to see something spectacular on that scale, but James is interested in something that is internally spectacular, not showbiz spectacular.

Burning Man
photo by Eve Coste-Maniere

TRANSPARENT MEDIA

James welcomes the erosion of media and branding as codified forms
developed by skillful designers to be repeated in the service of business
and profit. He has spent long enough in an office on the top floor of a
Manhattan high-rise; he is searching for a more ecological and communal
experience. He enjoys the prospect of people being empowered to create
things themselves, similar to the "creator" concept from Paul Saffo—
James calls it "transparent media."

I'm sort of throwing out ideas that entertain me, because I'm
allowed to be entertained by ideas at this point in my life. And
of course, what always happens is that some new experience
comes up, it finds a form, it becomes a brand, it gets
marketed as such, and then the life is sucked out of it. I'm just
interested in what happens in the early stages rather than the
later stages of that.

I was at Burning Man the last couple of years. At the end,
we left with about ten people in a little coach and everyone

was keeping the vibe going until we turned a certain corner when there was cell phone service, then everybody got their Blackberries out and they were gone: the community was broken. There's all this worry at Burning Man about whether commercial interests are going to come in and spoil it, and the simplest way to ruin Burning Man is to put a cell phone satellite above it. Suddenly you wouldn't have it: it would be lost, categorically lost.

I'm not really taking a moral position. I just feel that I'm noticing that media has stopped being material and has become transparent. Everyone can make a movie now with very simple software. So that is the end of a certain idea of media, and with that type of transparency will come new issues. And we don't quite know what they are yet. Right now, it's like hobby day at school—you stop getting lectured and start making crafts yourself. I don't know if that gives you the right to run the whole curriculum, but we'll see.

Media is in a very, very interesting phase. I remember years ago, how people would say that in the future technology is going to become invisible. I even remember fashion designers who would sew microprocessors into the lapels of jackets with some unforeseen future consequence of being wired and connected. So media was announcing the disappearance of technology, but what's happening now is that technology is announcing the disappearance of media. The word *media* implies something that intermediates—that mediates between an institution and the public, or an event and a reader, or whatever. That role seems to be less and less useful, and less and less needed.

News stories on the Web seem to be becoming the equivalent of the CDOs, those weird financial instruments that brought down the banking system, where many mortgages are sliced up and put back together. You read a story and find that it has a little bit of *New York Times* reporting in it, perhaps a little bit of *Los Angeles Times* reporting, plus a little bit of gossip, and then a little bit of something that someone made up. Underneath there is a response by a blogger that seems interesting, but you don't know if the blogger has actually been paid to write it by a big corporation or if it's what the author really thinks.

Traditional media offers a chaperoned experience—material is handed to you by people who were experts in a field and could claim some sense of objectivity and responsibility. New media mixes and matches material that is created objectively and subjectively, and it is difficult to tell the difference or hold anyone accountable. Wikipedia is being created as a community effort: different viewpoints are accumulated and policed. James sees this ongoing conversation as a replacement for traditional media, which was never conversational—it was authoritarian. Compare Wikipedia with a church magazine. You know the people who made the parish magazine, but you don't know the people who are contributing to Wikipedia, why they're making it, or for whom.

> While it is a community enterprise, it's an interesting phase of facelessness of who the instigators are. Who are the authorities in that? I feel that, just as CDOs went through the system and caused havoc, something is going to happen in this new technology that'll cause havoc.

> I was always fascinated by how it was a misunderstanding on the telephone that really started World War I, because the phone call should have been made after the assassination of the archduke, but people didn't understand the technology; it wasn't made and the war began. And I think there's going to be some misunderstanding or misuse of this new sense of media technology that will probably have some very contagious and dramatic effect in our lifetimes."

The Face
photo by Nicolas Zurcher

DESIGNING MAGAZINES

Soon after James arrived in New York at the age of twenty-two, he started writing for a new British magazine called *The Face*. It was the first magazine to combine a sense of style and glossy production values with gritty street smarts and a connection to edgy popular music. It was a break from the punk rock era, when musical magazines expressed themselves in newsprint, graffiti, and ransom notes for logos. People had their fill of punk rock and wanted to get dressed up again.

> I've become close friends with Malcolm McLaren, who managed the Sex Pistols. He concedes that what was wrong with punk rock was that it had no sex in it; that people didn't go out to meet romantic partners; they went out to offload aggression and that was not a sustainable model. So in reaction to that, I think this notion of style and glamour emerged.

Before that, people who were interested in rock and roll didn't read *Vogue*. They weren't interested in it; it belonged to the cloistered world of Paris. Street fashion, at which London had always been so marvelous, had no media to explain it, even if sometimes high-end designers would come and see girls in miniskirts in the East End and be inspired to create couture.

The Face understood that the street was glamorous, that the street wasn't just sort of angry, and dirty, and punk. In turn, the rise of that magazine started to make the conventional fashion magazines like *Vogue* suddenly start paying attention to the street. There had been a little bit of that with [supermodel] Twiggy because she's from the East End, but it was really all about pulling things off the street, putting them through the sort of glossy process, and then coming out the other end with a $1,000 dress.

In its own way, punk rock was fantastically glamorous. I remember seeing Malcolm and Johnny Rotten on Shaftesbury Avenue one day, before I knew either of them. I mean you'd never seen anything like it. They were wearing clothes that were ripped, but so beautifully organized and so beautifully designed. Vivienne Westwood had designed them. Cars were stopping and people were forming crowds around them. You saw that for them that was part of the arsenal, that you could shock and awe with the use of style.

Before *The Face* you could divide magazines by gender. The boys read grungy, poorly designed magazines printed on newsprint, with long tracts trying to explain the meaning behind the music, while the girls read fan magazines, with glossy pictures of the musicians. *The Face* brought girls and boys back together by making a glamorous magazine about music that featured fashion. Condé Nast noticed *The Face* and realized that it had something that they needed, and so they made an ownership investment. Those who had occupied the upper ranks of "Glossidom" accepted the underground world as potentially good business, bringing the street and the penthouse together during the eighties and nineties in publishing.

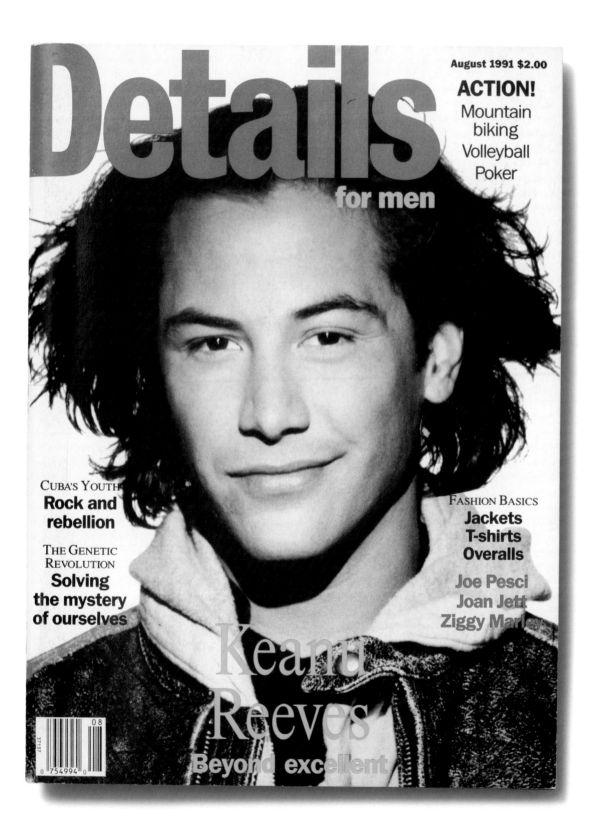

Details

for men

August 1991 $2.00

ACTION!
Mountain biking
Volleyball
Poker

CUBA'S YOUTH
Rock and rebellion

THE GENETIC REVOLUTION
Solving the mystery of ourselves

FASHION BASICS
**Jackets
T-shirts
Overalls**

Joe Pesci
Joan Jett
Ziggy Marley

Keanu Reeves
Beyond excellent

In 1990 James was made editor in chief of *Details* magazine. He remembers clearly the moment when the inspiration for the new design approach for the magazine came to him. He was in Pasadena, California, standing outside the Rose Bowl as the audience arrived for a concert by Depeche Mode. He had been expecting backstage passes, but they never came through, and he didn't have enough cash for the scalper tickets that were going for hundreds of dollars because the concert was sold out, so he just had to stand outside.

Depeche Mode was a weedy group from Essex who had sold out the biggest concert arena in America. I had this experience of watching people come in, and I'd never seen an audience like that in America. It was very gay, and it was very straight. It was very masculine; it was very feminine. It was very fashionable, but it was very street. And I felt this … it was like the first time I'd gone to see the Sex Pistols; you felt something was fermenting that was different and rich. It had at its heart a sense of style, but it was also fighting for a certain kind of social freedom, because there were a lot of Hispanics, a lot of Mexicans there, and there were a lot of white preppy kids as well. I felt that something was cooking; there was some congregation around this foreign group, who represented the beginnings of a Goth idea, certain style sensibilities, a certain kind of film noir quality, and that became my idea of what I thought the audience of *Details* should be.

It was the first magazine in America that ran stories about gay men and straight men alongside each other; we would have men together in fashion stories who were clearly not trying to be heterosexual. It was trying to broaden an idea of what a man was, and it was touching at the beginning of the technology boom. We had a lot of coverage of that. Then there was also psychological stuff about what it's like to be a man—what your relationships with your parents were like, what they mean to you. We were doing a magazine for sensitive young men who were not self-defined by their sexuality or by their class or actually by their ethnic origin. So it was kind of a rainbow magazine. Those magazines had existed but had always had a very small circulation, and the success of *Details* is that it went from being about 80,000 to 500,000 in a couple of years, so it had this explosive growth.

← *Details* magazine cover
featuring Keanu Reeves,
August 1991
photo by Nicolas Zurcher

Japanese schoolgirls
photo courtesy of Wikimedia Creative Commons

That surge in circulation did not happen immediately. James had always been fascinated by the edginess of rebellious music and street fashion, and he may have brought too much of that for his American audience to the early issues of *Details*. The art direction started with a rather punk-derived design, but on glossy paper. There was a lot of in-your-face imagery and non-beautiful type, which looked quite aggressive. It nearly went out of business in the first year because people just hated it, proving that a certain amount of sugar coating or prettifying is needed in the United States to communicate ideas, even if the ideas themselves are neither pretty nor chic.

Putting Keanu Reeves on the cover rescued the venture. It was his first cover in America, and in spite of the fact that it was supposedly a men's magazine, the circulation doubled overnight; 100,000 teenage girls bought it because they liked Keanu. James realized afterward that the first design had expressed hostility to the audience, expecting it to be galvanizing and exciting. He learned something about the people he was designing for, both for their gender and for their attitudes toward aggression:

If you come at an American audience with a kind of "fuck you," they're going to turn around and say, "I'm not going to pay two dollars to read that." I think it's the same reason why the Sex Pistols never worked here; the performative aspect of hostility is something the English relish, but Americans take more literally and actually are put off by.

Teenage girls know about everything before anyone else does. It's the same in Tokyo, it's the same in London, the same in New York. When I was at *Wired* we had this Japanese Schoolgirl Watch, which was what was going on in the streets of Tokyo, with the understanding that this was the best barometer you could possibly have of what was going to be happening in the USA in a year. We'd go and photograph, interview girls on the street in Tokyo and find out what they were thinking about.

Women have conversations. They say what they like. They share what they like. I mean, they are communicators, but men are monkish, and private, and fearful around a lot of things that really interest them.

We really shifted the design, which was an interesting lesson about design because design is not morally right or wrong. If it can communicate an idea to a larger number of people without spoiling the idea, then I think it's good design.

Details continued to be successful, reveling in the new mix of content that James had envisaged intuitively as he watched the audience in Pasadena. One month there was a ten-page feature on the biggest S&M parlor in New York, and the next month the first interview Carlos Castaneda had done in twenty years. It was a wildly eclectic offering, and perhaps the last time magazines had that freedom, as they got more and more reined in by competition among themselves and by the bigger voice that advertisers came to have in content. Magazines had been an adventurous and exploratory medium, but the mix of competition and the Internet forced them to become vehicles for serving the needs of advertisers.

In the seventies and eighties, the best graphic designers were cutting their teeth in magazines and would then go on to do other things, but as magazines started to become a little too static, a little too polished, and a little too bland for the really bright young talents, they chose product design or Web design instead. The downturn of 2008 caused drastic reductions in advertising budgets across most industries, impacting almost all magazines. Automobile or luxury goods manufacturers are much less likely to buy full-page ads in magazines in a recession, particularly as they can target their limited advertising budgets much more successfully on the Internet. Google has made media accountable for the effectiveness of advertising. Nielsen's ratings on TV give some indications, but magazines rely on blind trust. Information is available about the number of people who see an ad, but nothing is known about whether they acted on it, whereas Google can track actions in detail. James believes that there has to be a new model or a new technology of advertising that can satisfy advertisers and also keep the well-known brand names afloat, as they are not willing to pay comparable amounts to advertise on the Web:

> Banner ads haven't done it. Click-throughs haven't done it. I don't know what it's going to be, but whoever thinks it up is going to save an industry, because the model as it is now doesn't work. It's not complicated; it's just a question of real estate. How much real estate can you give on a Web page to an advertiser versus how much can you give in a magazine or newspaper? What happened, which was so unique with the Web, was that at the beginning the point of entry was so cheap; so much came online that didn't need advertising support that we aesthetically grew used to a vision of what a Web page should look like. If you put up a Web page that was seven-eighths advertisement, you wouldn't make it. People wouldn't stay with you, even though they had been acclimatized to accepting that in magazines and newspapers.

When James was given responsibility for overseeing all of the magazines published by Condé Nast, it was *Wired* that seemed distinct from the others. *Wired* was founded in 1993, early in the days of the surge of growth of the Internet. It showed that the technology of Silicon Valley was not just for nerds; it could appeal to everyone, offering a new sort of glossy excitement about all things digital. When Condé Nast bought the magazine, it was unable to include the Web site, because it was separately owned. The Web was using some content from the magazine, but without editorial control. James credits Chris Anderson, the current editor in chief, for keeping the magazine afloat after the dot-com crash, and bringing the Web and paper versions together.

> *Wired* was lucky in that it was in San Francisco instead of New York. There was a lot of talk about moving it to New York, but I think it would have essentially done in the magazine, done in its originality. I think it being in its own culture and being 3,000 miles away is vital. The head of Condé Nast saw that, too, and it was very smart of him to say, "It makes cost sense to move it to New York, but it makes no other sense. It stays in San Francisco." *Wired* was fantastically successful, then it was an absolute disaster after the bust of the dot-com boom, and now it's come back largely because Chris has done such a good job.

NEXT WE TAKE A CLOSER LOOK AT *WIRED* MAGAZINE in an interview with Chris Anderson. Chris is confident that the magazine format is here to stay, as long as it makes the most of the unique attributes of magazine design, energetically pursuing luscious images, diagrams, and illustrations, with dramatic layout and rich production values. He feels the ambivalence of working to create a magazine that is owned by Condé Nast and writing books that are distributed by Disney, while in his heart he wants to celebrate the possibilities offered by the Internet to serve individual needs and desires in niches of focused interest. He believes that the print side of *Wired* should strive to add value to the Web, while the Web serves the endless expanse of amateur interests, even as it relies on the printed magazine to pay the bills.

CHRIS ANDERSON

Interviewed November 17, 2008

CHRIS ANDERSON

When *Wired* was first published in 1993, Chris was working at the scientific journal *Science*, expecting that the Internet would continue to be used solely for communications within the scientific community. Reading this bold and glossy magazine full of ideas about the the way this technology would change the world made him realize that "this thing is a lot bigger than I thought," and he knew immediately that his career was going to be related to the Internet forever more. He spent the subsequent seven years with *The Economist* magazine in various editorial roles and was responsible for launching its coverage of the Internet. In 2001 he was approached by Condé Nast and asked to take over as editor in chief at *Wired*, a daunting task, as the magazine was reeling after the dot-com crash. He succeeded in resuscitating *Wired* as a magazine and it has been thriving since. Chris coined the phrase "the long tail" in an acclaimed *Wired* article, which he expanded into book form.[2] His 2009 book *Free: The Future of a Radical Price* examines the rise of pricing models that give products and services to customers for free.

← Chris Anderson
photos by author

2 *The Long Tail: Why the Future of Business Is Selling Less of More* (New York: Hyperion, 2006).

The *Wired* magazine offices are located in San Francisco, on the third floor of a rectilinear brick building, crisscrossed with steel reinforcements against earthquakes. Gene Celso and I set up the cameras for the interview in front of the metal-framed windows of Chris's office. As he walked in, he was already ranting against overused words, with "media" being his first complaint:

I think media is an expired word. I don't know what it means. It's a word that maybe once had meaning but that meaning has been fuzzied to the point that it means everything and as a result nothing today. I think in the twentieth century media meant something pretty crisp until Marshall McLuhan came and screwed it all up. Today I have no idea what media means.

A little worried that the title of this book was vanishing down the drain, I reminded Chris that McLuhan had been extensively quoted in *Wired* magazine.

When I took over at Wired, *Marshall McLuhan was the patron saint of the magazine, with a quote printed every month. At a certain point, about a year into my tenure, as I was rethinking things we do, it so happened that we'd run out of quotes from our McLuhan database and we were going to recycle them. I decided to take the opportunity to actually read these quotes and ask myself whether we wanted to do it. When I read them, I realized that not a single one stood up to scrutiny, for example, "The medium is the message." If it does mean anything, then unfortunately the word media doesn't mean anything I understand anymore, so I killed the quotes.*

This critical approach to semantics is one of the attributes that makes Chris such an effective leader in his role as editor in chief.

WIRED

Premiere Issue

Exclusive:
Behind the Inslaw
Scandal at Justice

Paglia and Brand
on McLuhan

"The Medium...

オタク
Digital Sex

Negroponte: What's
Wrong with HDTV

Bruce Sterling

Has Seen the Future of War

$4.95 / Canada 5.95

WIRED MAGAZINE

Wired was founded in 1993 by American journalist Louis Rossetto and his partner Jane Metcalfe and edited by Kevin Kelly. The magazine and accompanying Web site were immediately successful, with the print version intermingling fluorescent DayGlo colors with striking images and typography. The bold vision won *Wired* awards for both content and design in its first four years, showing that the Internet was not just for scientists but would change the world for everybody. The publication evolved alongside the host of new companies springing up in San Francisco during the dot-com boom.

Then various busts came. IPOs failed, the dot-com crash decimated the industry, and the magazine split with its Web site, HotWired, which was bought by Lycos and turned into an archive. The magazine went to Condé Nast. In 2001 James Truman invited Chris Anderson to take over as editor in chief.

I really had never had a media job before. *The Economist* is more of a think tank, and Condé Nast is largely a fashion company. I'm the geekiest guy by far in an otherwise very cool company.

The stock market crashed in 2001, and what with September 11, Enron, et cetera, it was a real challenge to figure out what to do. We decided that there are really two questions: One, this story about the power of the Internet to change the world and technology—is this a mirage? Is this a fraud? Was dot-com just a bubble? Is it tulips? I knew in every fiber of my being that it was not, that we were at the beginning of something, not the end. The dot-com bubble was all about the stock market, not about the underlying technologies. The second real question is, What should we do about that? What should this magazine be? Even if I was right and the

First edition of *Wired*, March 1993
photo by Nicolas Zurcher

revolution was won, what do revolutionaries do when they've won? Become counter-revolutionaries? Become the establishment figures? Sulk about the lost days of the long march?

So I decided that we would declare victory and join the establishment, if you will, be as revolutionary as possible within the establishment, but basically take the magazine mainstream. After a year and a half of flailing, we got traction. I was right. Everyone acknowledges that the Internet is here to stay, technology is now mainstream, it does empower individuals to change the world. No problem there.

We still want to blow minds twelve times a year, but that isn't so hard, because we're not really about technology; we're about how technology is changing the world. All we have to do is look out there somewhere. Technology is changing the world somewhere everyday, so the story is very broad and lots of fun. Two years ago we bought back the Web site, and we can now walk the talk and do the kind of experiments we've been advocating, but like everybody else, we are groping in the dark.

Chris believes that the acts of journalism, editing, and distribution are here to stay, but that the forms that are designed to contain the contents will vary to fit the vehicle. A magazine is largely a visual medium, whereas the Web is largely verbal. *Wired* has 8,000-word stories with lavish photography and design on high-resolution page spreads. On the Web, a story of this scale turns into sixteen pages of text, the photographs lose their richness, and the design is lost.

Our job on the print side is to add value to the Web. I think everybody's job in the information world, regardless of the industry, is to add value to the Web. The Web is the water we swim in, the air that we breathe—you need to stand out. So we do something the Web can't do. So now we come to the Web site. What should the Web site be? Well, it shouldn't just be a bad version of what we do in print. It should be something else. We have limited pages in the magazine and unlimited pages on the Web, but the cost structure is not right, because we're competing with amateurs who are creating an infinite amount of content on very narrow subjects for free.

Our challenge really is how to bring amateur energy into our domain. How do we use our brand, our kind of catalytic power, our leadership and our technology to incentivize people to create valuable content within our confines? You know, we have Reddit, which is like Digg, a user news-submission-andvoting mechanism. We have wikis, we have blogs, we have user-generated Flickr sets. We do it all. Some things work, most things don't – that's the normal way of things.

The magazine itself is not going to change. We'll continue to innovate, but I think Wired will look like Wired magazine for decades to come.

There are aspects to the magazine that may seem like virtues, but can also be seen as sins. It's got intrinsic hierarchy; it's got a cover; the stories have an order; the table of contents lists them in order. I have to guess every month at what the most important story is. I have to guess at how we're going to place our weight. I have to decide what the reader's path will be through the magazine. And every month, I'm wrong, sometimes a lot and sometimes a little, but the reason I know I'm wrong is because when I look at the actual user behavior on the Web, its never what I expected. What I thought was going to be the most popular story is often not the most popular story on the Web, and what I thought was not going to be the most popular story turns out to be a popular story. I hate having to guess, but I have to because we build the thing before we ship it, and once it's shipped we can't change it.

Chris is disarmingly modest in blaming himself for errors of judgment, given the number of people who want to know what he thinks, no matter how often or rarely he may be wrong. They value his selection of the most important stories. He is interesting and provocative even when he is not accurate. There is room still in the virtual world of the Web for editorial authority. The skills of editing are timeless. People are interested in the opinions of a good editor, expert, or curator, whether online or in print, without presuming that it has to be right, but believing that the opinions matter enough to compensate for the errors.

Wired covers

FREE

THE FUTURE OF A RADICAL PRICE

FREE!

840012 55480

CHRIS ANDERSON

AUTHOR OF THE NEW YORK TIMES BESTSELLER THE LONG TAIL

FREE

Chris wrote a groundbreaking article titled "The Long Tail" for the magazine and later found time and energy to convert it into a book. His next book, *Free: The Future of a Radical Price*, was written during 2008 and launched soon after this interview. He is sensitive to the irony of the clash between his content and the traditional medium of book publishing.

There are many ironies in my life. One of them is having coined the term *long tail* and described the phenomenon, as it has become our worst enemy, because we are the short head. I work for Condé Nast, one of America's biggest magazine publishers, and my book is published by Disney. I'm in the blockbuster business by day, and by night I celebrate the rise of the niche. I'm in a mass, top-down, one-to-many business, which pays my rent. And yet what excites me is just the opposite.

Many people misunderstand the lessons of "The Long Tail," assuming that it's the end of the blockbuster. It is very much not. Instead, it is the end of the monopoly of the blockbuster. The way I think about it from our perch in a skyscraper at 4 Times Square (Condé Nast headquarters) is that we big-media companies, using the traditional definition, owned the twentieth century. We owned the tools of production. You could not compete with our ability to produce and distribute content. Our factories are indeed factories. They are three blocks long. They are printing plants; they are massive. Our distribution channels are trucks. Our retail space is newsstand space, which you cannot get access to—but we can. We were unbeatable. And so too for television and radio.

All those supply-chain advantages have disappeared in the online version of our world, where everybody has exactly the same access to the consumer as we do and the same tools of production. And as a result our tradition of competing—big companies competing with other big companies—is now big companies competing with a zillion amateurs. They can't do

Free by Chris Anderson
photo by Nicolas Zurcher

what we do. They can't do mass-market glossy publications on newsstands everywhere. But what they can do is what we can't do, which is to focus with laser precision on narrow topics for niche audiences who care more about their niche than anything we do in our publications. So this army of ants is a real challenge and, to move from my last book to my next book, they're doing it all for *free*.

Chris has walked his talk, making the book *Free* freely available in its digital form. He uses free as a form of marketing, believing that it is the best tool to sell something that is not free, even if only 1 percent of the people buy the superior, physical form. Access to the free version will only extend the reach of the physical book and increase sales. He believes in books—meaning paper books, with covers, that you put on your shelf. He thinks books are here to stay and will be with us for his entire life, but he does not believe that physical books are the only way to consume the written word. There are many digital forms of books: the audio book, listened to in a car while you're driving; eBooks, for example the Kindle from Amazon, Que from Plastic Logic, or the Sony Reader; or Google Book Search, with everything scanned, accessible from any of the screens that we use. The digital forms offer advantages in terms of use and price, but the superior form remains the traditional book—it is immersive, easy to read and carry, offers high-resolution images and an excellent contrast ratio. A paper book is a delight to look at and browse through, but the free digital forms are a really good way to introduce ideas to the broadest possible audience, so they can make an impact and spur a desire among some people to read the superior paper version.

Those who want more, those who value the attributes of the traditional book, can upgrade to the premium of the "freemium" equation and pay $24.95 for the superior form. I think that's a small percent of a big number and a good model for books. I wish books were more designed. In the magazine industry, the reason why *Wired* magazine exists as a magazine is because we are a visual medium. If we were just 8,000 words of text, laid out in columns, I don't think we'd be in business. I wish books were more of a visual medium. I think that would preserve the book's specialness in the future.

Now comes the twenty-first century and we've got a new form of "free," based around digital economics. The difference between the economy of atoms, which was the twentieth century and before, and the economy of bits, which is the twenty-first century and beyond, is that the marginal cost of bits is zero. It doesn't cost anything to send those bits out to one more person—or so close to nothing you might as well round down. If the actual cost for a product is zero, then the price can really be zero; it doesn't have to be a trick. Now you have the ability to have what we call "real free," which is to say, get your products and services out there to as many people as possible. Let 95 percent of them take it for free, but find some way to offer a paid for version to the 5 percent who really want it and get the value.

This is the inversion of the old "free sample" model. If you're selling muffins, maybe you'll give away 1 percent of your muffins and sell 99 percent. In the digital world it's just the opposite: you give away 99 percent to sell 1 percent. And now free doesn't just become a marketing trick. It becomes the best way to introduce your product to the maximum number of people—not in a marketing form, but in an actual sample form, so that they can self-identify as the customers who really want it.

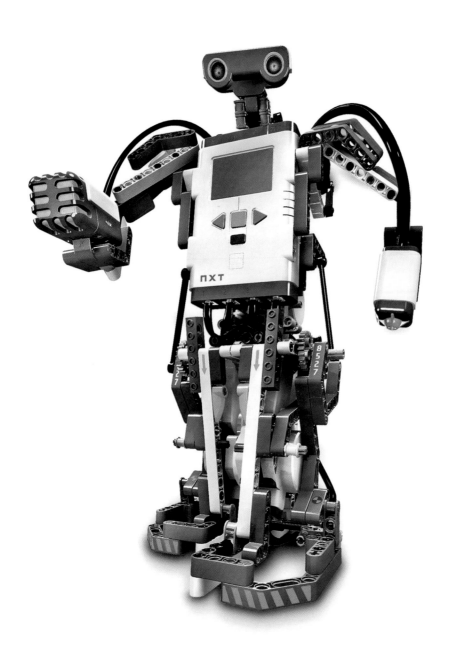

VOTES

Many people think of Wikipedia as democratic compared with
Encyclopædia Britannica, but Chris thinks that is misleading: the
significant difference is between credentialed and uncredentialed.
You can look up the credentials of the editors and experts who
contributed to Encyclopædia Britannica, but you can't do that
for Wikipedia. In the past, if you wanted to make television, you
needed to be in the television industry to have access to the channels
of distribution. Now anyone who buys a video camera and some
software for their laptop can make television. You browse YouTube
and discover millions of anonymous video makers, whose efforts are
structured by millions of popularity contests. Those of us who grew
up in the twentieth century make an instinctive assumption that
there is one popularity contest—one top forty, one prime time—
the new reality is that there are millions.

The videos that Chris watches are never going to make the front page
of YouTube, because he is passionate about Lego robotics videos, a
narrow niche, but still one that has enough material to need a hierarchy
of votes to bring the most popular ones to the top. People care in two
dimensions. They want to find material that has been filtered to satisfy
their own niche interests, but they are also interested in the hits that
have universal appeal, even if they tend to deliver content that is only
superficially entertaining.

All the successes of Web-based interactive media rely on counting votes.
Traditional media had no good way to measure the back channel, to say,
"Here's what we're doing. What do you think?" Instruments like Nielsen
ratings, polls, and surveys are really coarse, yielding little information
about what people actually think. Interactive media make it really easy
for people to express what they think, both in terms of what they say
and what they do, which produces data that is easy to act on with a
greater level of confidence in the results. Producers of content can stop
guessing now; they can just measure.

Chris makes connections between many different kinds of emerging
media companies based on the fact that they rely on votes:

←---- Lego NXT robotics
image courtesy of Lego

Google is an algorithm, yes, but it's an algorithm that's measuring human votes. That's what a link is: a link is a vote. Is there really a big difference between a Digg vote, a link vote, and a Wikipedia revert? I mean, they're all really votes. What their computers are doing is reading our collective opinions and then structuring the content around this latent information that was there all along, just not measurable. I think they all fall into the same category. They are markets of opinion, and we can measure those because they are substantiated in digital acts, and we use algorithms to parse them, rank them, and otherwise chop and channel them—to structure information in a way that's meaningful.

Google competes with media companies not just for advertising but also for attention. Google doesn't create content—it organizes other people's content. The reality is that we're competing for attention. We're all competing for attention. Google is competing for attention in a different way than we're competing for attention. We're all competing for reputation, as well, and by reputation I don't just mean page rank and incoming links, but brand, Q ratings, celebrity, all these kinds of things. The meaningful metrics are reputation and attention. Media have probably always implicitly had reputation and attention built in.

People care about reputation and attention, but they also care more about connecting to one another socially than they do about connecting to hierarchical structures or abstracted organizations. Social media are emerging as the fastest growing segment on the Web, as one-to-one communication is more important in people's daily lives than any other form of communication. Voting is useful in helping people find one another and compare notes about their common interests, but they can bypass the votes when they are communicating directly. The big change is not about the desire to connect socially—that is here to stay. Rather, it's the *scale* of connectivity that is changing, increasing drastically as technology enables it. The natural tribal size used to be around 120 people, but that number is much larger now and growing all the time:

We've gone from a small number of tight relationships to a large number of loose relationships. We're seeing a generational change. We're actually rewiring our species on some level. My capacity to multitask is less than my children's, and it doesn't just reflect their age. We are training a generation to consume information in a massively parallel way, and they are going to retain those skills forevermore. I think likewise, we're training a generation to build their social network differently than we did. Their ability to maintain many loose connections is something technology is only just now allowing.

I'm not really interested in the companies, and I'm not interested in the technologies. I'm interested in the collective experiment and figuring out how it is we want to engage with each other online. That's the social part, and we do it using whatever technology happens to be available at the moment—and those change over time. What people do on Facebook is interesting, but I don't think Facebook the company is as interesting. Not that I think anything bad about the company—I just think that ten years from now we'll be doing something else. MySpace, likewise. As yet, we have not figured out what the optimal form of this communication is, as we dash from Twitter, to FriendFeed, to whatever. They're just experiments in trying new things and seeing what sticks.

NEIL STEVENSON LAUNCHED A PERSONAL experiment in engaging with other people online. He started an anonymous weekly newsletter and Web site to publish scuttlebutt about the lives of celebrities, a venture that has stayed alive based on user-generated content. In the next interview he tells this story and also analyzes the consumption of various media. He contrasts "sitting back" to enjoy traditional media with "leaning forward" to engage with interactive content online. He describes some design rules for magazines and chronicles the emergence of reality television.

NEIL STEVENSON

Interviewed March 28, 2008

NEIL STEVENSON

After studying psychology and social anthropology at Oxford University, Neil gratified his passion for dance music and club culture by writing about DJs. Soon he became editor of the dance music magazine *Mixmag*. From there, he moved into more mainstream titles, helping to launch the weekly celebrity magazine *Heat,* and became editor in chief of the style magazine *The Face*. He became frustrated by the controls on publication of some of the most interesting stories, so he founded an underground email newsletter and Web site called Popbitch to distribute stories about celebrities that were contributed by amateur volunteers. In 2005 he joined IDEO and now leads the Kid+Play domain, a group focused on two distinct but overlapping content areas: children and play. His play projects include creating games for the Wii and the iPhone and developing ideas about how lessons learned from designing play can be applied to adult creativity and used to help companies become more innovative.

←···· **Neil Steveson**
photos by author

Neil brought a breath of fresh energy to IDEO when he joined us in 2005. He immediately delved into our history and discovered the backstory of our culture, assembling an amusing presentation about the history of the people behind the ideas that inform our process of human-centered design, rapid prototyping, brainstorming, and so on. I asked him for an interview as an early prototype in my own process of collecting material for this book, but I found his story so interesting that I ended up including it in the final material, recording it a second time for better quality, set in the San Francisco location of IDEO.

MULTIPLE MEDIA

Media are like the big bang, in that the number of choices on offer seems to expand continuously and rapidly. The number of television channels is now counted in hundreds instead of single digits, never mind the quality of the content, and you can watch an infinite number of videos online, again of mixed merit. We've gone from having newspapers of a few pages to a few inches of paper thickness. There are more books and magazines being published today than ever before, despite the arrival of email, mobile phones, and the Internet. The old media are here to stay, but there has been an absolute explosion of choice in both old and new.

When the publishers of magazines came to realize that they could benefit from distribution online as well as in print, they hoped at first that there would be nothing but synergies between analog and digital. They had content that they could send down different pipelines—the print pipe, the Internet pipe, the mobile phone pipe—and they thought that the more pipes they sent it down, the more value they would gain. They were wrong. This dangerously simplistic view didn't take into account how people consumed each medium and what mode they were in. The art of creating content that is tuned for consumption in each medium tends to separate the versions, so that the material prepared for a glossy magazine—rich with images and elegant typography—will not fit well on a pixilated screen of limited size, be it a personal computer or a PDA. Neil contrasts "sitting back" with "leaning forward" in this fashion:

The Pleasure of Magazines
photo by Getty/Thomas Northcut

> A lot of the pleasure of magazines is like taking a warm bath. You sit back, you open this beautiful thing, and you flip through it and luxuriate in all this color and energy. For a lot of titles, like *Vogue*, the differentiation between the editorial and the advertising doesn't register because you're getting these

beautiful images. It's just generally inspiring. Now, that's very different from being on the computer and wanting to go to a specific Web site. You have a specific goal in mind. You want to find out about something. You're "leaning forward" and accessing something. You're not going to lean forward and say that you want to look at a Prada advert. That's just not how you behave. I don't believe that you have the sense of time and broadmindedness to wallow in a picture when you're on a computer in that lean-forward mode. You tend to be after a piece of information.

All attempts to send the same content down these different pipes are utterly doomed. The magazines that have done well have optimized their content over a long period of time to deliver exactly the right magazine experience, which means that it is exactly wrong for these other media.

If you put people in a focus group and ask them, "Would you like more choice?" the answer is always an enthusiastic "Yes!" but it doesn't necessarily make them any happier. The explosion of choice in media has led to some odd behaviors. With TV shows, a lot of attention is paid to the name of the show, because it has to attract the viewer who is browsing an electronic programming guide with a sentence that is short enough to fit in the box on the screen and is succinctly descriptive. Hence we get, *When Good Pets Go Bad* and *The World's Funniest Animals.* The name needs to explain exactly what it is, leading to the death of nuance or ambiguity. The fear that people will leave also drives the design of material that is immediately obvious and gratifying but tries not to let people escape. You don't want to annoy people— otherwise they'll change channels, given the number of options just a few seconds away. You therefore try to avoid giving offense. In order to succeed in this global, over-choiced media world, you find yourself designing things that everybody will kind of like and nobody will dislike with any passion. The common denominator of design expression sinks ever lower.

DESIGN RULES FOR MAGAZINES

The editors who put together the golden age of British magazines, with winners such as *Smash Hits*, *Q*, *Empire*, *The Face*, and *FHM*, developed rules of thumb for design decisions based on their ability to capture the emotional drivers toward purchase. They had built up a body of knowledge by prototyping and repeated testing. Every month they put out a magazine and the sales figures would give them feedback about the level of success, so they would argue with one another about which elements were influential and arrive at a consensus about what had worked and what hadn't, leading to rules of thumb. Neil loved to engage with all these very fuzzy emotional attributes that attracted people.

Always have eye contact on the cover, because going into a newsagent is like walking into a cocktail party—you want to make eye contact with someone, and they need to be someone you are intrigued by. That's the person you'll go over and have a conversation with, and the conversation will be reading the headlines on the cover.

We'd get in these conversations about why Catherine Zeta-Jones would sell bucket-loads of women's magazines, whereas Cameron Diaz would not sell very well at all. Catherine Zeta-Jones, Cameron Diaz, both beautiful, successful actresses, both equally famous—why should one sell and not the other? And they would say that for the women's market, the magazine worked as a kind of idealized mirror: the readers would look at the cover, and it was as if the person on the cover was them on the best possible day with a nice light and everything working out well. They could be Catherine Zeta-Jones, whereas Cameron Diaz was just too hot, too blond, too perfect—that would never be them.

Catherine Zeta-Jones and Cameron Diaz
photos by Nicolas Zurcher

Some of the rules were quite distressing. The sad fact in Britain was that, even in this very racially tolerant society, with a lot of black people being aspirational celebrity figures for youth culture, if you put a black person on a magazine cover, it wouldn't sell as well. The way the editors talked about it was not in terms of absolute theories, nor psychological explanations as to why Naomi Campbell wouldn't sell. It was like "spook magic." This is the myth. Occasionally someone would come along and have a success despite breaking some of those rules.

The original purpose of those magazines was to deliver the secrets of the cosmopolitan elite to people living in provincial towns and to let the people living in the cities have listings of what DJs were playing at what clubs. Both of those values started to erode as the Internet became popular, as the secrets about a Finnish techno record or obscure Adidas trainer became available in greater detail at a specialist Web site— and every club had a Web site with listings and links to the DJs' Web sites. The magazines that had started as the hip voice of the streets had also been subverted by commerce, as they had attracted the attention of Italian, French, and American fashion labels wanting to buy into this edgy culture. A Faustian bargain had emerged: the magazines had taken their money, but now the owners of the labels needed to have plenty of photographs of expensive fashion, even though they also wanted the authentic voice of British street culture. Neil thinks that the magazines were caught in an untenable position.

In British culture, and possibly in American as well, there had been through the nineties an almost a binary culture. In the mainstream, people went to normal shops and bought normal clothes and records and listened to what was on the radio. Then there was "the underground." Even though the underground segmented into these broad tribes—of Goths, ravers, punks, and so forth—there was still coherence to it. You were either mainstream or underground, or alternative, if you like. If you were alternative, you would buy a magazine like *The Face*. If you were mainstream, you'd buy mass-market newspapers.

When the Internet arrived, it splintered the underground into an almost infinite number of tiny cells of passionate interest. If you were into weird Argentinean dub techno that sounded like someone had dropped a computer down a flight of stairs, there would be a Web site for you and a whole community of people you could connect with across multiple geographies. There was not longer a coherent underground but a mass of tiny, little undergrounds.

Culturally curious people no longer defined their set of tastes by being underground. Instead, something more like a mosaic was happening, where an individual would say, "I am into this particular form of arty music, this particular form of under-ground cinema, but I also like Justin Timberlake and Kylie Minogue, and I actually really like that blockbuster movie, and I will assemble myself a unique mosaic of both niche, obscure things and mainstream things." By having that mosaic, they asserted individuality and transcended the marketing men who attempted to put them in a box.

The Spice Girls
photo by AP Images

REALITY TV

In 1990s Britain there was a broad aspiration in society to become famous, causing people to identify with celebrities who seemed ordinary. The Spice Girls embodied that. They were a group of "girls next door" who had become famous. That's what was so attractive about them. The creators of media were suddenly made aware of the value of letting people identify themselves with the stars, and they developed a new type of celebrity journalism to attract those with aspirations to become famous themselves. This trend culminated with reality TV. Neil points out that there was some idealism driving this movement as well, as many people working in television thought that there was a moral good in appealing to a broader audience—a freshly democratic media:

Television in the past had been dominated by people educated at the best universities, who attempted to foist their own points of view on people with uplifting television shows that were actually arrogant forms of paternalism. Instead, all of these clever people started to make shows like *Big Brother*, creating reality TV. They devoted a lot of intellectual energy to creating the formats and told themselves that what they were doing was morally good because it was democratic. They were allegedly reflecting the will of the people.

Some think that is a delusion and that what really happened is that big business won, that all these clever people making reality shows actually were just serving the needs of big business, and that television has lost its diversity and lost what made it uplifting and interesting to people. You could certainly see really clever people making a lot of really trashy TV. Britain has become the source of almost all the reality TV formats that have become big around the world. Whether it be *Wife Swap* or *Pop Idol* (*American Idol* in the United States) or *Big Brother*, they all came out of Britain. It's kind of scary!

The change is toward format innovation rather than content innovation. For a drama, you have a well-known three-act structure, with some room for variation, but it's an accepted format so that people can exercise their creativity within it. For reality TV, you don't have to describe the content, you just have to say, "This is a format where a hundred women compete to be chosen to marry one guy." You can describe it on the back of a napkin in a trendy media bistro in Soho after a couple of glasses of wine and a line of cocaine, and your job's done. You can sell the format, someone else makes the show, and you can sell the overseas rights, so it works well with the globalization of TV media.

USER-GENERATED CONTENT

As Neil was working with magazines in London in the late 1990s, he gradually became more frustrated with the limitations imposed by the public relations agents of celebrities, finding that time and time again he would have access to wonderful stories but not be allowed to print them. His writing career had started with fanzines, in which you just wrote what you cared about, but now he was being controlled. As a cathartic response to these restrictions, he and his girlfriend, Camilla Wright, decided to start an anonymous weekly email and Web site called Popbitch, containing all the stories that they weren't allowed to print. They sent it to people in the music industry, with an option to sign up, and it soon became remarkably successful, with a thousand subscribers after six months of operation growing to six hundred thousand in three years.

What we got was an early experience of user-generated content. Stories started coming in from receptionists who worked at record labels, hairdressers, makeup people, and so on. My initial set of stories was quickly exhausted, but new ones came in. The email and Web site caught the imagination of people in the industry and sustained itself. Eventually there were enough new stories coming in that I couldn't handle the volume, so with the help of a volunteer, I built a primitive message board on the Web site, and suddenly people could have conversations with each other. Certain people were very active on the board, so I made them into editors and added software where they could flag any interesting stuff. At the end of each week, we could harvest all the best stories and that made the email.

I was working at the time for a magazine that spent £10 million a year to produce itself, with a staff of fifty working away feverishly. In the evenings I'd go home, and me and my girlfriend would collect a few emails off the Web site. In terms of the hard celebrity news we published and the reaction it got, the £50-a-month Web site was outperforming the £10-million-a-year magazine, because there were enough people scattered around the country sending fresh stuff in for free. The distributed network of idealistic amateurs was defeating the room full of professional journalists. It was a very exciting period.

The design was aggressively all text. The Web site itself, even the logo, was done with ASCII art. It was deliberately done to be as gritty and as cheap-looking as possible. With celebrity journalism in Britain, if you are in possession of a saucy story about the Spice Girls, you can go to a tabloid newspaper and sell it and make a significant amount of money. For this Web site to get people to give stuff for free, it was very important we made it clear we were an amateur operation. We deliberately designed it to look like a bedroom operation that was being done for love, not money.

We got famously sued by several of the Spice Girls, David Beckham, and people like that. It became quite notorious for a while after we were outed in the *Daily Mirror*. The legal challenges would evaporate once the lawyers saw a list of assets, consisting of a few unsold T-shirts and an old laptop.

This version of user-generated content has something in common with Wikipedia. If you want people to donate their own time to writing, editing, and overseeing something in this way, it won't work if you are coining it. If you're a big-media brand, people will feel like they are slaving away for you and your shareholders. Neil compares Wikipedia to Popbitch:

Wikipedia doesn't make money. It doesn't carry advertising. It survives through donations, and I believe that is not a coincidence. I think if Wikipedia was owned

```
POPBITCH         _    _ _
 _ _  __  _ _ | |_ (_) |_ __| |_
| ._\ / _\| ._\| ._\|  _/ _| ._\
| |_) | (_) | |_) | |_) | | || (_| | | |
| ._/ \__/| ._/|_._/|_|\_\__|_| |_|
|_|         |_|    16.06.09 ISSUE 457
Free every week: to subscribe/unsubscribe
go to http://www.popbitch.com
To send us stories Email: hello@popbitch.com

* When Lady GaGa met Lady BaBa
* 90s Retrospective: Popbitch goes back in time
* Charts: JLS are the new number one
_____

        >>  GaGa v BaBa  <<
        Lady G takes on Take That and loses

It was reported that the reason Lady GaGa cancelled
two Take That shows was due to illness. There
might have been a little more to it. Her crew
turned up with two lorries full of new lighting
equipment expecting to waltz in and set up a
whole new show. At Take That's carefully planned
stadium extravaganza. While GaGa obviously
cleverly controls everything she does, Gary
Barlow is known for his perfectionism when it
comes to The Thats shows. Lady Gaga v Lady BaBa?
There could only be one winner. Two shows were pulled
until the support act finally accepted reality,
and she recovered from her illness of course,
and then went on with the tour with reduced show.

_____

Today is the 50th anniversary of the moon landing.
Buzz Aldrin's mother's maiden name was Moon.
_____

        >> Big Questions <<
        What people are asking this week

Photos of which current celeb-magazine
hate-figure are circulating showing her on
a night out, with the spunk of a reality show
contestant over her clothes?

Another sometime tabloid hate-figure
was seen at a Reverend & The Makers gig
openly taking lines of cocaine at the bar
with his friends. At least he wasn't
the one jacking-off on the star above.

_____

According to his God-daughter, Michael Jackson's
favourite meal was fish and chips.
```

Popbitch screenshot

by Time Warner and had loads of ads round it, those people would go away, because otherwise they would feel cheated. If you're working for nothing and someone else is making money, it won't work.

That's the problem with these user-generated content models. If you're trying to collectively build something together, then the owner can't get rich off of it. It's a bit different with YouTube, as that's just a venue. It's just a bucket in which people can throw their stuff. But for Wikipedia, where there is a collective body of knowledge with its own voice, you can't expect everyone to jump aboard and do the work unless you are prepared to do the whole thing pro bono.

I experienced this with Popbitch. People will do remarkable amounts just for kudos, for a form of celebrity. For example, with Wikipedia, "I have written the entry on Napoleon Bonaparte, and it's mine, and I feel good. Within the Wikipedia community, it's recognized as a good piece of work." With Popbitch I had a bunch of people who were editors, not paid, but they had a high status. They could approve other people's messages, so if some bitter makeup artist from Los Angeles posted an interesting story about Christina Aguilera's terrible behavior, one of these editors would flag that as interesting. That person would receive points, and if they posted repeatedly interesting stories, those points would express themselves in tiny little icons that appeared next to their name. Within the community, they conferred status, and that was enough to keep people motivated. They were essentially getting badges for how knowledgeable or how insidery they were. Those things had social value within the community.

PAUL MILLER, AKA DJ SPOOKY: THAT SUBLIMINAL KID, operates fluently in multiple media, as music composer and producer, DJ, artist, writer, and impresario. In the final interview of this chapter, he talks about the new order of creative commons and shareware, which, he argues, is here to stay.

PAUL D. MILLER, AKA DJ SPOOKY

Interviewed October 21, 2009

PAUL D. MILLER, AKA DJ SPOOKY

Paul is a composer, multimedia artist, and writer who travels extensively to perform and give presentations. His writing has appeared in *The Village Voice*, *The Source*, *Artforum*, and *The Wire*, among other publications. His art has been shown in the Whitney Biennial; the Venice Biennale of Architecture; the Museum Ludwig in Cologne, Germany; Kunsthalle Wien (Vienna) in Austria; The Andy Warhol Museum in Pittsburgh, Pennsylvania, and many other museums and galleries. His work *New York Is Now* was exhibited in the African Pavilion at the 52nd Venice Biennale and at the 2007 Art Basel Miami Beach Fair. The MIT Press published *Rhythm Science*, his first collection of essays, in 2004, and *Sound Unbound*, an anthology of writings on electronic music and digital media, in 2008. Paul's deep interest in reggae and dub music has resulted in a series of compilations, remixes, and collections of material from the vaults of the legendary Jamaican label Trojan Records. The DJ Spooky/DJ Mixer iPhone app has been downloaded more than 1 million times.

I met DJ Spooky at the Indaba conference in Cape Town, South Africa, where we were both presenting. At that time I thought of him as a DJ but discovered from browsing his Web site that he has a fluent command of media, with music, video, speech, social media, and online representation all contributing to the communication of his ideas. I immediately wanted to interview him for *Designing Media* but found it difficult to get in touch. Eventually I made contact through the people who manage his engagements and found out that he lives very close to the IDEO offices in New York. The next time I was in New York, we set up an interview in the IDEO studio.

Paul Miller may seem a less interesting name than DJ Spooky: That Subliminal Kid, but he makes up for it with his erudite conversation, informed by his background in philosophy and French literature and his experience in art and music. He speaks fluidly on many topics, constantly branching off in new directions of thought. Here, I've presented his interview as long quotations to reflect his style.

CREATIVE COMMONS
ARE HERE TO STAY

With sound, I'm trying to open up the artist, like an open architecture operating system, and try and figure out ways to have people participate, but I just then guide the process. I'm the helmsman. I'm trying to figure out how do you walk on this liminal threshold, the razor's edge of creativity and individuality.

I do not feel emotionally connected to music once it's out of my brain. I think, "You know what, it's a file. Anyone can take that file and cut it, splice it, dice it, do whatever they want to it." Let's look at it as biomimesis, like mirroring, camouflage, and the idea of the mimetic function. There's a really good book [by Michael Taussig] called *Mimesis and Alterity* [Routledge, 1993] that I always chuckle over. It's like saying, if anybody can be a mirror of anybody, you have a hall of mirrors, with two reflective surfaces facing one another, but there is no there, there. That's what is going on now with the creative process and art online. Everyone is mirroring everything. And the problem is, where do we find the unique and human moment out of that? Like, you know, the sublime: the experiences of centuries' worth of art. In fact, you don't. It's the death of the sublime.

The shareware model assigns value to this idea that the artist is an open system font almost, like you're a font that just lets people take that font and use it to modify their own material. "Datacloud aesthetics"—that's a better nickname for it. Things where you have access to it all the time, like water in an urban economy. If you think about electricity and water, those are public goods, part of the commons. But, if you want "good" water, you're going to pay a certain amount of money for it. You'll pay extra for bottled water, but if you want part of the commons you're just going to turn on the tap, and that's it.

⟵ Good Water
photo by Nicolas Zurcher

Two of DJ Spooky's albums
photo by Nicolas Zurcher

The easiest thing to do is just rip it, mix it, burn it, and that's it: no one gets paid. You just do it for free, and you give it to your friends for free in an "informal economy." When I was in Beijing, I went by a couple of markets. They had bootlegs of everything from Chairman Mao's "[Little] Red Book" to the latest Madonna remix album.

People need to realize they are the creative person. Just because somebody buys a Shep Fairey "Obama Hope" poster or downloads one of my mixes doesn't make them me. It's like I'm a mask, or I am a font. And as soon as that idea, song, or image that I've come up with leaves my biological frame here, my skull, I have to say, "Whew, let's take a deep breath. People are going to run with it and do whatever they want." Now there's people out there in the world that will burst into flames over that idea because of the whole legal mechanism of centuries of copyright control, has just gone into entropy. But, you know, to be completely honest, that entropy is where the most creative stuff is going. I don't see it as something you can control.

I don't see it as something you can legislate in Congress. I don't see it as something that anybody out there in their right mind says that they can lock down. In fact, the illusiveness of it is what makes it interesting.

FROM VINYL TO DIGITAL

Paul's main interest is in layering multiple media in the dematerialized virtual world, but he is best known as a DJ. He is fascinated by the richness and emotional power of sound and music, our responses to acoustic environments from all kinds of sources, from cell phone rings and melodies to rhythmic relationships or motifs. These qualities are here to stay, even if the media of delivery are constantly changing. Everyone is wearing earbuds now, allowing them to always have their music with them. Paul contrasts this to previous media.

The interiority of the iPod and equivalent music players has really transformed the way that people listen. The iPod is less than a decade old, but it's changed everything in terms of people's consuming of music.

Let's look at the idea of the phonograph. If you're thinking about the idea of sound and interface, that's probably the most popularized image of how people think of recorded information. After a century of people living with what I like to call "the culture of the copy," you almost take access to music for granted. If everyone has the same records and access to the same memories of the records that are in vogue, then that's a social sculpture in its own right. It's people sharing and exchanging recorded memories—we could call it "the social life of information."

To me, records aren't dead media. What gives them a sense of social vitality is the exchange process and regeneration process. The notion of just pressing "play" on a phonograph, which happened for most of the twentieth century, has been flipped on its head by the playlist, allowing the consumer to participate in the process of distribution in a way that was never possible before. Nowadays everyone is their own radio station. We have our own specific data set of songs to relate to. There are list servers, Web sites, collating software, and collaborative filtering to help us choose: if you like this song, you'll like that.

The DJ operates somewhere between selection and analysis of song and decoding things that people will relate to. If I'm at a party, I play a sequence of songs that I've sampled, edited, collaged, and spliced. The interface between the phonograph and the digital media file is this kind of selection process, with the vinyl record here to stay as a form of interface.

Vinyl will outlast the CD because it's got more value, both as an interface for the DJ to control speed and transitions, and allow sampling and scratching, but also as a collector's item. The CD is just a vessel for data, so if you can have the same files on a digital device that you would have on a CD, why do you want the CD at all?

When you think about an album, it's usually meant as a coherent full-length sequence, but if you go back to the beginning of the record industry in the 1920s, you had a 78 vinyl with only enough room for a single. Now, with digital media, we're going back to the single as we have the option to purchase one song at a time online.

So, what makes a song? Motif, a melody, a genomic function of rhythm's relationship to the bass line, the keyboards, all these things are still eerily like old school, but they're all transformative. When I was working on my new album, *The Secret Song*, the pun was that albums are totally, utterly obsolete, so I decided to think about it as a collection of disparate singles that somebody might be coasting through on Pandora.[3] Given our recession and the kind of financial meltdown that happened in 2008, I was also looking at the intersection of politics and economics, and that led me to exotic forms of manipulation of currencies and toxic assets. I was trying to make an album that was about buyers and sellers.

In the twenty-first century, where's the Cold War except in the rearview mirror? We now have an economic tension based on globalization. For example, everything I'm wearing was made in China. The design might have happened in California, but

<--- Vinyl
photo by Nicolas Zurcher

3 See the interview with Tim Westergren, the founder of Pandora Internet Radio, in chapter 2.

that idea, that little zip file, or whatever you want to call it, gets sent to a factory in Guangdong Province or one of the other provinces that make up the factory to the world. I kept wondering how a musician could express that intriguing sense of globalization? If I make a song and send it to China, what would happen? Imagine if you sent it the same way that people send the design for an iPhone, which gets components from Malaysia, engineered in Indonesia, and compiled in Hong Kong, and then shipped to California, where it gets a little stamp saying "Manufactured by Apple."

The title track of *The Secret Song* exemplifies this globalization, with a sweetly feminine voice singing fragments of poetry about financial transactions in Mandarin. Paul also thought of expressing the new dematerialized world of music by throwing a Craigslist party, where everyone on certain lists would get components of the song, or putting an album's components on eBay and having people bid for the elements of the music, like the beats or the bass line.

COMMENTARY

I don't want to interrupt the flow of the stories in the interviews by stopping to discuss the ideas about designing media as they emerge from the narrative. Instead, I have added commentary at the end of each chapter to summarize and reflect on the significance of the ideas. I put the interview with Paul Saffo first because he gives an overview of the changes in media and the challenges faced by the people involved its creation and design.

Paul helps us understand the differences between traditional mass media and new personal media, contrasting characteristic differences. First is the nature of the experience. With mass media, we watch, but with personal media answering back is required, so we need to design the interactions for the participants, implying a tight feedback loop. Then there is the location. Mass media came into our living rooms, but we carry personal media with us everywhere we go, so we design for portability and mobile access. The nature of the dominant players has also changed. Mass media was the world of the few and the large, but the personal media world is dominated by the many and the small.

Saffo's law is a useful design principle to help us understand the personal media world. Ask for a message of not over 140 characters, a search string, or just a click, and you can create successful personal media.

Paul reassures the producers of mainstream media by his statement that old forms of media never die out entirely but get repurposed for new uses, implying that it will be important to work out what those new uses are going to be and how much value they will create. James Truman also expects traditional media to survive in repurposed forms, with luxurious versions of magazines and books standing a much better chance than inexpensive texts, because when people only want information in text form, they can find it for free online. Beautiful designs to enhance the reading experience for printed books and magazines will be more important. That's good news for the designers!

James sees a move from authority to conversation as exemplifying the change from mass to personal, with media becoming more transparent, implying that the participant can see through the medium because the tools of creation are accessible, so people no longer listen to lectures; instead, they make things themselves. Paul describes this as a new "creator economy." The manufacturing economy of a hundred years ago was about making things cheaply and well enough to overcome scarcity. After World War II the manufacturing economy was replaced by the consumer economy, where the central actor was the person who purchased, enabled by the credit card. In a creator economy people make and consume at the same time.

James wonders whether that gives the creators the right to run the whole curriculum, pointing out the need for a balance between democratization and a hierarchy of control. Traditional media offer a chaperoned experience, but new media mix material that is created objectively and subjectively so that it is difficult to tell the difference.

For more than a decade James had the most influential voice in the content of all of the magazines published by Condé Nast, and from his perch he saw the influence of the street converge with the penthouse, with new titles emerging that were eclectic, integrating diversity in adventurous and exploratory ways. Eventually, as the pressures of competition and the Internet increased, they were forced to become vehicles for the needs of advertisers. He noticed cultural differences within the English-speaking world between Britain and the United States, with the former welcoming an abrasive quality that the latter rejects. He believes that teenage girls have an uncanny ability to see what is coming next and recommends tapping their intuitions as a form of design research. He sees more of the young and talented creative designers and innovators focusing on the Web, as the opportunities are more expansive there than they are in print, but he also expects advertising and editorial content to continue to need each other in paper publications.

The clash between new media and traditional media is most obvious in the different financial models, which still have a long way to go before balanced new structures emerge. Companies like Google and YouTube caught the wave early enough to gain dominant market share, leading to easy financial success from advertising revenue. Traditional media companies, particularly newspapers and magazines, face the most difficult challenges because their advertising revenue is eroding and they have large existing overhead costs. James sums it up when he says, "There has to be a new model of advertising that can satisfy advertisers and also keep the well-known brand names afloat."

In his new book *Free*, Chris Anderson helps us understand the complimentary benefits of online material. As the marginal cost of bits is close enough to zero to round down, he sees "free" as a form of marketing to sell something that is not free. In the case of books, those who value traditional book attributes can upgrade to the premium version and pay the price for the superior form. The old idea of free samples is thus inverted: offering free access to everyone attracts the small number who take delight in the premium version and are willing to pay for it.

In 2001 Chris bet on the idea that the bursting of the dot-com bubble was about the stock market rather than the underlying technologies, and he designed *Wired* magazine to become a mainstream publication. He has been proved right, as many of the crash survivors have emerged as dominant new media providers, and *Wired* magazine continues to expand as it explains how technology is changing the world. He believes that the act of journalism, editing, and distribution are here to stay but that the forms that are designed to contain the contents will vary to fit the vehicle. I agree with him that everybody's job in the information world is to add value to the Web, as the "Web is the water we swim in," but that the design of online material should be different from print, bringing amateur energy into the domain and leveraging the interactive elements to vote, dialogue, and aggregate.

Neil Stevenson contrasts the way in which we consume media, either sitting back to luxuriate in the material that is offered, as in a beautifully produced magazine or a movie, or leaning forward to steer or click, as in a Web search or a message dialogue. His description of enjoying the luxury media as you would a warm bath is apt. And designing for those media is very different from designing for active participation—nobody sits back to watch Google.

It is dangerous to assume that the same version of content can be sent down different pipes, like print, Internet, or mobile phone; each pipe needs a design that suits both format and behavior. Neil Stevenson offers some design rules for magazines, illustrating the nature of consensus that evolves as a medium adapts to changing circumstances. He explains the roots of reality TV, wondering whether the motivation for creating the formats was financially driven or motivated by the moral good in democratizing television.

Neil tells the story of his own experiment with living in two parallel media worlds, one as an editor of a lavishly produced magazine and the other as the facilitator of user-generated content on an anonymous weekly email and Web site about the private lives of celebrities. He points out that this kind of user-generated content, like Wikipedia, has to be created without financial rewards for the creators, as people prefer to donate their time to contribute, edit, or oversee the medium when they know that the organizers are also donating their efforts.

Paul Miller, aka DJ Spooky, takes us into the world of music. As a disc jockey, he takes a piece of digital music and cuts, splices, and dices it to avoid the emotional connections of ownership, as music will be shared and repurposed whether or not the originator gives permission.

He feels more emotionally attached to the traditional media, like vinyl records. The repurposing of a medium that seems to be vanishing may keep it alive, but radical redesign will be needed. Scratching on turntables has different performance qualities than ripping digital files, but they both have value and are different from the purpose foreseen by the originators. The skill of designing a musical experience remains securely human, with no likelihood of the DJ being replaced by an algorithm or robot. The DJ is here to stay, continuously mastering the manipulation of new media.

THE FIRST INTERVIEW IN THE NEXT CHAPTER is with Jimmy Wales, the founder of Wikipedia. He explains how he harnessed the energies of a hierarchy of volunteers to manage user-generated content. For reasons similar to Popbitch, he kept the structure of the business a nonprofit foundation.

2 YES WE CAN

Interviews with Jimmy Wales, Craig Newmark, Tim Westergren, Blixa Bargeld with Erin Zhu, Airside, and Roger McNamee

As technology advances, it reverses the characteristics of every situation again and again. The age of automation is going to be the age of "do it yourself."

Marshall McLuhan, 1911–1980, Canadian educator, philosopher, and scholar

← Do It Yourself
photo by Nicolas Zurcher

YES, WE CAN DO IT OURSELVES! The tools for creating media almost always seem to be as close as your personal computer, given the appropriate software and a bit of additional gear. Take this book, for example. I was able to create nearly all of it with just my laptop. I used a word-processing program to write it, a page-layout program to design it, and a photo-editing program to manipulate the images, with the ever-present Internet to help me find content and check facts. Did you look at the DVD? That was created on the same laptop, using a video-editing program, a sound-editing program, and DVD-mastering software. And how about the Web site, Designing-media.com? I built it with some help from a colleague at IDEO, but again with software available on a laptop. The means of reproducing the book and DVD are still traditional (with thanks to the MIT Press) and the distribution is physical (with organizations for manufacturing and distribution that require expensive infrastructure), but the means of creation are available to anyone who has learned to use a computer.

In this chapter we meet people who have developed the yes-we-can attitude in extreme, developing innovations in media that rely on contributions from the crowd. First up is Jimmy Wales, the founder of Wikipedia, who has harnessed voluntary contributions from anyone with sufficient interest and time to create the world's largest encyclopedia. He has evolved a hierarchical structure that benefits from the combination of automation and human judgment; the software is enhanced through the emergence of social rules and norms for interaction, which bring members of the community together to do something enjoyable and productive.

Do It Yourself
photo by Nicolas Zurcher

The second interview is with Craig Newmark, the founder of Craigslist, who is so disarmingly modest that he makes his incredible success seem almost accidental. Newmark has developed a culture of trust between employees, volunteers, and end users. Craigslist thrives due to excellent customer service, moderation for discussion boards, removal of offensive material, placement of ads into the appropriate categories, and policing behavior and ethics.

Next we turn to music. Tim Westergren, the founder of Pandora Internet Radio and the inventor of the Music Genome Project, explains his two goals: (1) to build the world's largest radio station, with hundreds of millions of people listening to broadcasts that are personalized specifically for them; and (2) to build a musician's middle class, so that musicians can find their audience.

From methods of distribution we move to creation of the art form itself with Blixa Bargeld, who has been leading an innovative, Berlin-based industrial rock band for decades. In the interview with Blixa and his wife, Erin Zhu, we discover that a band like his can bypass the traditional music business, developing a self-supporting economic model based on subscriptions from fans and enabled by the Internet.

Alex Maclean, Fred Deakin, and Nat Hunter, of London-based Airside, have developed a fresh approach to designing media, working as animators, movie makers, graphic designers, illustrators, interactive digital media designers, and musicians. They like to develop strategic concepts and solutions, keeping the results engaging and lighthearted.

Roger McNamee is both a musician and a venture capitalist. With inventiveness and abundant business acumen, he has created a unique new combination of media to promote music and musicians. His band Moonalice was formed in 2007 with a yes-we-can attitude to promotion and financial support. In his interview, Roger describes his ingenious use of multiple media to finance the band while allowing free access to the music for those who don't want to pay. Roger feels that accessible tools for creating music are beneficial to everybody, much more fun, and entertaining to use—creating it in his estimation is even better than consuming it.

JIMMY WALES

Interviewed October 14, 2008

JIMMY WALES

Jimmy is an American Internet entrepreneur, best known to the public for his role in the founding of Wikipedia in 2001, now the world's largest encyclopedia. With degrees in finance, Jimmy worked in futures and options until, enamored with the possibilities inherent in the new technologies of the web, he shifted his career to Internet entrepreneurship. Jimmy has created a phenomenon in Web development that aims to facilitate creativity, collaboration, and sharing among users. Indeed, Wikipedia was one of the primary drivers of several related internet trends. And as Wikipedia's public profile grew, Jimmy became a spokesman of the Web 2.0 revolution. He founded and now serves on the board of trustees of the Wikimedia Foundation, the nonprofit charitable organization that operates Wikipedia, as the board-appointed "community founder." In 2004, along with fellow Wikimedia trustee Angela Beesley, he founded Wikia, with the aim of building "the rest of the library." In 2006 *Time* magazine listed Jimmy Wales as one of the world's most influential people.

←⋯ **Jimmy Wales**
photos by author

I was surprised that the first email that I received from Jimmy Wales was signed "Jimbo," which struck me as an intimate name that might be reserved for family members and longtime friends, but it turned out to be his online nickname. I had been trying to set up an interview with him for some time, corresponding with the people who managed his overfull schedule, and I expected a more business-oriented manner. I arranged for him to come to IDEO San Francisco for the interview, but during the afternoon before the appointment I received this terse unsigned message directly from him, "I need to be at the Wikia office … I'm under extreme time pressure." When we had set up the video-recording gear the following morning, we waited for some time while Jimmy talked energetically to people in the open offices of Wikia. The dichotomy between this intensity and informal familiarity continued, as once he was seated in front of the cameras, he talked in a gentle and friendly manner about his philosophy, seeming to have all the time in the world, until an hour later, when he looked at his watch and rushed off to another appointment.

WIKIPEDIA

English
The Free Encyclopedia
3 017 000+ articles

日本語
フリー百科事典
612 000+ 記事

Deutsch
Die freie Enzyklopädie
948 000+ Artikel

Español
La enciclopedia libre
507 000+ artículos

Français
L'encyclopédie libre
844 000+ articles

Polski
Wolna encyklopedia
630 000+ haseł

Italiano
L'enciclopedia libera
600 000+ voci

Русский
Свободная энциклопедия
426 000+ статей

Português
A enciclopédia livre
504 000+ artigos

Nederlands
De vrije encyclopedie
555 000+ artikelen

search · suchen · rechercher · szukaj · 検索 · ricerca · zoeken · buscar · busca · поиск · sök · 搜索 ·
søk · haku · cerca · пошук · keresés · hledání · ara · căutare · suk · serču · søg · 검색 · hľadať · cari ·
بحث

| | English ⇕ | → |

---

100 000+

العربية · Català · Česky · Dansk · Deutsch · English · Español · Esperanto · Français · Bahasa Indonesia · Italiano · Magyar · Nederlands · 日本語 · 한국어 · Norsk (bokmål) · Polski · Português · Русский · Română · Slovenčina · Suomi · Svenska · Türkçe · Українська · Volapük · 中文

10 000+

Afrikaans · Aragonés · Asturianu · Kreyòl Ayisyen · Azərbaycan / آذربایجان دیلی · 閩南語 · Беларуская (Акадэмічная ·Тарашкевіца) · भोजपुरी · Bosanski · Brezhoneg · Български · Чӑваш · Cymraeg · Eesti · Ελληνικά · Euskara · فارسی · Frysk · Galego · हिन्दी · Hrvatski · Ido · Íslenska · עברית · Basa Jawa · ქართული · Kurdî / کوردی · Latina · Latviešu · Lëtzebuergesch · Lietuvių · Македонски · മലയാളം · मराठी · Bahasa Melayu · नेपाल भाषा · Norsk (nynorsk) · Nnapulitano · Occitan · Piemontèis · Plattdüütsch · Ripoarisch · Runa Simi · Shqip · Sicilianu · Simple English · Sinugboanon · Slovenščina · Српски · Srpskohrvatski / Српскохрватски · Basa Sunda · Kiswahili · Tagalog · தமிழ் · తెలుగు · ไทย · اردو · Tiếng Việt · Walon · Winaray · 粵語 · Žemaitėška

1 000+

Alemannisch · অসমীয়া · Armãneashce · Arpitan · Avañe'ẽ · Bân-lâm-gú · Basa Banyumasan · भोजपुरी · Bikol Central · Boarisch · Corsu · Deitsch · ދިވެހިބަސް · Eald Englisc · Эрзянь · Fiji Hindi · Føroyskt · Furlan · Gaeilge · Gaelg · Gàidhlig · 贛語 · ગુજરાતી · עברית · 文言 · Hak-kâ-fa / 客家話 · ʻŌlelo Hawaiʻi · Հայերեն · Hornjoserbsce · Ilokano · Interlingua · Interlingue · Ирон Æвзаг · ಕನ್ನಡ · Kapampangan · Kaszëbsczi · Kernewek · ភាសាខ្មែរ · Коми · Ladino / לאדינו · Ligure · Limburgs · Lingála · lojban · Lumbaart · Malagasy · Malti · Māori · മലയാളം · مصرى · مازرونی · Māzeruni · Монгол · မြန်မာဘာသာ · Nāhuatlahtōlli · Nedersaksisch · नेपाली · Nouormand · Novial · O'zbek · ਪੰਜਾਬੀ · Pangasinán · پښتو · ਪੰਜਾਬੀ / Панjабी · Қазақша · Rumantsch · संस्कृतम् · Sámegiella · Sardu · Саха Тыла · Scots · Seeltersk · شاه مکھی پنجابی · සිංහල · Šlůnski · Tarandíne · татарча / Tatarça · Тоҷикӣ · Lea faka-Tonga · Türkmen · Uyghur / ئۇيغۇرچە · Vèneto · Võro · West-Vlams · Wolof · 吴语 · ייִדיש · Yorùbá · Zazaki

100+

Bahsa Acèh · Aŋɔya · অসমীয়া · Авар · Aymara · Bamanankan · Башҡорт · Bislama · ཚ་ལོ་ང་ · Chamoru · Chavacano de Zamboanga · Cuengh · Diné Bizaad · Dolnoserbski · Emigliàn-Rumagnòl · Estremeñu · Evegbe · ᏣᎳᎩ · Хальмг · Hausa · هَوُسَ · Igbo · ᐃᓄᒃᑎᑐᑦ · Inuktitut · Kalaallisut · कश्मीरी / کٲشُر · Kongo · Кыргызча · ລາວ · Ming-dĕng-ngṳ̄ · Mirandés · Мокшень · Молдовеняскэ · Dorerin Naoero · Nᴈhiyawᴇwin / ᓀᐦᐃᔭᐍᐏᐣ · Norfuk / Pitkern · Нохчийн · Олык Марий · ଓଡ଼ିଆ · Afaan Oromoo · ਪੰਜਾਬੀ · Papiamentu · Ποντιακά · Qaraqalpaqsha · Qırımtatarca · ᱥᱟᱱᱛᱟᱲᱤ · Romani / रोमानी · Gagana Sāmoa · Setswana · سنڌي · Словѣ́ньскъ · ᏣᎳᎩᎢ · Af Soomaali · SiSwati · Sranantongo · Reo Tahiti · Taqbaylit · Tetun · ትግርኛ · Tok Pisin · ᏣᎳᎩ · ꆈꌠꁱꂷ · Xitsonga · Удмурт · Tshivenda · isiXhosa · Zeêuws · isiZulu

Other languages · Weitere Sprachen · Autres langues · Kompletna lista języków · 他の言語 · Otros idiomas · 其他语言 · Другие языки · Aliaj lingvoj · 다른 언어 · Ngôn ngữ khác

---

📖 **Wiktionary**

 Wikinews

🔊 **Wikiquote**

📚 **Wikibooks**

 Wikispecies

Ⓦ **Wikisource**

🏛 **Wikiversity**

 Commons

🌐 **Meta-Wiki**

 WIKIMEDIA project

KING JIMBO

You can edit Wikipedia. You don't even have to log in. You don't even need a user account. You see an article, click on "edit," change it, and save. It's recorded as your IP number, so that you automatically become a registered user. If you log in, you get an account, and you instantly have a talk page where people can discuss things with you. Your identity develops over time. You don't have to use your real name. Users can create a pseudo-identity, but their reputations will be cultivated around their work and behavior. IP numbers identify people, but contributions identify them uniquely.

The next level of participation involves assistance with quality control; in other words, working as an administrator. Administrators, at least in the English-language Wikipedia, are elected from within the community by an open-ended voting process. If 80 percent of the other administrators vote for you, you are elected; with 70 percent or less you won't make it. Between 70 percent and 80 percent the "closing admin" will study it a bit more, gauge the sense of the discussion, and make a judgment call. Administrators can protect pages and block people or IP numbers from editing, but these actions are visible to everyone, recorded in the open block log. Administrators who abuse their power will soon be "de-adminned."

The next level in the hierarchy is the arbitration committee, whose members are chosen once a year with an open vote of administrators, so that everyone can see how everyone else voted. The last step is that Jimmy Wales personally appoints people based on the results of the election. He explains this monarchist approach:

> It's a little strange for the wiki environment that I have
> this final veto power over who makes it onto the arbitration
> committee, but the arbitration committee itself has been

← Wikipedia
screen capture

extremely supportive of this idea. They are quite staunchly monarchist, in the British sense. No one in Wikipedia wants a despot or an uncontrolled monarch, but the idea of constitutional monarchy actually suits us very well. And I think it's kind of interesting. Americans find it a little disconcerting compared to the Brits, who actually get some of the ideas of Wikipedia governance a little better. In the United States we tend to think of the Constitution written down and it's very formal, whereas the idea of constitutional law in the UK is much more open-ended. Lots of things are simply done by convention with no actual rules.

There's lots of things that in theory I could do but don't do and wouldn't do. The arbitration committee likes this, because we can be very experimental in our design of social institutions, and because there's a certain level of trust that I'm not insane. It allows us to be more democratic without being concerned that it's going to go haywire. My preference is, and we're moving in this direction, that over the years, like an accelerated history of the British monarchy, I will just be there to wave at parades and be symbolic.

DESIGNING FOR COMMUNITY

Wikipedia has emerged as the most successful encyclopedia in the world due to the unique combination of user-generated content, volunteer quality control based on both human judgment and algorithmic indicators, and an open voting structure with hierarchical leadership. The history of designing for usability on the Web has focused on understanding what people expect, to help people know where to find things and where to go next; well-known standards and principles for navigation have evolved and are accepted as classic design approaches. Beyond that, there is a layer that enables social interactions between people, but there is little recognition that the rules that are set down by the software of a Web site have major implications for the social norms and the social rules that come out of that interaction process. This is where Jimmy Wales has been ingeniously innovative in designing Wikipedia:

I consider my work to be in many ways primarily about what I call "community design." And what I mean by that is the design of the software, but then beyond the software the social rules and norms for interaction that let a community come together and do something that they find productive, enjoyable.

In the early days, when I first set up Wikipedia, I really thought we were going to have to lock everything down very quickly. I was thinking at that point really in terms of just being a slightly different software tool to do something in the traditional way, but because the traditional project that I had before to create a free encyclopedia had failed, I had this desire to say, "Look, I know what went wrong the first time. It was top-down. It was controlled. It was difficult for people to get involved. Now we have this other approach. I'm going to stay as open as we can for as long as we possibly can. Let's just try this." And so, I would get up in the morning convinced that everything was going to be all just curse words. Usually it wasn't. Occasionally you would find somebody had done something and then you would just revert it.

Very quickly I changed the software to keep all of the old versions because I realized that eliminates a major vulnerability. When the software was first installed, I think it kept five revisions. So people sometimes ask, "What was the first article in Wikipedia?" and nobody knows because for the first few weeks or so we only kept the first five revisions, so the very earliest history got lost. I know what the first words were. I typed, "Hello World," which is an old thing programmers always do.

Society simply wouldn't work if we were concerned about getting stabbed everywhere we went. We don't design societies like that, except for the airports, which is one reason that airports are such dreadful places. On a day-to-day basis we drive down the street with all kinds of maniacs driving around, and we eat in restaurants with knives. We assume people aren't going to stab us, and we're usually correct. The people online are the same ones you see walking down the street. They're all online, and most of them are basically nice people with friends and family—and the ability to restrain themselves around silverware.

Dangerous steak knife
photo by Nicolas Zurcher

When we think about designing any kind of space for social interaction, we need this kind of analogy to say, "Look, basically we need to go under the assumption that most people are good." We don't want to have systems that are designed around the worst people. At the same time we … have to understand that we need institutions as a society to deal with those problems. And so in terms of people getting stabbed in restaurants, we have ambulances and hospitals. We have the police to come and take the bad guy away. With the hospitals we try to fix the problem as quickly as we can. Obviously, when you're talking about getting stabbed in a restaurant, which does occasionally happen, you can't always fix things. Real damage does happen.

Fortunately, online, in most cases you actually can fix things. You can't stab people online. You can say mean things and those things can be deleted. Those things can be gotten rid of. That person can be excluded. There actually are solutions that are pretty straightforward in most cases.

The first design principle of Wikipedia is to keep the software open to let the users do things their own way. Don't decide how to do things on behalf of people. Let the software be flexible enough that the people who are using it can actually develop their own social norms around whatever it is they are doing.

Next in importance is to keep all changes visible, both at the content level, with all the versions of any entry remembered and accessible, and the administrative level, with open editing and voting structures. Watch lists help the administrators do their job; most active administrators have the option set to monitor by means of a watch list anything they touch or edit. When they log in they just click on their watch list and they see what's changed since they were there last. It's also possible to track versions, or "diffs." When you go to the history of any article, all the old versions are there. Of course, it would be tedious to reread every article every time you wanted to check on it. Instead, the changes are highlighted, with yellow for the paragraphs and red for the words that have changed. It makes it easy to see what other people are doing.

The provision of space for comments and discussion is limited to the wiki pages themselves; separate message boards aren't necessary. This may seem a little ponderous to new users, when they click on "edit" and everybody else's text is there—and they're not supposed to touch it? The advantage is that troublemakers are automatically under control:

> Right off the bat it avoids the problem of the one troll who comes in to stir up trouble. Maybe we're editing an article about the history of the chocolate bar, and somebody comes on the discussion page and they're not happy with the way it's going, so all of a sudden they launch into a complete vicious, angry diatribe involving Nazis and Hitler and calling people names, and so on. Well, what can happen at that point is then the very next person that comes along can simply remove that rant and say, "Rant removed." It's still in the history, you can still go look at it if you really want to, but it's not appropriate. The philosophy is that we don't attack each other personally. If you have a problem with the article, let's discuss that, but don't start tearing into other people.

We're just going to remove that. And then the next person who comes, well, if they really want to they can go and dig and see this angry attack, but more likely they're just going to see that something got removed and keep reading.

Another kind of example is that you might say, "I can't remember where it was, but I remember we had this discussion last year, maybe you should refer to that." The next person coming along says, "Oh, I remember where that was." And they go find that link and they actually change your statement; parenthetically they say, "Here, click here." Well, they've actually edited your comment, but they did so in a helpful, useful way that you won't mind. You'll say, "Oh, thank you. That's what I was talking about." Maybe they leave you a note on your talk page saying they found the discussion you were talking about. I don't remember that discussion so I linked to it there. It's so flexible and easy for people to do as they wish that it enables all kinds of good behavior. It also enables bad behavior, but that just doesn't happen that often.

A Wiki is an online social community where fans create content about their passions, aggregating a vast amount of information on any given topic. The idea was invented in 1995 by Ward Cunningham, but from then until the launch of Wikipedia in 2001, wikis remained a small, underground phenomena on the Web. In the early days, developers and users were really scared of vandalism, so they tried to hide themselves from the search engines. Few people promoted wikis because they were worried that malicious characters might discover and destroy them. In essence, wikis, despite their utility, were regarded as both vulnerable and fragile—a rather inauspicious combination. Jimmy's approach addressed these weaknesses and kept a complete record (a history) of changes.

For all of its original (and persistent) challenges, Wikipedia is remark-ably accurate and considerably more up-to-date than any printed reference book. Its history is driven by the interests of the hardcore Internet crowd, so there tends to be a bias toward geek culture topics. As the size of Wikipedia has grown, though, so has the breadth of its content. It's no longer just for geeks—it's about everything. You might still be tempted to poke fun at Wikipedia for having a longer entry on a video game character than on a battle in World War II, but you can also look at *Encyclopædia Britannica* and find a longer entry on an obscure Elizabethan poet than on Sir Paul McCartney. Wikipedia is an elitist meritocracy reflecting the culture of computer engineering and pop culture writ large. Yet the breadth and depth of the site's content continues to grow, at pace with the number and diversity of Wikipedia contributors.

> The experience from Wikipedia comes in to say, "Look, we actually can build large-scale social processes that allow lots and lots of people to come and work together." We know there are some troublemakers but let's not design around them. We can start thinking about transparency and openness. How is that process done? How can the public have an impact on that process? How can we complain about it? How can we fix it if it's broken?

Jimmy Wales has also helped communities of people to come together by developing Wikia, which provides a collaborative publishing platform that enables communities to discover, create and share content on any topic in any language. He founded Wikia in 2004 with Angela Beesley as a for-profit business funded by advertising, operating Open Source MediaWiki software and licensing all of its content under Creative Commons. People come together as communities and create Wikia sites to share knowledge and enthusiasm about subjects ranging from video games, TV shows and movies to food, fashion, and environmental sustainability. With over four million pages of content and 130,000 enthusiast communities, Wikia attracts more than 30 million global unique visitors per month. Examples include "Children's Books Wiki," "Family History and Geneology Wiki," and "World of Warcraft," about which Jimmy says:

> World of Warcraft wiki, for example, has over 80,000[4] articles all about this online video game. It's not a charity, and it wouldn't even occur to the people working there to think that it's a charity, but they enjoy it. It's a part of

4 84,526 articles as of August 12th, 2010.

what they do online. It's a part of what they have fun doing; they're fanatically interested in this topic, they like to share knowledge with others, and they like to help the community of other players.

People edit Wikipedia because it's interesting, they meet other people to either make friends or enemies with, and they enjoy the bond of sharing and comparing. The real question about community design is, "What is it that people are going to be doing that they'll find fun, and how do we make it interesting?"

IN THE NEXT INTERVIEW, CRAIG NEWMARK, the founder of Craigslist, describes his approach to developing his amazingly successful and ubiquitous site for want ads and for-sale postings. Craig believes that the community that he has created has a lot in common with Wikipedia and admires the achievements of Jimmy Wales. He sees similarities in philosophy, community spirit, technologies, and internal architecture.

CRAIG NEWMARK

Interviewed December 2, 2008

CRAIG NEWMARK

Who hasn't heard of Craigslist, the Web site that has dramatically altered the classified advertising universe with its largely free want ads and for-sale postings? Craig Newmark started it in San Francisco in 1994. Out of school, he landed a job at IBM and worked in the Detroit branch that served General Motors. When he later joined Schwab, his new job allowed him to move San Francisco, but he soon decided that he could have more fun, make more money, and take more time off working as a contractor, writing a mix of Perl and Java code. He started Craigslist as a "cc" list to a few friends about cool arts and technology events in San Francisco, like Joe's Digital Diner or the Anon Salon, and it took off from there. He started a pattern then of listening to suggestions, doing something about them, then listening more. He is a vocal advocate of keeping the Internet free and using it for investigative journalism. He lives in San Francisco's Cole Valley, where he blogs and tweets, and attends to his customer-service job at Craigslist, mostly dealing with spammers and scammers.

←···· **Craig Newmark**
photos by author

Craig invited us to interview him at his house in San Francisco, idyllically located at the edge of a magnificent eucalyptus grove. Craig works at his computer in front of a large window so that he can glance up at the trees rustling gently in the breeze and filling the air with scent for respite. Unfortunately, on the day of the interview Craig's girlfriend had her purse stolen, so there was a tense atmosphere in the house as they tried to deal with police reports while answering my questions. Perhaps the tension made Craig even more stoic than normal, but he talked in an even and succinct manner, emanating rationality in the face of the misadventure. He would never admit to having designed anything, insisting that his success is due only to persistent problem-solving as he built solutions, which evolved from an initial desire to provide information for his friends.

craigslist

post to classifieds

my account

help, faq, abuse, legal

search craigslist

for sale ▼ >

event calendar

S	M	T	W	T	F	S
6	7	8	9	10	11	12
13	14	15	16	17	18	19
20	21	22	23	24	25	26
27	28	29	30	1	2	3

avoid scams & fraud

personal safety tips

craigslist blog

craigslist factsheet

best-of-craigslist

job boards compared

weather quake tide

progressive directory

craigslist movie & dvd

craigslist foundation

system status

terms of use   privacy

about   help

SF bay area ^w sfc sby eby pen nby scz

community
activities
artists
childcare
general
groups
pets
events

lost+found
musicians
local news
politics
rideshare
volunteers
classes

personals
strictly platonic
women seek women
women seeking men
men seeking women
men seeking men
misc romance
casual encounters
missed connections
rants and raves

discussion forums
1099	gifts	pets
apple	haiku	philos
arts	health	politic
atheist	help	psych
autos	history	queer
beauty	housing	recover
bikes	jobs	religion
celebs	jokes	rofo
comp	kink	science
crafts	l.t.r.	shop
diet	legal	spirit
divorce	linux	sports
dying	loc pol	t.v.
eco	m4m	tax
educ	money	testing
etiquet	motocy	transg
feedbk	music	travel
film	npo	vegan
fitness	open	w4w
fixit	outdoor	wed
food	over 50	wine
frugal	p.o.c.	women
gaming	parent	words
garden	pefo	writers

housing
apts / housing
rooms / shared
sublets / temporary
housing wanted
housing swap
vacation rentals
parking / storage
office / commercial
real estate for sale

for sale
appliances	arts+crafts
antiques	auto parts
barter	baby+kids
bikes	beauty+hlth
boats	cars+trucks
books	cds/dvd/vhs
business	cell phones
computer	clothes+acc
free	collectibles
furniture	electronics
general	farm+garden
jewelry	garage sale
materials	household
rvs	motorcycles
sporting	music instr
tickets	photo+video
tools	toys+games
wanted	video gaming

services
beauty	automotive
computer	farm+garden
creative	household
event	labor/move
financial	skill'd trade
legal	real estate
lessons	sm biz ads
pet	therapeutic
adult	travel/vac
	write/ed/tr8

jobs
accounting+finance
admin / office
arch / engineering
art / media / design
biotech / science
business / mgmt
customer service
education
food / bev / hosp
general labor
government
human resources
internet engineers
legal / paralegal
manufacturing
marketing / pr / ad
medical / health
nonprofit sector
real estate
retail / wholesale
sales / biz dev
salon / spa / fitness
security
skilled trade / craft
software / qa / dba
systems / network
technical support
transport
tv / film / video
web / info design
writing / editing
[ETC]   [part time]

gigs
computer	event
creative	labor
crew	writing
domestic	talent
	adult

resumes

other cities
bakersfield
chico
fresno
gold country
hanford
humboldt
mendocino co
merced
modesto
monterey
redding
reno
sacramento
san luis obispo
santa maria
sf bay area
stockton
susanville
visalia-tulare
yuba-sutter

us cities
atlanta
austin
boston
chicago
dallas
denver
detroit
houston
las vegas
los angeles
miami
minneapolis
new york
orange co
philadelphia
phoenix
portland
raleigh
san diego
seattle
sf bayarea
wash dc

canada
calgary
edmonton
halifax
montreal
ottawa
saskatoon
toronto
vancouver
victoria
winnipeg
more ...

us states
alabama
alaska
arizona
arkansas
california
colorado
connecticut
dc
delaware
florida
georgia
guam
hawaii
idaho
illinois
indiana
iowa
kansas
kentucky
louisiana
maine
maryland
mass
michigan
minnesota
mississippi
missouri
montana
n carolina
n hampshire
nebraska
nevada
new jersey
new mexico
new york
north dakota
ohio
oklahoma
oregon
pennsylvania
puerto rico
rhode island
s carolina
south dakota
tennessee
texas
utah
vermont
virginia
washington
west virginia
wisconsin
wyoming

countries
argentina
australia
austria
bangladesh
belgium
brazil
canada
caribbean
chile
china
colombia
costa rica
croatia
czech repub
denmark
ecuador
egypt
finland
france
germany
great britain
greece
hong kong
hungary
india
indonesia
ireland
israel
italy
japan
korea
lebanon
luxembourg
malaysia
mexico
micronesia
netherlands
new zealand
norway
pakistan
panama
peru
philippines
poland
portugal
russia
singapore
south africa
spain
sweden
switzerland
taiwan
thailand
turkey
UAE
UK
uruguay
US
venezuela
vietnam

KEEP IT SIMPLE!

At the end of 2008, Craigslist operated in 55 countries and 570 cities, with approximately 13 billion pages per month and around 50 million unique visitors. The growth had come as more and more communities and countries added communications technologies and people welcomed the offering. The simple design of the site has kept it fast, and the use of text in columns allows it to scale very easily across platforms, working well on Smartphones, PDAs, and personal computers.

Originally, Craig started compiling his list of local favorites for a few friends, but word spread fast. More and more people starting asking to receive his updates; they wanted to be on this list and to make suggestions for additions—the inclusion of local events, items for sale, ride shares, all sorts of things. In the middle of 1995, the "cc" list mechanism broke, overloaded at 240 names, so he wrote a program to handle more people.

Craig was planning to call it SF Events, but his friends kept telling him that it was already called Craigslist, so he found that he had accidentally created a brand. He continued running it himself as it kept growing, slowly but surely, over the next few years. When a task threatened to take too much time out of his day, he would write some software to automate it. At the end of 1997 he hit a million pages per month and soon after was approached by Microsoft Sidewalk with the suggestion that he run banner ads for them, which would have generated enough income for him to live on. He said no since the ads are "often kind of dumb and slow a site down."

He agreed to bring in some volunteers to help deal with the growth but found it difficult to provide them with sufficient guidance while continuing to shoulder the bulk of the workload. So in late 1998 and

← **Sfbay.craigslist.org**
screen capture

early 1999 he made Craigslist into a real company. In 2000 he hired Jim Buckmaster. He soon realized that he had joined forces with an excellent manager, so he delegated the leadership of the company to Jim.

Craig's secret has been a consistent process of listening to customers, designing solutions to address the problems that he hears, testing his solutions, and then listening again. His modesty is deeply genuine. He gives himself little credit for his amazing success, but you can tell when you meet him that he is determined, rigorous, and focused and equipped with simple but strong values and beliefs that keep him always moving forward.

> The pattern from the very beginning of Craigslist was doing something, listening to feedback, acting on that feedback, and then listening some more. That pattern continues to this day under Jim Buckmaster. There's been really very little vision on my part, really none. It's a matter of actually listening. Jim runs the company in a much more businesslike and serious way, but the pattern remains: listening to people, doing something about it. We've always moved in small increments and that kind of growth is sustainable, and your community, if you listen to feedback, keeps you on course. Fortunately, I knew from the beginning that I have no design skills but knew how to keep things simple. And we've maintained the simplicity over the years.

> The people who run the company are paid employees, but there are also volunteers who help us understand how the site's going—patterns of abuse, that kind of thing. Depending on the context, you have to balance what the community is saying with the need to make an authoritative decision, particularly if there are legal matters involved.

> Jimmy Wales does a great job with Wikipedia. Our model isn't that different, and most of what happens is based on community feedback and guidelines. Wikipedia and Craigslist share the spirit of the community driving things, and for that matter we share some of the same technologies. Our internal architectures aren't a lot different. There's more in common than you'd imagine, and they do a great job.

> Now and then, there are tough situations, say when people are bickering, and then someone just has to make a decision. Sometimes Craigslist has to act as an arbiter. Just as in normal society, sometimes the courts have to step in. But I don't want to take too much credit for that. I act as a customer service rep, and sometimes I'll have to defer the decisions to my boss who runs customer service. It seems to be working out pretty well, but if we make errors, people may wind up looking for an alternative.

Customer service includes moderating discussion boards, removing racist material, moving ads into the appropriate category, and managing cases where people are posting just to pick a fight to get attention. Dubious ethics need policing, for example, when an apartment broker pretends to own a place to disguise the commission that will accrue when it is rented. Sometimes people flag items for customer service review in forums or email with a question. The strongest similarity to Wikipedia is that people rather than algorithms make the crucial customer-service judgments so that the sense of empowerment flows back and forth between administrators and the end users. Craig acknowledges imperfection:

> It is not perfect. Democracy is a lousy form of government; it's just better than anything else we've tried. Our culture of trust is based on our values, like treating people the way you want to be treated. At first it was implicit rather than conscious, but we've come to recognize it. That was true from the very beginning. It was not a conscious action until recently, and we just took that attitude and practiced it, and then followed through more, and people saw that it was sincere on our part. It's a matter of consistency and persistence. It just works, and works consistently, and that works for us.

On a typical day Craig works on customer service as soon as he gets up. After the early tasks are done he gets coffee and reads the *New York Times*; then he goes to the office down the street, works some more, has lunch; then more customer service. Depending on circumstances, he may meet some people, or go out for dinner, but when he gets home, he usually catches up with customer service before bed, to fix any urgent problems and to avoid a painful start to the next day. This

SF bay area craigslist > jobs > art/media/design jobs

[help] [pc

all SF bay area | san francisco | south bay | east bay | peninsula | north bay | santa cruz

search for: _____ in: media jobs ⇕ (Search) ☐ only search titles
☐ telecommute ☐ contract ☐ internship ☐ part-time ☐ non-profit   ☐ has image

[Thu, 10 Sep 15:24:22] [craigslist is hiring!] [jobs forum] [craigslist vs monster vs careerbuilder] [**PERSONAL SAFETY TIPS**]
[**AVOIDING SCAMS & FRAUD**] [success story?]

Thu Sep 10

Part-time Newspaper Graphic Artist (financial district) - (financial district)

Seeking Designer to Help with Adobe Illustrator Project - (san rafael)

Technical Illustrator -

Kitchen Sales / Interior Architect- Designer / Design Build Firm - (mountain view)

Wed Sep 09

INTERIOR DESIGN ASSISTANT/PURCHASER/PROJECT MANAGER - (lower nob hill)

Picture framing - (San Francisco)

Graphic Artist - Temporary - (berkeley)

Senior Flash Actionscript Programmer - (sunnyvale) img

Design Savvy Sales Manager Needed For Custom Window Treatment Store - (pacific heights)

Information Visualization Designer - Stanford University - (palo alto)

Senior Graphic Designer - (redwood shores)

Web Based Visual Merchandise Supervisor - (fremont / union city / newark)

Paid Adobe Study - Professional and Casual Photographers - $150 - (san jose downtown)

Redfin Senior Designer - (downtown / civic / van ness)

UI Designer - PC World & Macworld - (SOMA / south beach)

User Interaction Designer - CREATIVE CIRCLE -

Camera Equipment Rental Store Need Operations Help. Access to Gear. - (san mateo)

unpretentious lifestyle matches his humility and has allowed him to appoint the right people to lead the company.

> For me, it's not a matter of modesty or humility—it's just a matter of being realistic, and that works for me. About twenty years ago at an IBM course we read an article about how people who are good at starting things are often pretty bad at continuing them, and that big lesson, which was a good one, actually stuck with me.

> I do want to remind people that I don't feel there is anything altruistic or noble about Craigslist. We're just doing what feels right and that means we are doing well as a business by doing some good for people. It just feels right, and it's a successful business strategy. My basic design approach is to keep things simple, keep the site fast, and remember to treat people like you want to be treated, which means to provide good customer service, knowing that as imperfect humans there will always be lapses. But do what you can—take that seriously.

Craigslist will to grow incrementally as it adds more languages and locations, but its guiding philosophy will ensure careful enhancements of functionality and a focus on quality control, with implementation of better tools for fighting ad spammers and any new forms of exploitation that may emerge. The only source of revenue is paid job ads in select cities, with a charge of $75 per ad in the San Francisco Bay Area, and $25 per ad in eight other major cities in the United States. New York City has paid broker apartment listings for $10 per ad. There is a $5 charge per erotic services listing, but the site donates the revenue from this to charity, suggesting that the fees are intended to deter illicit activities by requiring posters to create information that could be used in legal proceedings. The company does not disclose financial or ownership information, but commentators have reported annual revenues above $100 million, with Craig believed to own the largest stake.

The most important technology developments for the business will be the increasing deployment of smart phones with Internet access.

<- Craigslist job ads
screen capture

As wireless infrastructure is a lot cheaper to deploy than wired, eventually almost everyone in the world will find it cost effective to get a good mobile device, on which the simple design of Craigslist will thrive; indeed, the site already has the third largest amount of traffic from mobile phones. Craig strikes an optimistic note:

> Right now I think we're living in a time of enormous change, where the way people get stuff done is changing, not in a small way, but everywhere. The Obama election is a manifestation of that, but we're seeing a lot happening right now where people again are giving each other a break in unpredictable ways. I seem to have stumbled onto being a part of that. We'll see much more as the Obama administration gets inaugurated and gains momentum. For example, there seems to be a new generation of civic engagement, where people are rededicating themselves to service—national service as a job versus occasional volunteering. I think we're seeing all this and in a big way.

TIM WESTERGREN, THE FOUNDER OF PANDORA Internet Radio, shares Craig Newmark's ideals of community service and civic engagement. Tim wants to create a middle class for the community of musicians and personalized radio for the music listener.

TIM WESTERGREN

Interviewed February 24, 2009

TIM WESTERGREN

In 2000 Tim founded Pandora, the personalized Internet radio service. Based on his Music Genome Project, Pandora selects songs and artists with similar musical qualities to examples that you choose and creates a "radio station" just for you. Tim loved music as a little boy, starting off playing jazz and blues piano, gaining skills with lots of different instruments, and learning more about theory and composition in college. At Stanford University he became more interested in the intersection of music and computers, but after graduation he spent about ten years as a performer, playing shows and touring. He became interested in composing for film and developed a niche in Hollywood by building on his understanding of how the structure of music matches the needs of films. When he realized that this kind of music profiling could be turned into a taxonomy of musical attributes, he began working on the Music Genome Project, which led to his starting a company that eventually became Pandora.

←···· **Tim Westergren**
photos by author

Tim was very busy at the beginning of 2009, what with promoting the company and trying to sort out difficult licensing agreements for the music. It took several canceled appointments before we found a date and time that stuck. It wasn't far to go, as the Pandora headquarters is in downtown Oakland, where the office space is less expensive than on the San Francisco side of the Bay Bridge. The office space has an open plan, except for an acoustically controlled music performance room, so we set up the cameras to record Tim with the music analysts working at desks in the background. Tim is charming, talking with an engaging openness and enthusiasm that is infectious.

MUSICIAN'S MIDDLE CLASS

Tim articulates an ambitious and idealistic vision for Pandora:

> I think about the vision for the company in two ways. One is to build the world's largest radio station—to have hundreds of millions of people listening to Pandora all over the world and connecting cross-culturally, discovering music from all over the place, communicating with other listeners, and completely redefining radio from the ground up.
>
> The flip side of that—which is very near and dear to me—is to build the musician's middle class, so that you can quit your day job when your song gets added to Pandora, because you get unleashed in a targeted way to this enormous audience of people who like your kind of music and they become your patrons. That's what I hope for!

One great benefit of the digital revolution for musicians is that it makes complex recording affordable. It empowers individuals to create and record music that could previously only be performed by large ensembles. It allows everyone to think, "Yes, I can!" With a decent computer and a little bit of outboard gear, you can get into heavy orchestration, arranging, layering, and multitrack recording. Tim has harnessed this creative explosion. In Pandora he has created a new promotional tour for these emerging musicians, while providing a new medium for personalized listening for the rest of us.

The first phase of the Web gave people access to an unlimited inventory of music. You can go to a virtual record store that has six million songs or a video site that has hundreds of thousands of independently produced videos. The problem is finding what you like within that big collection. Broadcast radio can't curate that experience for you on a

<----- Concert
photo by Laura Ashly/Morgue File

personal level because it has to serve and retain an audience that is a viable size for advertisers. Pandora uses the Music Genome to help you find just the stuff that you want.

If you are an independent content producer, you now have access to the tools to make your music, but you can't find your audience. The state of the art for recommendations has been "collaborative filtering," as practiced so effectively by Amazon ("People who like this also like this"), but that doesn't solve the problem for somebody who isn't known. If you are an independent band on a site that relies on historical data, you might as well be a bottle of shampoo since nobody knows you. Nobody's already liked you, or bought you, or reviewed you, or done what is needed to pop you up into that kind of virtuous cycle of "people who like … also like … ."

That's where the story behind Pandora starts. Tim had too many years of the nomadic life as a performer and turned his hand to composing music for films. He was interested in the connection between the digital realm, the demands of the film's storyline, and the qualities of the music. He also liked the problem-solving aspects of designing the music to fit the needs of film and television.

> It's a very intentional form of composing. You have an objective in mind, which is "to make the door slam scary," or "make the romantic scene more compelling." You think about song structure, and sounds, and instruments, and harmonies in a very applied way. You also spend a lot of time trying to figure out somebody else's musical taste. Film composers are good at quickly deducing or gleaning the taste of a director, or producer, or whoever is calling the shots. You get pretty good at music profiling, taste profiling. I developed that skill as a film composer and found myself just thinking about music, and taste in terms of these musicological attributes. I was doing it all the time, and it started to crystallize into this idea of a taxonomy.

> There was a moment when the idea of the genome came to me. I was reading an article about a musician named Aimee Mann. She was a talented artist who had a reasonably sized following but not large enough to warrant investment from a

Aimee Mann CDs
photo by Nicolas Zurcher

big record label, so she was sort of stuck in this no-man's-land. Her records weren't being released, and she was frustrated by that. And it occurred to me that what's missing is a way to cost effectively connect her with folks who we know like her music, her kind of music. The Web had developed quite a bit of energy in the music space that was ostensibly a perfect mechanism for doing that and this taxonomy that I had in my head. I immediately thought, "Wow, if I could take this process that I've developed to profile music taste, apply it to her music, and use that to make people aware of a record she was going to make, it could solve the problem that she was having."

I had also spent many years among independent artists, so I'd seen a sea of incredibly talented musicians [who] were essentially invisible because they had no access to a big audience.

iPhone Pandora player app
photo courtesy of Pandora

You name the art form—it's feast or famine. And so I was amply aware of all this great talent that was one decent promotional tool away from a great audience of patrons. Those ideas all came together as I was reading this article, and the idea of the taxonomy for the genome popped into my head.

Tim had never written down a structure for his analysis. He would play CDs to film directors to get their reaction. As they gave him their thumbs-up or thumbs-down, he would interpret their responses over the course of the interview, like the musical equivalent of a Myers-Briggs test. After his inspiration from the article about Aimee Mann, he sat down to record it in writing and it just came pouring out since the information was already in his head.

He set about building a taxonomy of musical attributes for every aspect of songs, including melody, harmony, rhythm, tempo, instrumentation, vocal performance, vocal harmony, and even softer values like feel. He ended up with four hundred attributes. Each one of those musical dimensions was broken down into basic building blocks and positioned on a ten-point scale. For example, there are more than twenty-five attributes dedicated to understanding the sound of the voice, so that you can describe any voice, from a low, gravelly male vocal to pristine, soprano operatic voice. Tim analyzes Aimee Mann's music:

A lot of her music is acoustic guitar based, with nylon strings or sometimes steel. She has a high alto voice that's fairly airy and pretty nasal too. She definitely has a nasal quality to her singing (the nasalness of the sounds is an attribute in the genome), with almost no vibrato. She is very melody-oriented, so if you think about her form and structure, she does have very identifiable, strong melodies. Her instrumentation is very sparse, so if you look at the supporting instruments, they tend to be on the thin side. The structure is fairly typically pop, you know, A-B-A kind of songwriting. Rhythm and tempo are fairly straightforward, occasionally three-quarter but mostly in four—moderate stuff. If you step back and look at her music in the abstract, what is it really about? It's lyric- and melody-focused. She's got a distinctive sound as a singer, but she's not a virtuoso singer. It's not about the vocal acrobatics. It's really about delivering a melody.

Tim realized that his experience in writing music to fit the needs of film had taught him enough about the structure to allow him to describe the music of Aimee Mann as a set of attributes, and that this analysis could help her find the audience that would like her work.

MUSIC GENOME PROJECT

Before he started building the genome, Tim had been watching the explosion of entrepreneurship on the Web, a good portion of it in music. He watched musicians gain access to the tools they needed and still remain invisible—they were part of a huge, almost dizzying virtual inventory; they were needles in a haystack. He shared his ideas with John Kraft, a friend from college who had already launched and sold a company by that time. John said, "Let's turn this into a business," so they wrote a business plan and started looking for venture financing.

The original idea behind the company was to build a recommendation engine to allow clients to say, "I have a customer who likes this song. What else would he or she like?" They didn't need to understand the idea of the genome; they just had a query for the engine. There were lots of online music Web sites that needed help navigating the catalog of musicians, so Tim thought, "Wow, we'll license it to all these people."

0:10 ⬤▭▭▭▭▭▭▭▭▭▭▭▭▭▭ -2:39

Stations

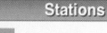
QuickMix

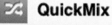
JJ Schultz Radio

Jessica Stone...

56 Hope Road...

Ill Mondo / Nea...

Dynamic Radio

Cara Jones Ra...

The Finches...

Michael Zapru...

Now Playing:

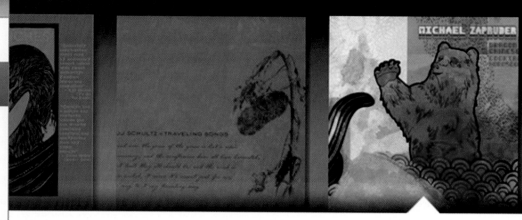

Michael Zapruder
Happy New Year
Dragon Chinese Cocktail Horoscope   Menu

About Michael Zapruder

San Francisco-based singer/songwriter and guitarist Michael Zapruder first gained attention as a member of Patty Spiglanin's band the Naked Barbies, which self-released three albums (Dancing with Vacuums [1994], Tarnished [1996], and Living Independently [1998]) before reconfiguring and renaming themselves the Vagabond Lovers for the 2000 album When I Was You, released by Monarch Records. By then, Zapruder had embarked on a solo project, writing, recording, and posting on the Internet one song a week for the entire year 1999 (www.52songs.org). On September 17, 2002, Zapruder released his debut solo album, This Is a Beautiful Town, on Explorable Oriole. He then formed an orchestra dubbed Michael Zapruder's Rain of Frogs from existing San Francisco bands, the principals including Nate Query of the Decemberists, Jonathan Segel of Camper Van Beethoven, Scott Pinkmountain of Pink Mountain, Scott Solter of Tiny Telephone, and Jon Bernson of Ray's Vast Basement. Zapruder's second

Will Glaser joined them as the third founder, bringing computer science and mathematical expertise to the group.

Another early contributor was a classically trained musician and a musicology PhD from Stanford by the name of Nolan Gasser. He had a rigorous academic background. Gasser helped to make the genome more polished, moving from Tim's informal and intuitive approach to something with a stronger theoretical framework. There is no computerized way to capture the information, so musicians, who listen to the songs and assign values to the attributes, enter it manually. An important aspect of the whole endeavor is language, as words are needed to describe attributes, and the whole team of analysts needs to understand and interpret the words consistently.

Their timing was unfortunate. They launched the company at the beginning of 2000, months prior to the dot-com crash. Internet optimism plummeted, leading to a long and painful period of trying to survive. They took the opportunity to improve and improvise their business. They searched for someone willing to pay something for the technology, but at the same time they continued chipping away at the genome, adding songs to it, growing the database even though they hadn't quite figured out how to make a revenue-generating business out of it. More than forty people in the company worked without salary for nearly three years, which had the surprising side effect of imbuing everyone with a strong sense of ownership and desire to turn the sacrifice into something. At last, in 2004, Tim managed to raise the first large round of investment, outfitting Pandora with a decent reservoir of cash as well as the great piece of intellectual property that he and his colleagues had spent many years building.

← Pandora screen
photo courtesy of Pandora

Soon after the investment, Tim hired Joe Kennedy as CEO. His experience was in consumer marketing. "Radio is an interesting category. It's much bigger than retail!" he said. Lo and behold, the genome was perfectly suited for the task of creating and manipulating playlists. Under Kennedy's guidance, they left the business model of the subscription-based recommendation engine and shifted entirely to a consumer-facing radio application. Pandora Internet Radio was born:

> "Radio" is shorthand for something that's close to what we do, even if there are substantial differences. It's such a well-understood word, so it's a kind of shortcut for us. The principal

difference is that radio has historically been a broadcast medium, with one station streamed to many people. The Web offers you the ability to do unicasting, where you stream a single channel to one, or two, or three people. It's also two-way. Listeners can give stations direct feedback, where broadcast is just one-way without feedback. I mean, you can pick up the phone and call a DJ, but that's not an effective personalization tool. On the Web you can react directly to what you're listening to, so it offers the ability to personalize.

The thumbs-up/thumbs-down concept is designed for feedback, inspired by the analogy of a conversation between a film composer and a director. It's not enough for Pandora to know that you like a song or an artist. To really be good at personalizing playlists for you, they have to know what you like about that song. Two people might both like Elvis Costello, but that doesn't necessarily mean that they have the same musical taste. One might be focused on lyrics and the other on musicianship, or the sound of the singer. Pandora's secret is to be really good at suggesting the next piece without knowing anything about you, without you having purchased anything beforehand. The genome can take the most independent of bands and know exactly where to position them relative to other artists and performers and play pieces for you that have the musical attributes that match your initial choice. Then you can refine the choices by voting with the thumbs-up or -down interaction.

VIABILITY?

There was no obvious way to create a viable business based on the Music Genome Project. Tim and his colleagues launched Pandora Internet Radio as a subscription service in the fall of 2005, thinking that people would be willing to pay $3 a month for radio, but nobody signed up. This forced them to relaunch for free, which was a risky step—they had seen other people have problems with monetizing an online music stream, and they didn't know how to attract advertisers. People listen to music, so there is no obvious way to provide visual advertising, which is still the bread and butter of advertising money online. Salvation came from the combination of personalization and interactivity.

After we launched, we learned that because of Pandora's personalization capabilities, it causes people to interact with it a lot. You get rewarded for going in and thumbing songs, engaging with the listening. And as a result people come back steadily, about six times an hour, to do something; whether it's to create a new station, thumb a song, skip a song, add a new artist, or find out about an artist they've heard but don't know. Seventy percent of our collection is independent, so there is a lot of discovery. That drives engagement, and once we had that, the equation became pretty simple. You've got these advertising impressions and opportunities.

You've got to sell enough of them at a high enough price to make the business work, and that's all about building a great sales team. There's a lot of education involved. The first year was predominantly about introducing the company and the product to advertisers. You're talking to advertising agencies and clients who are used to buying terrestrial audio advertising, and you have to explain to them the benefits of Web radio that don't exist in terrestrial. For example, you have the ability to target because you know who each listener is, and because you're connected you can offer someone the opportunity to do something, like clicking on an ad.

We sell a ton of music. We're one of the top affiliates, if not the top affiliate on both Amazon and iTunes, but it's not a big part of the economics of our business as it's a very thin-margin, low-per-unit-transaction business.

Pandora operates under a statutory license, which limits them to not more than four songs by a single artist in a three-hour period, no pre-announcement of songs, and allows the listener no more than six skips an hour. The limitations are designed to make sure that they really are radio; if it gets too interactive and close to "music on demand," they no longer qualify for the license. Tim is optimistic about the outlook:

Advertisers are becoming a lot more discerning and demanding about the results for their money, for their campaigns, but Pandora can deliver on those. We're doing really well, year on year right now [interviewed in February 2009], and I think it's because there's a bit of a flight to quality. Even though it's harder over all, the money is trying to find the sites whose advertising products really work.

When you can get into your car and plug in an iPhone and have Pandora streaming personalized radio to you, there's really no reason for you to go back to a broadcast music station because it doesn't play music you like. It can't. It's got to please a half million people simultaneously.

Pandora is particularly attractive in social situations. If you are entertaining and you want to choose a mood for the moment, or you know that your visitors like a particular kind of music, you can select one of your stations, or create a new one on your smart phone or computer and plug it into your sound system. You can then leave it unattended as you look after your visitors, feeling confident that the music will continue in the same vein. This advantage does not help the viability of the advertising model, though, as that depends on your paying attention to the source, returning to your Pandora station to see who composed or performed a piece that you are enjoying or to add a thumbs-up or -down.

BLIXA BARGELD HAS BEEN LEADING an innovative industrial rock band based in Berlin for decades and has accumulated a loyal and enthusiastic community of fans. Working in the traditional relationship to music publishers, he was never able to do more than cover the costs of production and even that level of support was steadily eroding. In the next interview, with Blixa and his wife, Erin Zhu, we learn how a band like his can bypass the traditional music business, developing a self-supporting economic model based on subscriptions from fans, enabled by the Internet.

BLIXA BARGELD
WITH ERIN ZHU

Interviewed December 1, 2008

BLIXA BARGELD WITH ERIN ZHU

Blixa Bargeld, former guitarist with Nick Cave and the Bad Seeds, leads an innovative industrial Goth-rock band called Einstürzende Neubauten, based in Berlin. Band members work with whatever readymade scrapheap objects they can find to act as musical instruments, hence the label *industrial* rock. Blixa's wife, Erin Zhu, an American originally from China, has extensive experience working in Internet start-ups. Soon after their marriage, Erin was able to help the band develop an elaborate Web-based fan subscription experiment that bypasses the traditional music business, allowing them to release the album *Alles Wieder Offen* in 2007. They have continued to develop this model because without the sponsorship of a record company they rely on fans to donate subscriptions for exclusive editions of the CDs and DVDs plus privileged access to the musicians and the entire creative process.

⟵···· **Blixa Bargeld and Erin Zhu**
photos by author

I read a piece in the paper about the way that Blixa Bargeld and Einstürzende Neubauten were able to survive by fan subscription, thus avoiding the traditional perils of the music industry. I sent an email request for an interview to Blixa through the band's Web site and was surprised to receive a reply from his wife, Erin Zhu, who pointed out that as the webmaster for the site she was responsible for most of the design decisions that they had made as they developed an Internet-based model of direct fan financing. She added a postscript at the end of her message, "This might be too much of a coincidence, but would you happen to have a beautiful architectural house in Woodside? If so, we were actually seated next to each other on a flight from London to SF a few years ago; you gave me your card and showed me some pictures of your house on your laptop." What a coincidence! Blixa and Erin own a house on one of the steepest hills in San Francisco, so I was able to interview both of them together there when they were next in town.

Alles Wieder Offen (pronounced: *ah-llus vee-der off-en*):

Current News

Album release dates:

October 19th in Europe;

Nov. 6th in North America.

If you would like to follow our progress in self-releasing this album, please check out the blog here.

Digital Single: "Weil Weil Weil":

single release on iTunes Germany

We are pleased to announce that there will be a digital single release coming one week ahead of the full album release date. The single will be called *Weil Weil Weil* and include a radio mix and remixes of the song from each member of the band, plus a karaoke version (for the German speakers).

The album version is now available for download here (right click to save), or for listening on the neubauten.org listening page. You are welcome to link to it from your own website or blog, if you also include a link to either this album site or neubauten.org.

Supporter Project, Phase 3:

Phase 3 of the neubauten.org supporter project is now closed for new subscriptions. The final supporter CD and DVD are now in production, and we are getting ready to start the shipping process as of end of September. If you are a supporter please make sure that we have your current mailing address, as it's painful to both you and us when we can't get the item to you on the first shipment.

Press/Media:

If you would like to review the album and have not been in touch with our PR contacts, please write to promo@neubauten.org and let us know where and who you are.

THE FANS CAN HELP!

In 2000 the record industry was consolidating, with labels being swallowed up by big production companies, which in turn were being bought by the investment arms of huge corporations. Pressure from the owners forced the less well-known musicians off the labels, even if they had a consistent record of creativity and a loyal fan base, as Einstürzende Neubauten did. This left Blixa and his band in limbo, wondering how to find the financing to produce another album. Erin suggested that they take advantage of the Internet and develop a new model for supporting and marketing themselves independently of any record company. Here is the story as Erin and Blixa told it to me:

> **Erin:** I thought that I could use my Internet experience to give them a different option, to use a Web site to go directly to their fans and have the fans help pay for the band to have the means for production. Before, the band would get an advance from the record label for the next album, they would take the advance, spend all the money on producing the album, and then the album would usually not recoup the advance, and that would be the end of the story.

> **Blixa:** These albums would eventually recoup, but the band still wouldn't see any money, because there were too many gangsters and corrupt record companies that we had contracts with. We had a contract with an English record company in the eighties, Some Bizzare, and we still haven't seen any money from any of the records that we've done with this company.

> We were all Internet novices, but Erin gathered us around a table, put a laptop there and showed us what we could do. Everybody was skeptical, but we couldn't get advances from a record company anymore; we couldn't even pay the production

⟵ Neubauten.org news
September 2009
screen capture

costs from what we could get from a company, so we really didn't have any other options than trying something different.

Erin: I arrived at a 1,000-people break-even point by asking Blixa what he would expect to get as an advance from a record label, and he gave me an amount of $35,000, so I said, "Okay, how about we try to get a thousand people to each put in $35?" Unfortunately, that was not quite an accurate estimate of what it actually took, but that is what we started trying to do instead of normal marketing. We went to the existing fan lists and otherwise just word of mouth, and I think we hit the 1,000 in about four months.

We made it clear that they were paying not to just get something in return, but that they were really supporting the band through their contributions: you know, this was a way they were enabling the band to actually work and produce a next album, so there's definitely an element of more than a commercial transaction happening.

Blixa: I think there were two sides to the basic idea. One was to take what is known since the beginning of book printing, to do a subscription to a book that will come out in the future; you buy something like the complete works of the Marquis de Sade in twelve volumes, you get them bound in leather, and you get one volume after another as they come out. The other side is that we have taken some things that are only possible through the use of the Internet, in connecting, broadcasting, and communicating with the supporters through a lot of different channels.

Normally you work in a recording studio, where everybody is trying to be separated from the rest of the world. It changed the process having webcams in the recording studio and people watching you, but we had to play with the ideas for a while to figure out how to use it to artistic advantage, and how to make a living for the band out of using different ways and means of production. We have done three of these periods over five years. Phase three ended last year, and for that we had 2,500 supporters.

Einstürzende Neubauten performance
photo courtesy of Einstürzende Neubauten

We refined the models as we were going along. First was an album, and the second one ended up to be an album and a DVD only for the supporters. The third one ended up being an album for the supporters, a much smaller version for the public, a DVD for the supporters, and a monthly track that they could download. We would love to see it being a general solution for bands, or groups, or artists in similar situations. How do we end up having a phase four, which is rather going to be public, where that model is open to everybody? That's what we are doing now.

Erin: The Web site didn't change that much, but the offerings did. We started with the concept that the site was there not just to make this offering but to encourage interaction—that the supporters should be able to interact with the band and also among themselves as a self-selected group that have a

Blixa performing
photo courtesy of Wired *magazine*

lot of common interests. So in that sense we had a very active forum on the Web site and a real-time chatroom where people could spend time. That took off much more than we expected. The chatroom was inhabited most of the time for purely social reasons that really had nothing to do with the band. There were people who would make a habit of just coming online each evening, their time. We had people from more than forty countries as supporters on the site.

There were some surprises. My original vision was for it to be an Internet-only project, as all the results were going to be digitally distributed. But as it turned out, a big piece of what we offered the supporters was intimacy—or at least access to the band at work in a way that they normally could not have—so that we did several webcasts a month, where the supporters could log in and actually see the band rehearsing or recording, with live chat going on simultaneously with the webcast.

Blixa: We would have their comments on our monitor. If they started talking about the weather, then you knew that whatever you were doing was not really interesting. But sometimes it went into crazy situations where they were singing along on the monitor; you could see it scrolling.

A moderator would sit at the live chat and tell us what they're saying. In the same way that in old times I would play a rough mix of the piece of music to my friends, we were opening this up to our supporters too. I didn't ask them what we should do, but they sometimes rescued pieces that we had already given up by saying, "We really like that!"

You play something three of four times, you are focusing on particular details, and then you notice that you are losing them, but that they all refer to the second time you were playing. And probably three days later you listen back to the tape and you find out that, yes, they were right. It's the same situation with actually having people in the studio.

I was born in 1959 and I've seen many changes of formats— from 78 rpm, through the 45 single, to the long-playing stereo record, the diverse labyrinthine technical new things have all disappeared, from quadraphony, to reel-to-reel, to the cassette, to the compact cassette, to the CD. I saw all these different formats coming, happening, and going. I know that each one of them, now that I look back, had and impact and an influence on how the music actually developed. The twenty-minute noodling is a product of the vinyl long-playing record. The pop song of three and a half minutes comes straight from the 45.

I find the format change that's happening now very interesting! What is it going to support? What is it going to force? And what is it going to suppress? There is no longer a preferable form or length of a song. There will be a continuous flow, and everything else will be rather related to the body and to the human being. The classical "band," a group of usually male people that get together at a very young age to play music, has been for a long time disappearing, because you cannot be lucrative working with four people in one room recording. So it becomes more and more garage land, garage band. You own the program. You own the computer. At maximum you're going to be a duo, and most are just going to be alone. They're all going to work with their own computer in their own environment, and it's going to be dictated by their imagination, with no particular format that binds all these things together.

Erin: I think there will be a virtual library of music of everything that you could possibly digitize out there in the cloud. You can access it with your mobile device or any other device that can access the Internet. I suspect that the subscription way of paying for access—that you just pay a monthly or annual fee

Johann Strauss
photo courtesy of Creative Commons

for access to anything you want in that cloud—is probably the direction that things will go, because I think that's what people want. At the same time I think that live performances are going to be a significant way for artists to make money. And "live" could be facilitated over the Internet to be able to reach places where it doesn't make sense to actually go and play a concert.

Blixa: Do you know who was responsible for the whole idea of publishing music? It was Johann Strauss, the famous waltz composer. He just hated to see his compositions being played in every *Weinstube* in Vienna, so he started that whole publishing-rights thing.

THE INTERVIEW THAT FOLLOWS with the partners in Airside, a London-based creative design agency, demonstrates a fluent approach to using multiple media platforms. Fred Deakin is both a musician and a designer. He brings a rich combination of media to the support of his band Lemon Jelly. Nat Hunter thrives on developing algorithms and communication design; he relaxes by knitting "Stitches." Alex Maclean combines a flair for animation with a whimsical wit.

AIRSIDE

Interviewed July 2, 2008

AIRSIDE

Airside is a creative agency working in moving image, graphic design, illustration, and interactive digital media. They like to develop solutions that work across all media, such as TV commercials, Web sites, and billboards. Founded in 1998 by Alex Maclean, Fred Deakin, and Nat Hunter, Airside's unique approach has won many awards, including recognition from D&AD, Bafta, Design Week, and Apple. The twenty people in the team have diverse backgrounds, from fine art to programming and knitting to English literature. They bring a whimsical wit to their designs and prove themselves masterful in the use of multiple media. Alex started in architecture and interior design and has moved into animation and Web design. Fred began his music and design career by creating promotional material and visuals for the clubs he was running; he still performs as half of the band Lemon Jelly. Nat moved into graphic design from a background in human computer interface design and psychology.

Airside
photos by author

A visit to the Airside Web site is the best way to form an impression of the creativity and humor of their output. On the "About" page you find a Venn diagram, somewhat disguised as a flower, that shows the overlap in their work between digital design, graphic design, and multimedia productions. In spite of the varied backgrounds of the founders, there is no mistaking that they are a design firm.

I recorded my interview with them on a warm July afternoon in 2008 at their offices in London. They are located on three floors of an old brick row house on a busy street in Islington, so the interview was interrupted by vibrations in the structure whenever a heavy truck went by outside as well as a thunderstorm with dark clouds and dramatic lightning flashes, visible across the rooftops from the top floor. Before I left, I was flattered that Nat allowed me to adopt one of the "Stitches," a small knitted individual named Griffin, with eyes askew and arms akimbo. Griffin accompanied me back to California, where he seems to enjoy the sunshine.

NAT HUNTER

Nat spends long hours in front of computer screens, writing code, designing Web sites and interfaces. After a while she feels worn down by the limited dimensionality of the virtual world, and she is always keeping an eye open for chances to surf fluently from writing code, to media work, to design for print, to participating in Fred's music, or enjoying tangible physical experiences. The "Stitches" give this physical relief. They originated when Anne Brassier, a member of the Airside team since 2001, started knitting little creatures with slightly wonky personalities and Nat found them increasingly engaging. Eventually she realized that they had to be adopted, to go out into the real world and have real parents, and those parents had to communicate with one another. A Web site provided the vehicle for the adopters to form a community, and the tangibility of the hand-knitted dolls was a refreshing contrast to the computer screen. Nat explains the value.

> I'm uber-digital, but I enjoy knitting a Stitch. After the knitting, you sew up the sides and add the arms and legs. Then you put the eyes in, and there's this moment when it comes alive. Suddenly it's so real that you start projecting onto it, "Oh, he's a bit hungry."

> We send these Stitches out in the real world, and the new parents who look after them write us emails saying, "We've taken our Stitch on holiday" or "Our Stitch is training to be a DJ." We've always been very interested in how you get people to relax, play, and have fun, whatever the medium is. These Stitches really seem to do the trick.

← Demos: The Power Gap
screen captures from Airside's animated film for the Northern Gallery of Contemporary Art's "Think-Tank" exhibition

The contrast between whimsical little hand-knitted creatures and logical lines of code may be stark, but all three Airside partners have confident yes-we-can attitudes to operating in multiple media in the service of good design. They have always tried to ignore the actual format of media, looking to find the best way to communicate with people in each design context. Nat remembers when they started.

> The thing that united the three of us ten years ago was not thinking about the media but thinking about the experience of someone. Fred used to run clubs, so he'd think about the experience of someone walking in the door, what they were going to feel, how they were going to be, what was going to jolt them into having fun. I was a computer person, so I'd think about someone turning on a computer and having a bit of software, or Web site, and how they would know where they were going, what they were going to do. Alex was into virtual worlds through his architecture background, so he'd be thinking about virtual space, about walking into a real building and how it would feel.

> We were never really interested in the detail of what that Web site or club was. It was more about how to make someone feel something; how to make someone react; how to create an emotional response. When it comes to actually designing in old media or new media, I personally don't see that there's any difference at all. It's always been about problem solving and exploring and about having fun with it. Wherever media goes, we'll go there and always be among the first to explore.

THE PET SHOP BOYS

Nat led a team to design the new Web site for the Pet Shop Boys in 2007, keeping the design clean with simple navigation to allow access to the large amount of material that the Boys have written and performed in their twenty-year career. She and the team were proud of the easy-to-use content management system, the uncluttered appearance, and the thumbnails that made browsing easy and attractive. The most difficult challenge was to find a way for them to easily update the content. Neil and Chris, the Pet Shop Boys, are very busy people, touring around the world almost constantly. Nat was worried that the content management system would never be used since by the time they got to their hotel

Petshopboys.co.uk
screen capture

room they'd be too tired to sit down in front of a computer, so she developed a way for them to use their camera phones.

We thought, "What are they going to do?" They've always got a phone in their hand and are waiting around. They are in airport lobbies for four hours at a time waiting for the next plane, so we developed an application to allow them to take a photo with the phone, add a bit of text, and send it directly to the site.

The site really is for the fans, for the "Pet Heads" as they call themselves, so you want the shortest possible communication between Neil and Chris and the fans. You want to get them as close together as possible. The great thing about the mobile is that it's very intimate—they've got it on their holiday, they've got it at the weekend, they've got when they're waiting for the plane—so the content is very personal, very different from sitting down at a computer to use the content management system. They might say:

"Here I am on my holiday in my swimming trunks."

"Here I am with the band and waiting for the next plane."

"Oh, I went to this fantastic exhibition at the weekend. Look, here's a picture of it."

The design process starts right at the beginning, moving all the way back to ask why the brief exists in the first place? In this case the brief was a content management system for a Web site, but you rewind and say, "Hang on a minute, no one's going to use it!" Seeing them with their phones, sitting in your meetings talking about the content management system, but there they are fiddling with their phones all the time.

The actual designing of the solution and then the programming is just problem solving. With all interaction, whatever the media that your interacting in, you've got to remove as many barriers as possible, because everyone is so busy, everyone's got too much [going] on, so you've got to make it as easy and as intuitive as you can, whatever you're trying to do.

FRED DEAKIN

Fred started the Lemon Jelly band with Nick Franglen. His skill as a designer made him interested in working across the conventional barriers between media. He led a team at Airside to design the packaging, create the advertising and visuals to support the performances, and come up with illustrations to replace conventional press photos. They also produced their own videos and designed the Web site for the band, so they were able to keep a consistent spirit across media.

Fred was determined to create lavish packaging for the Lemon Jelly releases, as he was painfully aware that CDs are an ephemeral medium, easily bypassed by digital downloads and storage devices, so he wanted to add value through the design of the presentation materials. For their third album, '64–'95, he developed a DVD with animation for every track to offer something more for the purchase price than the music alone. He believes that if you buy a record or CD in the real world, there should be depth to the communication and interaction, so that the packaging, imagery, and extra materials, such as a DVD or digital booklet, should make you feel that your £10 is well spent. By contrast, when you download a file from iTunes, at best you get a small square image that pops up in your iTunes window, and at worst you just get a lot of type.

It doesn't seem impossible that a new media format for music will evolve that embraces the functionality of the digital age. Creating an album where every track was animated was an

Lost Horizons by Airside for Lemon Jelly
image courtesy of Airside

attempt to create a coherent piece where the whole album had a corresponding visual narrative. The online digital media that are evolving are just as interesting and "sticky" as real-world media, but for some reason record companies haven't yet found a way to nail that particular problem. They normally use specialist talent, saying, "Okay, you want a video—who makes a good videos?" or "I want a sleeve—who does great sleeves?"

We did the lot, right across the board, so there was a much more coherent feel to it all, and that was very satisfying. The imagery around Lemon Jelly is very reflective of the music, in that I'm doing stuff with a lot of repeating patterns, which is meant to echo the repetitive beats and loops. There are filters and plug-ins that you use for graphics programs that you can also use for making music. I was trying to create a visual language to fit with the way of composing that has evolved since people started making music with computers.

For us as a design company, it was a real chance to diversify. We did bags and T-shirts and played with the crossover between

real-world media and online media for live events. We had a
very strong fan base already on the Lemon Jelly Web site, so
we announced the concerts online. When people applied for
tickets, we sent them tickets in the form of T-shirts, with the
instruction to wear the T-shirt to get into the concert. On the
way to the concert they would start to see each other on the
tube, on the bus, or walking down the street; they'd spot other
people with the same T-shirt and they'd know who was going
to the concert.

When they got into the concert, they were all there wearing
exactly the same T-shirt and thus they created a pattern. That's
one of the things I'm really into with the Lemon Jelly album—
patterns of repetition, like you hear in the music. Halfway
through the concert—there was a secret UV pattern that was
also printed on the T-shirt—we turned on the UV light [and]
the pattern appeared. Weeks, months, or years later, they might
be wearing their T-shirt and see someone else who was at that
concert, and say, "Oh my goodness! You're wearing the Lemon
Jelly T-shirt. You were at the concert!"

It's a replication of what happens online, but it doesn't have
to only be virtual, it can be in the real world as well. You get
that kind of community feel. You get links with strangers
who you meet in a very different way. So it's a similar kind of
interactivity, but in the real world.

Fred is always looking for ways to expand the perceptions of his audience.
He likes Nintendo's Wii because it makes people interact with a screen
with the freedom of bold gesture and movement rather than by fidgeting
with a mouse or track pad. In 2007 Fred and Nick did a performance
at an IMAX cinema for the BFI Electronica Festival. They created the
IOTA (Inventions of the Abstract), an hour-long performance of abstract
imagery with a minimalist musical element, thinking of it as abstract art
that included movement and sound. Fred sees the possibility of ambient
art of this type becoming part of the living room.

Your huge flat TV screen can suddenly turn into a work of art,
with visuals that don't necessarily draw you in on a narrative
basis, but whenever you look at them they're beautiful and

ever-changing, with a sound track to match. Perhaps you don't want to watch the news because it forces you to sit back—you're almost pinned to the wall by watching traditional television. You don't really want to do computer stuff because that draws you in. You want this kind of ambient interactivity where it adds something to your experience but isn't the whole of your experience.

ALEX MACLEAN

Airside was commissioned by Panasonic to promote a new range of handsets. Alex describes his concept for customization in multiple media.

We designed graphics for the covers of the phones. We produced a minute of animation to the music that Fred wrote, based around animating the grid of LED lights on the covers. We designed the packaging for the customization kit, containing the covers and the coupons to download the ringtone and animation. Fans could also buy a T-shirt that went with it.

They did it as a limited edition of 2,000 to just promote the launch of the new handset. The package delivered the whole look and feel, almost like an operating system for the hardware. They let us do anything we wanted for the animation on the screen of the phone. It had silly ghosts and animated hands, and a little dog who lived in a sewer, who came up and did a lot of poo. It was just ridiculous animation, synced to the music Fred had written. Each version had its own little scene, its own T-shirt, and its own little cover that went on the phone.

Japanese people seem to absorb Western culture much more completely than people do here. They know more about things like Sesame Street or Winnie the Pooh. They know more about its creation, genesis, and characters than anyone in the West does. That's why we love working in Japan.

Blue Cat wallpaper by Airside
image courtesy of Airside

VIRAL MEDIA

Airside was asked by another Japanese company to come up with concepts for toys that plug in to a USB port on a laptop, so that you just plug the toy in and it does something engaging. They came up with lots of nice ideas about how it might play music or change color in a beautiful way, but then the subversive side of Alex's personality inspired him to say, "What if you had a memory stick that you plugged into your computer and it was like an animal that just humped your computer while you downloaded files?"

The idea was accepted and implemented and is being produced at a rate of about 100,000 a month. If you go to YouTube and enter "Humping Dog" in the search box, you find that there are 2,815,000 hits, as of November 2009, for a little movie of the dog in action. Alex is interested in the viral element of this success.

It's a project we almost didn't publicize because we weren't particularly proud of it, but it has such a viral element to it that it seemed of interest. We are constantly asked to produce virals for people. They come to us with a script and say, "Can you make this viral for us?" We have to say, "That's not a viral! You're making a short animated commercial you want to put on YouTube, but the idea isn't viral. Also, you need to take away the branding, because people won't forward it to their friends if it's covered in your advertising material." To be truly viral it can't be overtly commercial. The idea itself has to be viral. You almost have to take out the commercial element until it is a viral idea.

This idea of plugging a dog into your laptop and it humping your laptop is an end in itself. It doesn't need to do anything else. It doesn't need to work any harder than that. It's stupid and pointless and crass, but that may be why it's viral. There are a few examples that are both beautiful and also succeed in becoming viral, but there are many more successful instances that are full of raw sexual content, or toilet humor, or they contain some sort of outrageous violence that you can barely bring yourself to watch.

The BBC know this from their news Web site. If they were to go purely with the stats of the news items people actually watch, they would only ever publish the skateboarding dog stories, or the celebrity caught naked on the beach stories, because those are the ones that people click on. You have to draw the line somewhere. If you went purely with what is viral in terms of news media, then you know what sort of news you'd get.

That's funny, because the humping dog thing was all concept and no design. In fact, we designed something, but then the client went away and had somebody else design the final look and feel, so it's not really an Airside project. It doesn't even look like an Airside project. And yet, it's probably one of the most successful viral things we've ever really done, just because of the idea. It is more satisfying for us to come up with the design concept, as we are closer to the client's needs and helping them rewrite the brief. We're not taught traditionally in art school that that is design. Design is, "Look at this record cover that I designed," not, "Why is it a record cover?"

When the Internet became ubiquitous, Alex was very enthusiastic about the potential use of the new online media for public debate. He set up a charity to help people communicate with their members of Parliament, putting them in direct contact with their public representatives. He learned a lot about the Web and communications but became disenchanted with the medium as a democratic forum for debate since it became obvious that the loudest people are the ones who get heard the most. The people who want to disrupt or rant are the ones who grab all the attention and drive the other people away.

We're still a very long way from being able to hold our public representatives accountable for their actions through an Internet-based forum, but the Internet has become so much more interesting in so many other entertaining and fun ways. It's a lot less worthy than I thought it was at first. Also, technically, it's become a minefield now. I'm not very technical so I fell out of love with the Internet and fell in love with all forms of traditional storytelling and narrative. You have a lot more control I think that way as well. Crafting, writing, and storyboarding, and being able to create messages that way is very, very rewarding. The nice thing about Airside and about me, Nat, and Fred is that we all want to be creative. When clients come to us with really interesting projects, that's when we get those real "a-ha" moments!

GREEN MESSAGES

Alex also gets excited when he has a chance to contribute to more idealistic projects. Airside was recently commissioned to create two short films for Al Gore, for the worldwide Live Earth concerts, to illustrate issues around climate change. Alex felt that it was important to avoid getting preachy and worthy, as people are suffering from compassion fatigue when it comes to the environment. They've heard the messages too many times. The partners looked for entertaining ways to persuade people to change their behavior to help alleviate climate change.

We made two films, one about a penguin on an ever-decreasing ice flow who eventually has to jump ship; when he dives into the ocean he finds a city that's completely submerged. The other has all the animals teaching people lessons, with silly cartoon characters and one idiot bloke who represents your average consumer. And every time he does something wrong the animals have to teach him a lesson about how to put it right. By using these little cartoon characters and making silly scenes, it came across as pure entertainment. It was a really big lesson for us: entertainment first, message later.

A lot of the new work we're doing at Airside is more narrative-based, short form, short film–making animation. "Narrative-led" is the new thing for us, really. There's so much user-generated content out there. There's so much proliferation of messages, blogs, and opinion. We keep finding that it's worth coming back to well-written, entertaining, and fun bits of messaging. There is value is in those old-fashioned attributes of quality, care, and craft.

The interest in original narrative and environmental issues led Airside to pitch a project to the BBC, which was picked up. It's an animated series about environmental issues, with each episode in bite-size two-minute chunks containing some messaging, some information graphics, and a tiny bit of ludicrous violence and entertainment, plus some music and dances. They are crafting each of these episodes to be divided into smaller tidbits, which you can then download to your phone for use as a ringtone or to send to your friends. TV executives are changing the ways of commissioning animation, moving away from the traditional 11- or 20-minute pieces toward smaller chunks that will translate easily across media, into the ever-expanding world of cell phones, SMS, and Twitter.

ROGER MCNAMEE HAS USED HIS INVENTIVENESS and business acumen to create a unique new combination of media to promote music and musicians. His latest band, Moonalice, was formed in 2007. He has supported the band through the sale of posters, books, T-shirts, CDs, and DVDs while making material available online for free and keeping the price of concert tickets very low. He feels that accessible tools for creating music are beneficial to everybody. He tells this story in the next interview.

ROGER MCNAMEE

Interviewed November 25, 2008

ROGER MCNAMEE

Roger is both a musician and a venture capitalist. He plays lead guitar in Moonalice and has developed a unique combination of new media to promote music and musicians. The band has virtuoso performers, including ex–*Saturday Night Live* guitarist G. E. Smith. They perform live at affordable ticket prices but supplement their band's income with accessories and publications, promoted online and through social media, including MySpace and Twitter. The other half of Roger's life is dedicated to his role as a founder of Elevation Partners, a private equity firm that invests in intellectual property and media and entertainment companies. They have a major stake in Palm Computing, where he has guided many of the development decisions for the Palm Pre and has publicized it enthusiastically. Roger got his start on the business side, helping the Grateful Dead to stay viable after Jerry Garcia's death through direct sales to their fans.

Roger McNamee
photos by author

Roger has a day job as a venture capitalist and is very connected around Silicon Valley, so I have friends who know him well through both Palm and his musical activities. He came to the IDEO office in Palo Alto for the interview and talked enthusiastically about media in general and his approach to promoting Moonalice in particular. He believes passionately that it's more fun to create music, art, and design than to consume it, but his business acumen helps him bring interesting insights to the questions of financial viability that confront people who hope to make a living in the arts. He is also familiar with the leading edge of new technology, readily adopting the tools that can change people from consumers to creators.

MOONALICE

HOME   MUSIC   TOUR   NEWS   BIO   FORUM   FLIGHT CREW   STORE   CONTACT

CLICK HERE TO JOIN THE MAILING LIST

WOULD YOU LIKE TO ORDER OUR STUDIO ALBUM?

Produced by T Bone Burnett and optimized to sound like vinyl on any playback medium, "Moonalice" is now available!

We are offering a bundle of extras to those who are so inclined!!!

CLICK HERE TO ORDER

Upcoming Shows

+ 09/17/09   Jewels in the Square (Union Square)   San Francisco, CA
+ 09/19/09   Fox Theatre   Redwood City, CA   Supporting Marshall Tucker Band
+ 09/20/09   Lodi Grape Festival   Lodi, CA
+ 09/26/09   Earth Dance @ Black Oak Ranch   Laytonville, CA
+ 09/27/09   EarthDance @ Black Oak Ranch   Laytonville, CA
+ 10/4/09   Hardly Strictly Bluegrass   San Francisco, CA

The Moonalice Channel

Sightings

+ Moonalice Zombie Twittercast #MZT45 - Listen here!
+ Sept. 18 Berkeley, CA show to be rescheduled
+ New Philly date added in October!
+ Jack Casady planning to be with Moonalice September 11-20
+ New October Dates: NYC, Millerton, Baltimore, Va. Beach, Tampa!
+ Give It Away - Chubby's Op Ed essay for Billboard Magazine
+ Robin Sylvester sits in on bass in Sebastopol!!!

Moonalice Legend

Moonalice is a Native American tribe that dates back to the beginning of time. According to Moonalice legend, the tribe descends from Piltdown Woman, or possibly from a couple of naked, snake-charmed gardeners who liked to hang around with friendly dinosaurs. In later times, the tribe evolved into two major clans. One was agricultural, the other nomadic. The farmers were known as hippies. They cultivated many things, but their specialty was a native American crop: hemp. Over the years, the hippies found many uses for hemp and built an advanced culture around it.

Read more »

CREATIVE USE OF MULTIPLE MEDIA

Roger has performed in bands since college, where he claimed to be the worst performer in a very good band at Yale. Since then he has practiced consistently to enhance his craft, but he kept his performing career strictly separate from his venture capital work in the early years. When he started out, there was excitement and danger in the drugs and adventures associated with touring. More recently the music business has become separated from its audience, and newer bands have created the image of danger with body piercing, tattoos, and hip clothes. Then suddenly the onset of music file sharing crashed the financial structure of the record companies and the recognized bands.

The business basically died once Napster started in '97, so a lot of great performers suddenly became available. My old band, The Flying Other Brothers, started to become a magnet for really great players who were between gigs—first Pete Sears, then Barry Sless, then Jimmy Sanchez, then G. E. Smith. At that point T-Bone Burnett, the producer, was helping me on a project. And so T-Bone goes, "Look, I really like what you guys are doing but I think you need to start over again. You need to create a band from scratch. The business is dying and you ought to figure out what's gonna work here!"

←···· Moonaliceband.com
screen capture

So we started Moonalice. We picked the name because our poster artists thought it had fantastic imaging associated with it, so we could build art into the theme from the beginning. The legend is that Moonalice was an ancient native tribe that was everywhere, and that wherever we go, we discover pieces of the legend from the local community and share it at each show.

Moonalice posters
Screen capture

Before we even put out an album we put out a book. It's a
book of all the posters from the first year and all the legends
and set lists. In the first year and a half, we played 150 shows
and created 135 posters.

It was a bold move to start all over again, but it gave them a chance to
involve the fans right from the beginning. They decided to be accessible instead of remote, self-deprecating instead of arrogant. They were
committed to trying wild experiments as often as possible. Sometimes
G. E. Smith gets up at the beginning of a song and says, "This one's in E."
It's not just that they don't know what song he's going to play—they've
never even heard the song. They switch instruments constantly, so they
don't have the same people playing the same instrument on the same
song two nights in a row. If you're a fan, you can talk to the musicians
before and after the show. They felt reinvigorated:

You talk to famous musicians and they tell you, "Ah, I remember the days in the clubs. That was the best time." But they don't perform live in intimate venues anymore. Moonalice started from scratch. We've put up all the live shows on the Web, so that people can listen. The posters are all on the Web, but people want to buy stuff, so now we record and video every show, so we typically sell the prior ten shows each night, not that night because it takes about two weeks to get it done.

We charge practically nothing at the door because the economy sucks, and we want people to participate. It's better to play free shows and then those who have disposable income can buy T-shirts and albums. When we play to a couple thousand people, we'll sell hundreds of items. You can make really good money doing that, but you let people choose what they want. Everybody loves the posters, but because we do one for every show, we quickly overwhelmed people's ability to buy the whole set. And so we decided to put the complete set out in a nice-looking paperback book.

It is not yet clear whether the multiple media approach to marketing will be scalable, but it is working for Moonalice. As the tools for media production become more and more accessible, it seems likely that there will be a yes-we-can effect. On-demand publishing makes the book production easier, many artists are excited to hook up with a band and create a poster, and the Web is readily available to everyone. It's a form of ecosystem, with all of the participants benefitting from one another's success.

In April 2009 Moonalice held its first live Twitter-integrated concert in San Francisco. Following each song during the show, the sound team digitized the song's audio, uploaded it and then tweeted about its availability, all before the end of the next song. The sound team used TinyURL to tweet a link to a site where users could listen and download the song. Because of the live Twitter integration, Moonalice has seen an upsurge in downloads. It's likely to only be a matter of time before this trend becomes viral.

A record company executive approached Roger and said, "Look, this band is really good. This is a T-Bone Burnett album. I can give you 'sell in' of 23,000 units on the first day!" That is better than the Grateful Dead could do today, but they realized that there's a high risk that a lot of the CDs would get returned, as most people don't buy CDs in retail distribution any more, so instead they decided to market the album independently, through Amazon, at the shows, and with free downloads from their Web site. Roger explains that free downloads can help the band reach more people:

> If people want stuff for free, there are hundreds of our shows available online, but if they want the band's version of it in nice packaging, they can buy it from us. There are some people who sit there and go, "Well, wait a minute. I'd like to contribute." We effectively have a fan subscription but it's free, and in America *free* is a very powerful word.

IT'S CHEAPER TO CREATE THAN TO CONSUME

Roger believes that democratizing the creative process is inherently good for society, that it educates all of us and makes us realize that any of us can put up an idea, by blogging or adding an entry to Wikipedia. Just as in desktop publishing, where people quickly developed an awareness that more than two fonts on a page was an inherently perilous avenue to pursue, they've come to appreciate that democratization creates risks in other areas as well. What's really exciting is that we're right at the beginning of a revolutionary surge in accessibility of new digital tools.

> I grew up in a world where media was something that was created by others and then presented to us in some sort of broadcast fashion. In the last five years, a behavioral change has taken place, and people are returning to the notion that it's more fun and entertaining to create media than it is just to consume it. My sense is it started with digital photography, but now you see it everywhere.

> I asked one of the guys at MySpace. They have seven million bands on MySpace. I don't think that there is any way that

more than a million of them have ever given a live performance. So you say, "What about the rest of them?" Well, the answer is that the tools required to make recorded music and videos are available to anyone. They're really easy to use. There's almost no greater joy one can have as a musician than going through the process of creating music, recording it, mixing it, and preparing it for distribution; and so it doesn't surprise me in the slightest that there are six million bands for whom that is the objective. To me that's a wonderful change!

Roger studies people to determine how and where they spend their time. He tries to evaluate their priorities. Of Chris Anderson's "long tail" concept, he has the following to say:

Putting it in temporal terms, it is very clear that passions fragment very quickly as you get down the long tail of the curve. Where people place their time is where they place value. The conventional media world had a forty-year period where they could buy the population in large chunks. Now those chunks are not only being whittled down, they have less value because people are paying attention to things that have less economic value. I think it's getting easier and easier for people to put time and attention into the things they love, especially in a tough economy where it's a lot cheaper to create than it is to consume.

My parents, who grew up during the Depression, were part of the World War II generation. By the time they were twenty-five they had made three decisions: where they were going to live, who they were going to marry, and where my father was going to work that effectively put them on rails for the next thirty years. And the way I think about it is that they had very few choices from that point forward, but they had this marvelous safety net. Now the situation is reversed. All the safety nets are gone, but we always have choices. Oddly enough, the problem for many people is that they are overwhelmed by choice. You know the great joke about Starbucks is that it forces you to make seven or eight decisions before you're even awake. Everyone's trying to balance their family, their career, and their personal finances, and there's not enough time in the day because you don't have a support infrastructure.

COMMENTARY

I still find it amazing that Wikipedia works so well. There is genius behind the simplicity of the design that Jimmy Wales created, with a self-correcting structure that allows open contribution with just a little bit of police work by the volunteer administrators. In his interview he talked very philosophically about the values of community, collaboration, and sharing, so it seems ironic that he started Nupedia and Wikipedia with money made from financial futures and a men-only Web portal.

He evolved the design with surprisingly few twists and turns, claiming, "We actually can build large-scale social processes that allow lots and lots of people to come and work together." The success of these social processes is based on a simple hierarchy in four levels, which he describes as a benevolent monarchy:

1. An open architecture that allows anyone to contribute material, identified by an IP number and a screen name.

2. Volunteer administrators, elected from within the community, who police the behavior of contributors.

3. An arbitration committee, elected by administrators, to resolve difficult issues.

4. King Jimbo, holding the board-appointed "community founder" seat, to personally appoint officers for key roles.

This structure relies on the combination of automation and human judgment. Jimmy thinks of it as community design, where social rules and norms for interaction enhance the software, bringing members of the community together to do something productive and enjoyable.

As Wikipedia has evolved, a set of admirably simple design rules has emerged:

1. Leave the software as open as possible to let users do things their own way.

2. Keep all versions of an entry remembered and accessible, to ease policing.

3. Make changes easy to see by color-coded version tracking.

4. Keep comments and discussions within the Wiki pages, for visibility.

5. Don't attack people personally; discuss but don't accuse.

Wikipedia is surprisingly accurate and up-to-date, initially limited only by the founding culture of an elitist meritocracy of computer engineers. Contributors are the volunteers, so they have chosen the topics that they enjoy participating in and contributing to.

Craig Newmark is simple, elegant, and effective. Anyone involved in evolutionary design development should remember his pattern of listening to feedback, acting on that feedback, and listening more. He doesn't call it design, but I see it as embodying the most important elements of successful design. He is constantly aware of what people want and endlessly trying to make improvements by iterative prototyping.

He says, "Fortunately, I knew from the beginning that I have no design skills but knew how to keep things simple. And we've maintained the simplicity over the years." Craig, I beg to differ! In my opinion, keeping it simple is in itself a powerful design skill. He has also developed a simple set of design principles or guidelines:

1. Listen to customers.

2. Design solutions to address problems.

3. Try out the resulting designs with customers.

4. Listen again (and repeat the cycle of these four steps).

5. Always move in small increments to maintain sustainable growth.

6. Delegate roles, including leadership.

7. Avoid complexity.

8. Be consistent and persistent.

The culture of trust at Craigslist is based on values, such as treating people the way you want to be treated. The strongest similarity to Wikipedia is that people rather than algorithms make the crucial customer-service judgments.

Craigslist thrives due to excellent customer service. As with Wikipedia, some measures of policing and control are needed for quality and truth.

Pandora Internet Radio doesn't seem like radio to me. It seems like a new medium because it offers a lot more personal choice and control than traditional broadcast radio. The tortuous path that Tim Westergren went through in order to arrive at this innovation fascinates me. He started as a performance musician, then composed music for film and television, and discovered that he could define a taxonomy of musicological attributes. Next he patiently developed the Music Genome, tried offering it as a recommendation engine, and at last realized that it could be used for creating and manipulating playlists, something that might be called radio for the Internet. What a journey, and so rewarding to arrive!

Tim has a vision of two goals for Pandora. One is to build the world's largest radio station, with hundreds of millions of people listening to personalized radio. The other is to build a musician's middle class, so that musicians no longer need day jobs. The digital revolution has made it possible for musicians to create music with heavy orchestration, layering, and multiple tracks. The tools to make music are there, but it is still difficult to find an audience. Collaborative filtering, as practiced so effectively by Amazon and iTunes, does nothing to solve the problem for unknown musicians since it works on the "people who like … also like …" model. The Music Genome Project solves this dilemma by analyzing the attributes of each piece as it is included in the Pandora repertoire, so that music can be matched to preference without previous exposure.

As with Wikipedia and Craigslist, the secret ingredient is combining algorithms with human judgment. Pandora employs analysts who are trained to position each incoming piece of music on a genome of four hundred attributes, covering melody, harmony, rhythm, tempo, instrumentation, vocal performance, vocal harmony, and even softer values like feel. Tim evolved this design when he realized that he could describe his instinctive judgments explicitly and started the Music Genome Project. Advertising revenue followed once the tipping point of scale was reached, as advertisers are attracted to the ability to stream a single channel to each listener.

Thank you, fans of Einstürzende Neubauten! Here's another way to give hope to impecunious musicians. How ingenious of Erin Zhu to realize the potential of a subscription model enabled by the Internet—and thoughtful of Blixa Bargeld to see that the community of fans could be rewarded by closer connections to the performers. Blixa has led his innovative industrial rock band for decades, but even with an expanding and loyal fan base, he was unable to support the expenses of production using the conventional contract system with record companies, so he and Erin developed a new economic model based on subscriptions from fans, bypassing the traditional music business.

The breakthrough came when Erin said that they should go directly to the fans for contributions toward the next album. This simple idea has worked for three iterations of new material. In return, supporters have had more intimate access to the band, with webcam views of rehearsals and recording sessions; the opportunity to comment in real time online through a moderator; and access to one another through the chatroom on the Web site. The first time that they did this they created an album, the second time an album and a DVD just for the supporters, and the third time an album for the supporters plus a smaller version for the public, a DVD for the supporters, and a monthly track to download. By this time they had expanded to 2,500 supporters.

Blixa likens this subscription model to the tradition established for books, where members of book clubs purchase work in advance of publication. He is also interested in the evolution of formats and the way they influence musical structures, with the twenty-minute session dictated by the vinyl long-playing record and the short pop song coming from the 45. How will the unstructured possibilities of the Internet influence change? Perhaps the design will relate to people instead of formats. Erin sees a future with an infinite virtual library of music in the cloud, accessed by subscription from any device that is connected to the Internet.

The output created by Airside appeals through lively humor and slightly subversive charm. They agree with Blixa that a new media format for music will evolve that embraces the functionality of the digital age, but when it comes to designing in old media or new media, they don't see any difference at all. They think that design has always been about problem solving, and exploring, and about having fun with it. As Charles Eames put it so succinctly, "Design is a method of action," whatever the media or disciplines. They focus on people, and the subjective qualities of design solutions, saying, "We are interested in how to make someone feel something; how to make someone react; how to create an emotional response. With all interaction, whatever the media that you're interacting in, you've got to remove as many barriers as possible, because everyone's got too much on. You've got to make it as easy and as intuitive as you can." Try, try, and try again, until you have designed a solution that is simple and intuitive.

They have combined music with animation to enhance the flow, using visual as well as audible narratives. Creativity in one medium can be supplemented by linked designs in other. They are fluent in design skills across media, so some of their more serious underlying philosophies can be supported with a light touch and engaging style. For example, when they were commissioned to create two short films for Al Gore to illustrate climate change issues, they avoided getting preachy. They looked for entertaining ways to persuade people to change their behavior.

They made two films featuring cartoon characters and silly scenes that came across as pure entertainment, proving the value of "entertainment first, message later." Thank you, Alex, Fred, and Nat for your contribution as entertainers, with the meaningful messages there as well.

Roger McNamee is both a musician and a venture capitalist. Combining his inventiveness and business acumen, he has created a unique new combination of media to promote music and musicians. His band Moonalice was formed in 2007 with a yes-we-can attitude to promotion and financial support. They perform regularly and often, keeping their ticket prices low. They created posters for almost all the concerts, offering them for sale individually and compiled into a book, together with Moonalice legends and concert set lists. Every show was recorded on audio and video, with carefully packaged CDs and DVDs released two weeks later and the previous ten shows available for sale at each concert (along with T-shirts). Free downloads of the shows and videos are available online, but people can pay for the nicely packaged physical version if they want it. In April 2009 Moonalice held their first Twitter-integrated concert, with each song being uploaded during the show and tweets sent out about the real-time availability. This combination of offerings has proved more financially viable than the traditional record contract.

Roger feels that accessible tools for creating music benefit everybody. He believes that democratizing the creative process is inherently good for society, that it educates all of us and makes us realize that anyone can put up an idea, by blogging or adding an entry to Wikipedia. This change challenges the conventional media world, after a forty-year period when the population could be accessed in large chunks. It's getting easier and easier for people to put time and attention into the things that they love.

WE CONTINUE WITH THE MUSIC THEME for the first interview in chapter 3, "New Connections," with Jorge Just. Jorge masterminded the promotion of the band OK Go, making them famous through viral videos published on YouTube.

3 NEW CONNECTIONS

Interviews with Jorge Just, Chad Hurley, Alexandra Juhasz, Bob Mason with
Jeremy Merle, Ev Williams, and Mark Zuckerberg

Making connections may be the noblest work of man.

Ralph Caplan, author, public speaker, and designer

EVERY MEDIUM RELIES ON some kind of infrastructure, but the enabling technologies are often in flux, and the introduction of new technologies affects the experience of all end users. Consider the early decades of the telephone, when people relied on human operators, who patched cables at each local exchange, to help them connect. Compare that to modern phones, with automated exchanges, message services, Internet access, and thousands of unique applications.

Transmitters used to broadcast television and radio signals to audiences by pulsing analog electromagnetic waves from antennae perched on towers, but now digital signals are received from satellites or networks of fiber optic cables. Printed newspapers, magazines, and books reach their audiences through an infrastructure of physical delivery, but now they are also available online or as e-books. Music has been connected to listeners through an ever-changing series of delivery vehicles, including radio, vinyl records, cassettes, and CDs—now more likely using online distribution and digital storage.

Digital technology and the Internet have suddenly opened up a dramatic flood of new connections and connectivity that's confusing in its intensity and reach. Traditional media are being challenged by unexpected new media that have been spawned by these new connections. This chapter looks at a few surprising examples of these new media, discussed by people who have ridden the wave of change.

Jorge Just masterminded promotion for the band OK Go, making them famous through viral videos published on YouTube. Jorge is still young, but he has already made a lot of new connections. He learned digital audio editing in order to land an internship at *This American*

←---- **Noble Connection**
photo by Mel B./Creative Commons

Life. He connected with the band's fans by writing them personal notes that invited them to engage with the musicians. He developed a Web site that connected with journalists and advertisers professionally and with fans intimately. He made the connection with YouTube before any other musician, band, or label had ever contacted them. The members of OK Go came up with music videos that were intricate dance routines, a hybrid of boy band dancing and cheerleading. Once on YouTube, these videos turned viral, and total strangers around the world began emulating the videos with their own creativity and fantasy.

Chad Hurley, the founder of YouTube, describes how he designed the Web site and developed his company. Chad had noticed the success that Flickr was having in connecting people to share and publish photos and saw a similar opportunity for video. He knew that inexpensive video cameras and editing software were already available, but it was difficult to share video online because of varying formats, large file sizes, lack of standardized media players, and limited bandwidths. He put together a team to solve the technical challenges and designed the Web site to make it sympathetic and accessible, with an architecture that keeps connections open. By the end of 2008 YouTube was receiving more than fourteen hours of video every minute.

Some people are disturbed by the nature of the connections encouraged by YouTube. Among them is Alexandra Juhasz, who teaches media studies and is interested in the political and artistic uses of media. She leads a course called "Learning from YouTube," teaching the class both about and on YouTube. As a scholar and activist, she is instinctively repelled by the YouTube experience, believing that the communal building of knowledge can't happen on this medium and that the idea that the site is democratic is untrue. She sees a need for teachers and educators to raise the level of video creation skills, so that most people are competent to participate rather than just consume.

Online video is expanding exponentially, fueled by inexpensive video cameras and desktop editing, combined with the arrival of adequate bandwidth for viewing on personal computers and handheld devices. This means that video content of all types is becoming available online as well as in traditional media, so the door is open for new connections. Entrepreneurial offerings are springing up for a host of specialist applications that complement the dominant YouTube. Among them are subscription services such as Brightcove, which encodes video, uploads, launches, and presents it in a branded player on a Web site in less than thirty minutes. Cofounder and CTO Bob Mason explains how this works in his interview, along with Jeremy Merle, the leader of the company's team of user-interface designers.

Twitter is the most puzzling of the new connections. Even founder and CEO Ev Williams was surprised when he tried using the first prototype, finding it engaging to get that human connection in a fun, lightweight way. Ev is a serial entrepreneur and relates the sequence of ventures that led him to Twitter, including the adoption of *blog* as both a noun and verb and the use of the term *blogger* as a brand name for the tool that he was developing. He arrived at the design for Twitter via attempts to develop podcasting, upstaged by Apple, and ideas for creating a social status broadcast system, which were first inspired by real-time connections from dispatchers to couriers. Ev has been amazed by the growth of Twitter and tweets: initially the minimal format seemed odd to him, but it appears that the very simple structure makes it flourish.

For the final interview in this chapter, we talk with Facebook CEO and founder Mark Zuckerberg, who has developed a design approach for social networking that looks for empathy and openness, offering much more visual richness than the minimalism of tweets. Mark was only twenty and still studying at Harvard when he founded Facebook, exhibiting a prodigious ability to create software balanced by a surprisingly mature philosophy and idealism about sharing connections and information. Facebook looks like it will be a dominant player in social media, with more than a thousand employees and a potential market valuation approaching $5 billion in 2009. Mark is shy, but his ability to think deeply about the future and drive the strategic direction for the company shines through.

JORGE JUST

Interviewed December 9, 2008

JORGE JUST

While at Williams College studying history and political science, Jorge fell in love with the public radio program *This American Life*, so he taught himself to edit audio, moved to Chicago, and applied for an internship with the program. Ira Glass gave him the opportunity and helped him learn the art of storytelling. During his time with the program, Jorge developed a friendship with the members of the band OK Go and became interested in finding creative ways for them to communicate with their fans, and for the fans to connect with each other. When OK Go began experimenting with music videos as an art form, Jorge helped them reach an expanded audience through an ingenious viral campaign that leveraged social networking and YouTube. OK Go won a Grammy award for the video that accompanied the song "Here It Goes Again," which featured members of the band dancing on treadmills. Jorge also writes, sometimes with pen and paper, and enjoys delving into television and radio. His work can be heard on *This American Life*, and he is a frequent contributor to the Canadian radio program *WireTap*. Jorge has also applied his insights about creative collaboration to another kind of social venture, leading an open source technology project called RapidFTR that helps reunite families in emergency situations.

←···· Jorge Just
photos by author

When I was talking to Ira Glass (see chapter 5) on the phone about setting up his interview, he recommended that I also talk to Jorge Just, who has interesting ideas about viral media. I therefore set up an interview with both of them at the IDEO offices in New York and discovered that Ira had done a lot to help Jorge advance his career. Jorge was very thoughtful during his interview, often pausing to consider his replies before responding—I could see his thoughts racing forward to consider the implications of a statement before he made it. I was impressed by his maturity and wisdom, expecting that he would continue with a career as a radio journalist, writer, and music promoter. I find it admirable that he has instead decided to hone his creative skills by returning to school in 2008 to study design and media at the ITP program at NYU.

CONNECTING TO FANS

After he left college, Jorge spent a week in a musician friend's one-bedroom apartment, which was filled with the equipment needed to torture materials for sound effects and experiment with electronic music to teach himself audio editing. Once he felt confident with his new skills, he set off for Washington, D.C., in search of newsworthy material. He recorded interviews at a political march to use for his very first story. Armed with his edited audio sample, Jorge then flew to Chicago and knocked on the door of the radio station where *This American Life* was being produced by Ira Glass and his close-knit team. He talked his way in, met Ira, applied for an internship, and was accepted. There he learned the craft of radio, especially how to tell stories and engage an audience emotionally.

The internship didn't pay very much, so Jorge started earning some extra income by freelance writing. Damian Kulash, the lead singer of a band called OK Go, approached Jorge and asked him to help write the band's biography.

Damian came over to my apartment one day and we thought through the biography—not just as a standard timeline of what the band represented, but also thinking about the audience for this document, and what it could be, and who was going to read it. The collaboration between us was clearly going to work.

Bit by bit he and the band kept asking me to do small things and help them in a myriad ways. I started doing their merchandise and shipping things off for them, doing little bits and pieces of the infrastructure of what you need to keep a band going. That led to the Internet. I started thinking about their Web site and how people were going to use it and interact with it and what it would mean to have a band Web site. Slowly but

← Music editing
photo by LiquidMolly/Creative Commons

OK Go band members
photo by Danno Nugent/Creative Commons

surely I got enmeshed in the world of a band that was trying to make it and trying to grow—trying to understand the motivations of their fan base.

The fan base is a rabid audience. It's people that, in a lovely way, are very interested in what you are doing. I think the experience that people have when they listen to music is immersive, and it's hard for them to define why it's important to them. For a certain breed of fans, that translates into wanting to know everything, or wanting to engage with the artists themselves in a way that doesn't happen in a lot of other media.

The biography was aimed at local writers, reporters, and editors—people who would help the band get more exposure and attract audiences from a broader community. This was back in 1999, before the popularity of the blogosphere, when the local press offered the best form of publicity. Appealing directly to the fans was a very different challenge, as they hanker for intimacy rather than the factual information that will help a journalist put together a description quickly. A reporter who is writing a story about a band needs to read a bio. Somebody who works in advertising and wants to license a song needs contract information. They may listen to some music, but they're not there to form an intimate connection with the group.

When OK Go went on tour for the first time, they invited Jorge to tag along to help them sell their merchandise. He discovered that he had a natural talent for selling T-shirts to teenage kids. He liked talking to them and had very strong memories of what it means to be a fifteen-year-old who's really excited about buying a concert T-shirt. He learned a lot from these one-to-one conversations with individual fans.

Between shows he was stuffing envelopes to mail T-shirts and CDs, but he felt frustrated that the communication was cold and anonymous, with nothing interesting or creative about it, so he started writing personal notes to include in each package.

> I got this school pad of Little Princess paper, and with every order I would send a note, probably about a hundred words, with a few sentences about whatever I was thinking at that moment, or the fact that my plants were dying, or some sort of stream-of-consciousness riff.
>
> It was just to say, "Hello, somebody is on the other end of this, and thank you for buying something." On the back of each note I wrote, "If you go to a show and find a band member, sign and date this note, and they'll buy it back from you, for basically anything you ask." I don't think I told the band that I started doing that, and they started getting people coming to shows with these notes that were from me and demanding payment.
>
> So this remote interaction between a fifteen-year-old kid somewhere, and me, a guy who's stuffing envelopes in Chicago, that turned into an actual interaction between that kid and a band member, becoming a real personal interaction. It's not, "Hi, can I get your autograph? Can I take your picture with you?" It's, "I have this note. I'm here at your show and it says that you have to buy it from me." You're a band member and you've just performed, so you probably don't have anything on you. Your wallet is backstage. You have to figure out ways. … My friend Damian had a tennis ball. Somehow he had been playing with his dog after the set and the tennis ball was all chewed up, and whoever it was got incredibly excited about it and traded a note for it.
>
> I think I did it for a year just because it was such a challenge to write these notes, but that was another lesson in what it means to get people excited about a band. It's marketing in

OK Go performs
photo by Bradi/Creative Commons

retrospect, but it's not marketing at the time. At the time, it's reaching out. It's creating some sort of actual interaction and engagement, something surprising.

VIRAL DANCING

The band members and a filmmaker friend created a concept called "The Federal Truth in Music Project." It was a series of one-minute skits in the form of public service announcements. They were funny vignettes, each ending with a snippet of a song, for example, about payroll forms. They put up a Web site with no reference to the band, telling the story about this project that never existed, and they fell in love with video as a medium.

When *This American Life* did its first tour, Ira Glass invited OK Go to go along as the house band. It was strange for a rock band to be playing songs to a seated audience as part of a public radio show, so they looked for something to add that would be entertaining and different. They ended up creating an intricate dance that was one part choreographed boy band dance and two parts cheerleading routine. When preparing for their own next tour and planning their stage show, the band decided to replace encores with a new version of this type of dance routine, which proved to be very popular and turned into a signature element of their shows. Jorge remembers how the dance performance was recorded on video.

There is a video of them in Damian's backyard where they're rehearsing; it's the last take. They borrowed a camera and recorded it and sent it around to me, and some friends, just to show us the work in progress, and it happens to be this fantastic, perfect piece of viral video. It's just the sort of thing you see and immediately want to see again and want other people to see. It makes you feel good. You look at it and think, "I've never seen anything like this, and it's fantastic." It was clear to the band and to everybody around that it was something the fans should see.

By this time they had a record company sponsoring their tour, but the professionals behind the label did not want to release the video to the fans, thinking that having a boy band pirouetting around in a dance routine was not the right kind of promotional material. The band did what any self-respecting band does in that situation; they burned a few DVDs and handed them to fans at shows. They were in the habit of going out front after they had finished playing, to meet fans, take pictures, and talk to people, so in every city they'd give out a few DVDs. The video started to propagate and soon showed up on YouTube.

We knew about YouTube, but it was sort of nascent. You could tell it was something that was going to be fun to play around and experiment with. I was visiting a friend for a weekend in San Francisco, so on the plane I wrote an email to the contact address on YouTube. I got an email back asking how long I was going to be around, and if I wanted to come in and have a meeting with them, because, as they told me when I went, no band, musician, or label had ever contacted them.

The backyard dance routine for "A Million Ways"
screen captures

OK Go was still a relatively obscure band, but just the act of contacting them and saying, "There's something very cool that you're doing and we have ideas for it," was enough to get them excited. There were bands that were putting videos up, and the editorial team at YouTube was trying to feature them, get them placement, send them messages, and reach out to them, but nobody was paying attention. I went and talked with them about what a band might want, and why MySpace at the time was interesting to bands, and get their ideas of what they were going to do. They had videos, and they wanted to share videos. That was a tougher thing for bands, because having your music used in a video and sending it all over the world doesn't necessarily mean there's any connection being made between you and that video.

The first one that spread in a surprising way was this video of OK Go dancing in their backyard. Someone sent us a video of a re-creation of that dance at a wedding. The OK Go video is really fun to watch, but it was even more amazing to watch four chubby, middle-aged guys doing this dance for their sister at a formal wedding.

The band members and the fans loved this example, so they seized the opportunity to make something of it, setting up a dance contest. They asked people to re-create the video in whatever imaginative, creative way they could. This turned viral, with the derivative videos popping up everywhere. They were compelling, funny, and even sometimes cool. A magical new kind of connection happened, with the band inventing this new kind of entertainment that could

"My Sister's Wedding," a remake of OK Go's backyard dance video
screen captures

easily have just been an embarrassment but turned out to be both charming and engrossing. Total strangers around the world joined in with their own creativity and fantasy.

> The question that's interesting to me is whether you can do something that people want to pass along but then also want to engage with in some way, or interact with, or make part of their lives. People of all ages devoted significant amounts of time to learn a dance, which is both goofy and hard. The choreographed two-minute thing in the video is a single take. You can't fake it, really. People worked weeks and weeks to do this because it was fun, but it wasn't because payoff was going to be great. It wasn't the record company giving a million dollars. The thing about a viral video is that you can make something for $11 and get the exact same reach as you could with a Super Bowl advertisement! That's nothing to scoff at.

The first video had been inspired by the kind of dancing that you see in music videos, combined with cheerleading routines. The next video, which really made them famous, showed them dancing on treadmills. Damian's older sister Trish was a professional ballroom dancer. She loved goofy ideas and grand gestures. One day she went to the gym and came back with a fully formed notion in her head of the band dancing on treadmills and convinced them to do it. They loved the idea but couldn't find anywhere to rent treadmills, so they decided to buy them with a thirty-day return option. They installed them in Trish's house for a week, came up with choreography, filmed the video to the music of the song "Here It Goes Again," and then returned the treadmills.

OK Go dancing on treadmills
screen captures

There was tension with the record company about whether or not it would be of value to post the video on YouTube, so the band held on to the video for a very long time, until it was clear that the record company was done with them. They had been seeding YouTube and getting fans involved, so they knew that this new video would fly. It turned out to be a dramatic example of viral media success. The fan base for OK Go was there and ready—the open competition to emulate the first video had become popular—so the moment they put the new video out, it floated to the top of the YouTube ratings. The band went from obscurity to worldwide fame with the help of an ingenious connection to a new medium, combined with inspired performances that engaged and charmed people by their unselfconscious vitality.

IN NEW YORK THERE ARE OFFICE BUILDINGS full of experts who are trying to create viral videos, hoping to gain the exposure of enormous promotional campaigns at negligible cost. There is nothing new about the concepts of narrative and emotional engagement that people find interesting or surprising in an appealing way, but that is not the only ingredient of viral success. The medium for distribution must allow an easy way for enthusiastic viewers to pass a recommendation along to an ever-expanding audience. YouTube was the place where the virus spread, where the charming vitality of the video was noticed by so many and emulated by some, providing a key element in helping OK Go emerge from the musical wilderness. In the next interview, Chad Hurley, the founder of YouTube, helps us understand how the most successful video Web site came to be and what video sharing may mean in the future.

CHAD HURLEY

Interviewed December 2, 2008

CHAD HURLEY

Chad is interested in art and design. He studied graphic design but got interested in computers and taught himself some basic HTML and Web design. His first job took him to California in 1999, during the Internet bubble, where he was the sole designer in a start-up encryption company that later became PayPal. He is now CEO and cofounder of the video sharing Web site YouTube, the biggest provider of videos on the Internet. In October 2006 he sold YouTube to Google for $1.65 billion. YouTube was born when the founders wanted to share some videos from a dinner party with friends in San Francisco in January 2005. Sending the clips around by email was a bust, as the emails kept getting rejected because they were so big. Posting the videos online was a headache too, so Chad and his friends got to work to design something simpler.

←···· **Chad Hurley**
photos by author

Chad Hurley lives close to the IDEO headquarters in Palo Alto, so I was able to invite him to record the interview in one of our studios there. We set up the cameras in a large space with a high ceiling. In the background is the IDEO bicycle park, where people hoist their commuting bikes up under the ceiling with ropes and pulleys, leaving the space below uncluttered. Chad arrived early in the day, carrying a large cup of Peet's coffee, but he spoke so fluently and continuously that I don't think he had more than one sip of his drink during the entire interview, which lasted over an hour.

Search | Browse | Upl

Categories

Autos & Vehicles
Comedy
Education
Entertainment
Film & Animation
Gaming
Howto & Style
Music
News & Politics
Nonprofits & Activism
People & Blogs
Pets & Animals
Science & Technology
Sports
Travel & Events

Shows
Movies
Trailers
Contests
Events

Recommended for You

Videos Channels

In: **All Categories**   **Popular** | Most Viewed

Spotlight

Collateral Murder? HD
An in-depth analysis of a leaked
military video showing a U.S. arm
helicopter firing on Iraqis.
5,780 views   AlJazeeraEnglish

Flying Puppeh!!

637,586 views
RayWilliamJohnson

**Mascot Falls off
Dugout at Tripl...**

500,198 views
TripleAReno

**How To: Becom
Hottest Woman**
182,670 views
sxephil

**B.o.B featuring
Eminem & Hayley ...**
193,469 views
kingmuzikalbum

**Chinese Guy is NOT
A HOMO!**
139,398 views
pyrobooby

**US Senator Gra
asked to Admit.**
42,375 views
ALIPAC1

YouTube allows everything and all of us to be a spectacle, at least for a moment. But a moment is all we are after, or all we have time for—or so the world of YouTube would lead us to believe.

Carrie Brownstein, *Morning Edition*, National Public Radio, December 28, 2009

CONNECTING VIDEOS

Chad was the only designer at PayPal, so he designed everything, including the logo, credit cards, flyers, the Web site itself, as well as all the ways of dealing with payments online—sign-up flow, sending money, receiving money, auction features, building payment buttons, and eBay transactions. The dramatic success of this last feature led to eBay acquiring PayPal in 2002, so Chad was able to leave with enough resources to take time to work on his own ideas. He stayed in touch with some of the guys back at PayPal, so they could brainstorm about new potential opportunities in the Internet space. Chad remembers where the idea of online video came from.

← **YouTube homepage**
screen capture

This video piece came up as something we found quite interesting just because we had video files on our desktops. We had cameras that could take videos, but there weren't any services that would allow you to seamlessly share those videos with your friends and family. We thought there had to be a market! Flickr was allowing people to share photos, making them publicly available. We found that pretty intriguing and thought there was an opportunity to create an equivalent in the video space, with videos telling richer stories. I mean, photos are intriguing, but video is much more engaging to communicate an idea or experience.

When we first started designing the site, we were looking at the video world, trying to define a design around one experience or one type of content—for example, video profiles, so people could connect with one another. But at the end of the day we realized that we didn't want to box ourselves into a specific category. Coming from PayPal and eBay, we thought that video [would] be a perfect way to describe your products. Initially we had features that allowed people to take a video of a product and put in to an eBay auction, but people didn't use the site in that way.

We decided to create a platform that was pretty general and would allow the users to define the experience, so we provide the tools and sit back to observe how they are using it. It became a generalized platform where people were sharing their experiences, sharing events, and then evolved into creating their own entertainment to distribute to one another.

When we started designing the site, it was difficult to share a video online. We looked at the problems that frustrated us—dealing with different formats of videos, files being too large to share through email, having the person receiving the video be unable to play it, because they had the wrong media player or lacked the correct bandwidth to stream it back at a reasonable rate.

Chad started working on the site in early 2004 with a group of friends who were willing to collaborate for almost no pay, with the promise that they would have equity once funding came through. They met at his house and sketched out ideas on a whiteboard in his garage. A few months later they had a site up and running that people could use, but it wasn't until the beginning of 2005 that they launched officially and raised a round of funding.

They focused on simplifying the experience of uploading and viewing video, solving the challenge of different file formats by reencoding hundreds of video codecs (*coder-dec*oder) into Flash. Once reencoded, the videos could be served through Flash players, already installed in 98 percent of browsers. The person uploading files doesn't need to think about the format: YouTube does all the work and processing, reducing the bit rate of the video so it streams for every bandwidth. The viewer can watch using built-in Flash, without thinking about whether they have the right kind of media player.

YouTube logo
photo by Rego Korosi/Creative Commons

Behind the scenes they built architecture with an infrastructure that would scale at reasonable cost, affording them good financial control. They also made the video portable, so that anyone could embed a link to a YouTube video in HTML and put it on their own Web site or blog. This provided a marketing hook to drive people back to YouTube, so that their traffic would grow as the use of the videos spread across the Internet. This business concept was inspired by the portability of the payment button that had made PayPal so successful in the eBay application.

YouTube happened at the right place and time. Video cameras were cheap enough for the consumer market, and video editing programs were inexpensive and easy to use, so that huge numbers of videos were being created. People just needed some way of sharing them that was easy and cheap, ideally free. At that time bandwidth costs to host and push the data out were plunging. In the 1990s the rates to deliver data made it prohibitive to create a video site, but after the Internet bust too much capacity was available, and Chad was able to find some hosting services with extremely low rates and uncapped bandwidth limits. He signed deals that got them started, but the hosts quickly realized that their business model wouldn't be able to sustain a site like YouTube, so Chad and his team started to build their own architecture to serve the data. They were determined to create a neutral platform, so that anyone could participate with any type of video.

> We weren't going to define the experience for the people who used the site. We wanted the community to rate, share, and view videos, and thereby vote on what was engaging or entertaining to them. We figured this was going to be a much more scalable solution. There was no way we were going to be able to keep up with the amount of video that we were receiving, so we needed to allow the community to populate the pages, bringing the most viewed and highest rated pages to the top.

> The catalog of videos we had at the time was relatively small, but it was already hard to navigate. We continue to have these problems to this day. We receive well over fourteen hours of video every minute on our site. There is no way you can consume all of that video in your lifetime. We had to use the power of the masses to view the content, to curate the site, and now we have millions of people doing that on a global basis for us.

> We still struggle with that! We feel that there can be better ways to sort through the sea of video that we've hosted. Search takes you to a certain point. You can search titles, descriptions and key words, or any other element of the metadata associated with the video, to try and find what you're looking for. You can also use the community to define things by entertainment, or engagement by numbers of views and ratings. We are still looking for new ways to catalog and categorize videos, so that people have an experience that they can dig through.

I think a lot of services struggle with this, even iTunes. They have millions of songs. People primarily consume the head of the content. They have search, but also they have an editorial team that's trying to program pages for them and feed content to people. We have a much broader pattern of consumption than the head alone, so we're always looking for ways that don't just focus on a narrow segment of content but also unlock the entire tail beyond views and ratings. There's probably an approach to get the community more involved, but we just haven't put our finger on it yet.

DESIGNING THE YOUTUBE WEB SITE

Chad wants to build both a platform and a community. YouTube is winning against the competition because people who are creating their own content are allowed to interact with others in their personal networks and interest groups. YouTube has become the de facto standard for freely shared online video. It also makes tools available to content providers to help mitigate copyright infringement. Chad believes that in order to create a successful design for a community, you have to design an interface with a look and feel that people can relate to and trust.

I designed everything—the YouTube logo, the interface, and the design of the entire Web site. If someone is trying to create something in a very professional way, they sometimes make it overproduced and too slick, so that people don't want to participate in the community because they don't trust it. It feels corporate. I think that eBay, Craigslist, Google, and potentially YouTube have been successful just because they look basic; they look like the community designed and built them. I tried to apply that idea when designing the site. I didn't go for any slick kind of new HTML code that would give fancy rollovers; nor did we build the entire site in Flash, even though we are serving Flash video. It was a basic kind of HTML construction with blue links.

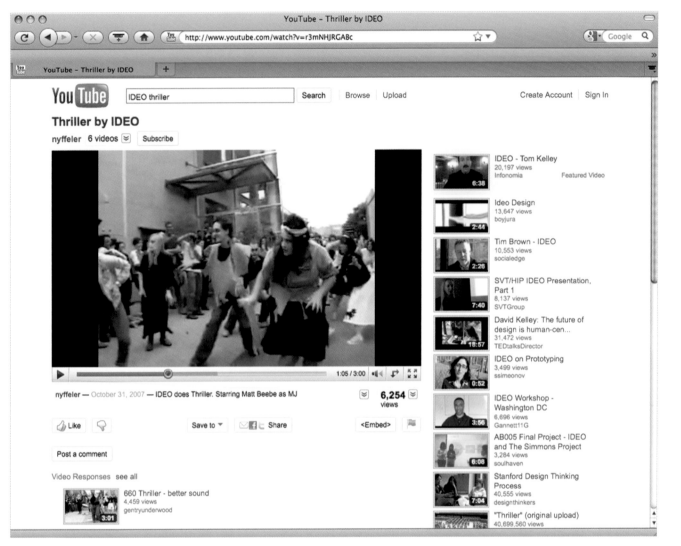

"Thriller" remake by IDEO, YouTube
screen capture

I did worry about branding, because I think branding is very important in the world of design, in that you want people to remember the product they used, so I tried to come up with an easy-to-remember name. It took me about a week just trying to think about the name. We were trying to express this idea of personal television. The name YouTube is a play on that—a playful kind of word that people could relate to, wrapped into a simplified logo, so that people could get a sense of what our site is about.

NEW REVENUE MODELS AND LEGAL RIGHTS

By the end of 2008 YouTube had grown to nearly three hundred people at its headquarters, plus a similar number shared with Google around the world, but it was still lean and mean compared with the overall size of Google. Being acquired by Google has given YouTube access to talented people to help build the site as well as more resources to build the architecture that they need to improve the speed and quality of the videos they're serving. They are also encouraged to preserve the start-up culture of the company and the kind of the environment that they work in. When Eric Schmidt, Larry Page, and Sergey Brin approached Chad about acquisition, they assured him that they wanted the people at YouTube to be empowered to make their own decisions. Chad is still focused on progress:

> I still feel like we're taking it day by day. I guess we haven't had much time to reflect on everything that's happened because there's so much yet to be improved, and we're trying to build a new model for media distribution. There are services coming out that are just replicating the past, by building traditional distribution models for network consumer content. We want that to be part of our platform, but we want everyone to compete on a level playing field. Everyone should have the same stage, and we don't want to be biased and make decisions toward one type of content versus another.
>
> We feel that there should now be an opportunity for creative individuals around the world to produce content and support themselves. We're already starting to see that, with users on our site making hundreds of thousands of dollars. These are individuals in their homes that have an opportunity to support their creativity. It's just the tip of the iceberg, as people now have access to the tools, distribution, and audience that we provide. They'll be better at telling the story, better at creating a piece of entertainment, better at sharing their experiences through the power of video. Look at Smosh, for example. They're some college kids who create goofy little comedy

skits. They're making pretty good money creating short pieces of entertainment that generate massive audiences, the same audiences that you might typically associate with TV shows.

People still like to throw YouTube in a box in terms of just being about silly cat videos, implying that user-generated content is useless because advertisers don't want to associate themselves with it. I think we're seeing a dramatic shift, that advertisers who associate themselves with this kind of grassroots media have higher engagement. Users are more responsive to ads that are placed against user-generated content than traditional, professionally produced content.

Google has helped YouTube develop more sophisticated business models for advertising support, allowing them to continue with a free service to consumers. They offer a "partner program" for ad placement, with thresholds for time in the system and number of views to trigger ads. Some are in a separate window on the page, others on a small banner along the bottom of the video window, plus pre-roll or post-roll videos. This combination yields enough revenue to keep YouTube profitable and also to share with the partners who created the video. It works like AdSense for Web sites, where Google makes some revenue from the ads that are placed on the sites, but the majority of the revenue goes to owners of the Web sites.

The new revenue models that are emerging for online distribution are in conflict with the complex mechanisms that have evolved in the past, particularly for music, but also for video. In music many different people own a piece of just one song—the songwriters, publishers, labels, artists, and rights-collecting organizations. The new models that are emerging make it difficult for them to adjust. Family members often inherit rights after the original creators are long gone. Nobody knows who owns what, and the record labels have no incentive to sort it out because they don't want to pay anyone. The television networks are similar: they have large catalogs of content that just sit there because it's too expensive to sort out the rights for online distribution.

YouTube has tried to approach this morass of confusion about rights from a new angle. Instead of just identifying music through audio fingerprinting and taking it down, they've created opportunities

YouTube
photo by Thomas van de Weerd/Creative Commons

for the record labels to have a new revenue source. As each video is uploaded, it is run through a content-ID system for music, which makes a fingerprint of the audio file and compares it to the YouTube music catalog. All the major record labels have subscribed to this catalog and defined rules about how the music should be used, so it's either taken down because the user doesn't have the rights associated with the video or left up for marketing reasons. The motivation to leave it up could be to generate sales though links to online retail sources, to allow ads to be placed against it to generate revenue for the record label, or just to expand awareness of the music. Now the users have a free and legal way to be creative with music within their videos that didn't exist before.

All these complex issues of revenue generation and legal rights seem far away from Chad's background as a graphic designer. He may have started off designing approachable Web sites, but now he seems to be a successful entrepreneur designing revenue streams. He thinks of this as a natural evolution.

> Design for me is always about just trying to solve problems, whether it's visually, conceptually, physically, or virtually with a Web site. You're trying to relate to people through the way that you put something together. At first I was designing the essence of the site, from the logo to the interface. That evolved to building the team that we needed to make the company successful, building it into a sustainable business. That transition from designer to CEO is something I have viewed as the same thing. You're still trying to solve problems.

> Everything we've done from the beginning has just been based on trusting our instincts. When you're trying to move at speed, you just have to make decisions. You can't hesitate. Too many times people create companies for the wrong incentives. Instead of thinking about the problem, the product, service, or site that customers want to use, they're thinking about the business model and what's going to make them a lot of money. We knew our service was going to be ad supported. That was our business model. We knew that if we had a large audience, a global community, that we'd be able to build a great business off of that, so we focused on the design for the people in that community.

Different forms of moving-image media are no longer easy to distinguish. Film, television, and online video are all digital, where the same content can be delivered across a wide variety of platforms, scalable in size and resolution. Inexpensive tools for creating content have made for endless supply, as anyone, anywhere, can create a piece of video at anytime. Chad welcomes this democratization.

> You used to have scarce distribution. Not only were the select few controlling the creation, they were also controlling the distribution, and both of those things are disappearing within our world. I think that changes things tremendously because everything from the theater, to your TV, to your computer, is going to be connected to the Internet. Every device is going to be IP-enabled, and you're going to be able to receive any

piece of content, at any time, through any device. This new world is approaching faster than anyone ever expected.

People have talked about IP TV for a long time, but they have been thinking about it in the wrong way. For example, the telcos have been building libraries of content to deliver on demand to the television set. I think there's just going to be video that people access from anywhere that it resides in the cloud, delivered to any device. There won't be specific libraries that are defined as IP TV.

I think there's probably going to be an evolution to a media RSS feed, a more intelligent way to index video content across the Web. When you access a piece of video, not only will you stream it to your device, but it's going to be wrapped in some type of rule or rules around its usage. Either you're going to be paying a per-play rate for what you or your service consumes, or that content may be wrapped with some kind of rule for advertising. The ad can be pulled from the person who owns the content, from a third party, or from a site like YouTube.

THE DOMINANT POSITION enjoyed by YouTube and Google has some detractors, as many people have concerns about big companies creating monopolies and being motivated by business values rather than social conscience. Alexandra Juhasz teaches media studies and is interested in the political and artistic uses of media. In the next interview, she describes her studies of YouTube and her misgivings about the cultural change that is radically altering society and the landscape of media.

ALEXANDRA JUHASZ

Interviewed October 28, 2008

ALEXANDRA JUHASZ

Alexandra is a professor of media studies at Pitzer College in California, where she teaches video production and film and video theory. She is interested in the political and artistic uses of media and in theories as well as the production of media in relationship to political or personal issues. In the mid-1980s she was producing AIDS activist videos in New York and then writing about the processes for her PhD in cinema studies from New York University. Since then, the themes have changed, but her commitment to projects that involve both creating material and theorizing about its rationale has been consistent throughout her work. She has taught courses at many universities on women and film, feminist film, and women's documentary. Her current work is on and about YouTube and other more radical uses of digital media. Her "video-book," *Learning from YouTube*, about her course and YouTube's failings more generally, will be published by the MIT Press in Fall 2010. She also recently produced the micro-budget feature film, *The Owls* (Cheryl Dunye, 2010), which premiered at the Berlin Film Festival.

⟵ Alexandra Juhasz
photos by author

Alexandra lives in a tree-lined residential neighborhood of Pasadena. I flew down from San Francisco with my video gear a week before the November 2008 election and found her wearing a T-shirt printed with Obama's face and the words "Another Mama for Obama" with the *O* of Obama modified as the peace symbol. It was a beautiful day, so we sat in the garden, with the shade of the trees occasionally changing to dappled sunlight. As we talked, we were interrupted every now and again by a low-flying plane overhead or one of her dogs barking.

WHAT'S WRONG WITH YOUTUBE

Alexandra has given a lot of thought to the social impact of YouTube. She teaches a class both about and on YouTube, studying it with her students to try to understand the cultural implications of the new level of connectivity for video. During the run-up to the 2009 election, she was looking at how the broad circulation of people-produced media was affecting the outcome, feeling optimistic about the positive impact for the Obama campaign. She is more critical about other aspects of the emergence of YouTube, disappointed that the potential for democratization is not fulfilled.

←···· **Alexandra's YouTube channel**
screen capture

I study YouTube, and I think YouTube fails to deliver the promises of these new technologies, namely, the ways in which they really could enhance our ability to communicate, open up channels of discourse, and allow people to build things together. When I tried to do something serious there, teaching a college course, we all found that that the communal building of knowledge simply can't happen on YouTube, and I am interested in studying why not. For instance, my students and I learned that the idea that YouTube is "democratic," which is one of the ways it sells itself, is simply untrue. Instead, as is true for many of these social-networking applications, the structure of popularity is how YouTube is organized. The more something is voted for, the more visible it becomes, and it dominates the terrain.

Everything that is not popular, what I call "NicheTube," is almost invisible; it's very hard to find. And so you get a kind of democracy of the loudest voices, and not even just the loudest voices. The videos that tend to rise in popularity on YouTube express very hegemonic understandings of our world in a loud and clear fashion. These are things that already make us feel comfortable, usually jokes, parodies of things we're already familiar with, or reiterations of popular culture. In a democracy, you don't want to only hear things in the public sphere that you already know, that you're already comfortable with, that you've already seen. That's not the democracy I want to live in.

The invisibility of the underlayer on YouTube is of great concern to me. Because the search function is so poor and the site always pushes the most popular into your face, you probably will only rarely see the people who are expressing alternative viewpoints. It's not exactly a flattening of culture. It's like there's two layers, really. And they don't ever speak to each other.

With her background in political activism, Alexandra thinks a lot about counterculture and what it feels like to view mainstream society from the outside. Her work has been committed to people who are critical of society and who occupy that analytical or oppositional space comfortably. She finds the idea of popularity extremely troubling because in her eyes it only offers a limited and juvenile way to organize life. She came to YouTube as a scholar and maker of activist media, wondering why she felt instinctively repelled by the YouTube experience.

People kept sending me clips through email saying, "Oh, go watch this video on YouTube." And I'd go and it was always just some ridiculous piece of fluff; some thirty-second joke about popular culture which I'm not particularly invested in anyway … and half the time I didn't get the joke, and if I did get the joke, it was at somebody's expense. It was this really low form of media production and for a while I just ignored it. I said, "You know, I don't understand what's going on here. I don't really care. This isn't what I meant when I said there was going to be a revolution."

And after maybe six or nine months, I thought, "It's ridiculous that I'm not paying attention to this," so I devised this innovative course, "Learning from YouTube," where I thought my media-savvy students and I could work together to study, analyze, and name in real time components of a cultural change that was radically altering our society and its media landscape.

Alexandra recorded all the class sessions on video and only allowed the students to present their work on YouTube, so that they were continuously experiencing the medium as they developed their research. She asked them to consider why, with the opportunity for people to make and share video, the resulting material is so uninspiring and insipid.

She realizes that, although we've been raised in a culture surrounded by images, most of us are not fluent makers of images. We are better equipped as writers of words because of the literate nature of our education, so the sudden access to the tools to make video has not been paired with access to education about media production. You don't have a rich vocabulary to express yourself in sophisticated ways with the new tools just because you have access to a camera and an editing system.

> Typical YouTube videos, the bad ones made by ordinary people, are uncut, without concern for framing, lighting, or the quality of the cameras. We've never seen such bad video, really. What would those video blogs be like if we could imagine a small amount of visual sophistication?

> The other question for me is one of content and not just of form. What kind of education do regular users need to express things profound, or things personal, or things critical? You hope that people will gain the ability to think about formal complexity and to learn from what's around them, but at the same time, that has to come with the belief that they have something valuable to say themselves. (I do, of course, believe everyone does!) Most of what you see on YouTube is mainstream culture, either repeated or parodied, and gives us no insight into the daily thinking of regular people, outside their fascinations with media.

> There really are two YouTubes. If you think about book publishing, or film, or other previous forms of mass media, it wasn't so strongly just one or the other: people-made (badly

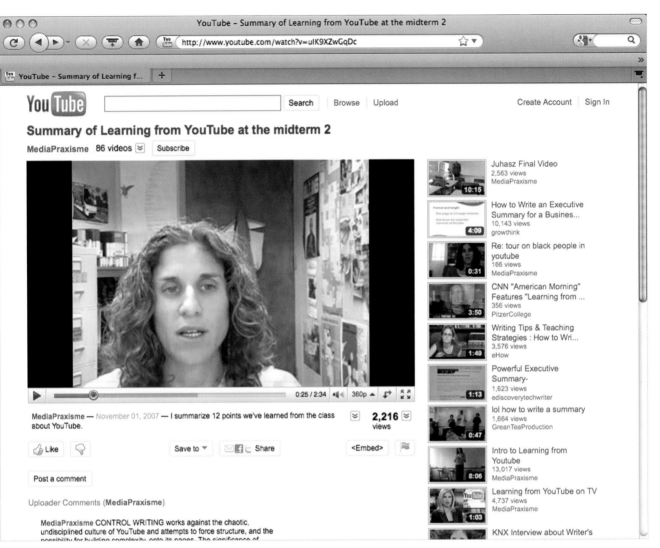

Alexandra's MediaPaxisme, YouTube
screen capture

made) and corporate (well-made). There was all of this
finessed space in between a Hollywood blockbuster and a
micro-budget avant-garde art film where very sophisticated
work occurred, for example, indie films.

The research completed for the "Learning from YouTube" class up to the
end of 2008 concluded that at least half the content was professionally
produced, making corporate produced media predominant in an
environment that is thought to be democratic. The vast majority of
videos are made to sell things, often music, and people often repurpose
this corporate media for their own production. Fans can make

inventive and self-expressive material by hacking, reformatting, or repurposing mainstream content, but Alexandra is more interested in productive and critical expressions that step away from the production of some corporation and provide a personal vision of the world. She is exploring what else is needed, besides access to the tools, which simply facilitate recutting professionally produced corporate video, to grow ideas, abilities, and possibilities that will make our society better. She believes that teachers are needed to provide structure and give the leadership to organize the discourse.

> You need people to say, "For today I'm going to 'discipline' this space." I use this word with quotes because it's been very hard for me to realize that I want someone coming into this anarchic space to discipline it. If you're hoping to reach goals at the end, there is some taming, defining, and purposing that needs to occur. Wikipedia is probably the most successful model of these user-generated learning communities, and YouTube is not, because it's at once completely anarchic but then actually controlled very fiercely by the corporation that owns it. There's only the artifice of user control. We might want to imagine a real community where users are producing everything.

> It's the imperative of corporations to make money. I see that particularly on YouTube. The result of my analysis of the site is simple: what they want you to do is move as quickly and unpredictably as possible from one thing to another, because that is how they are going to get your eyeballs to ads. It's a perfectly viable model for making money, but it's not a viable model for moving expression and art through a culture. You can see in YouTube the profound constraints that are written into the system because it is organized first to make money, not democracy, culture, community—and certainly not revolution.

NEW CONNECTIONS FOR VIDEO

Google purchased YouTube in 2006 for $1.65 billion. That in itself was a powerful vote of confidence that Chad Hurley had led the company to a position of dominance and that YouTube would withstand competition to stay in a lead position. By 2009 the services had been improved with effective search and the introduction of high definition, eroding the validity of many of the criticisms about YouTube being designed for the lowest common denominator and showing that Chad's philosophy of trying to encourage independent video producers had some legs. Google and YouTube are dominant financially, making them seem like big bad business to many radicals, but there is an element of idealism in their philosophy that separates them from previous generations of dominant businesses, and the services that they offer for free are irresistible to almost everyone. *(See the interview with Larry Page and Sergey Brin in chapter 7 of my book* Designing Interactions.*)*

Online video is emerging in a hockey stick joyride curve of expansion *(see the interview with Paul Saffo in chapter 1)*, fueled by inexpensive video cameras and desktop editing, combined with the arrival of adequate bandwidth for viewing on personal computers and handhelds. This means that video content of all types is becoming available online as well as in traditional media, so the door is open for new connections. Entrepreneurial offerings are springing up for a host of specialist applications that complement the dominant YouTube.

One of the more elegantly designed Web sites for delivering TV shows and movies is Hulu.com, offering both short clips and full-length videos for free. The site is ad-driven, with integrated video ads and banners played during the streaming of content. Hulu was founded in 2007 as a joint project of NBC Universal and News Corp., partnered with several consumer portals, including AOL, Comcast's Fancast.com, MSN, MySpace, and Yahoo! Consumers can enjoy lots of popular TV shows and movies from content providers, leveraging the material owned by NBC Universal and News Corp. Vimeo is another cleanly designed video sharing Web site that allows people to publish their videos for public consumption or just for friends and family. Hulu and

Vimeo may not be a competitive threat to YouTube or iTunes, but they offer attractive choices for consumers to gain more access to video content. Apple is educating consumers on the benefits of watching video through iTunes Movie Rentals on iPhones, iPods, and Apple TV devices, and companies like Netflix have pioneered the movement from physical DVD rentals to downloading streamed versions on demand.

THERE ARE ALSO OPPORTUNITIES for subscription services, offering business-to-business solutions for integrating video onto Web sites. An early innovator in this space is Brightcove, founded by Jeremy Allaire and Bob Mason. In the next interview, Bob and Jeremy Merle, who led the user interface design team, explain their approach.

BOB MASON WITH JEREMY MERLE

Interviewed November 12, 2008

BOB MASON

Bob Mason cofounded Brightcove in 2004 with Jeremy Allaire. They saw the possibility of a complete end-to-end solution to deliver video from any creator to any customer, across diverse devices, allowing content owners to have the same breadth of communication that had previously been limited to major corporations and media companies. Jeremy took the role of CEO and Bob CTO as they set about designing an online video platform to be used by professional publishers. Bob provides leadership for Brightcove's vision, design, and architecture. Before founding Brightcove, he was a founding member of the product team and a software architect at ATG, an innovative and market leading e-commerce software provider.

←····· Bob Mason
photos by author

JEREMY MERLE

Jeremy Merle is the Director of Product Design and User Experience. He leads the team that defines Brightcove's visual identity, user experience and product design, focusing on developing designs for the unique needs of individual groups of users while at the same time achieving consistency across all the different modules.

← **Jeremy Merle**
photos by author

The offices of Brightcove are located across the street from the MIT Press, so I was able to interview Bob Mason when I was in town to talk to Doug Sery, a senior acquisitions editor, about publishing this book. After recording a conversation with Bob, he suggested that we set up my cameras to capture a demo of the product, including his commentary. I could tell that he had presented that demo many times before, as his descriptions were obviously well rehearsed. Afterward he asked if I would like to meet Jeremy Merle, the leader of the interaction design team, so I was also able to record a short interview with Jeremy as well.

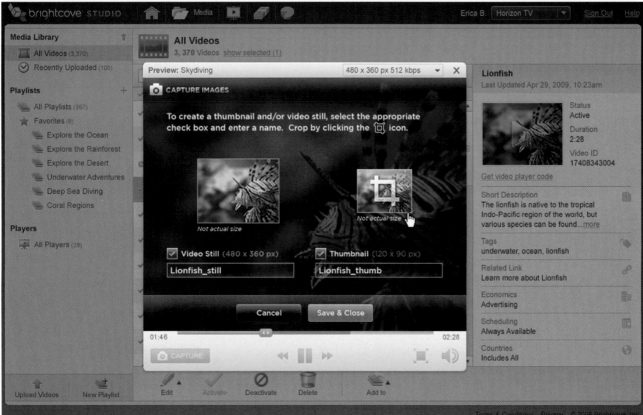

ONLINE VIDEO

Brightcove offers an on-demand video platform that allows content owners to publish, distribute, and deliver content to their audiences. It provides back-end tools connected to front-end user experiences, so that customers can use the Brightcove authoring tools to bring video to consumers in specifically tailored solutions that are fully integrated with the rest of their businesses.

> **Bob:** We have to have really good design of the usability of our back-office tools, be cognizant of the latest consumer trends and of what's happening in the social-networking space, and try and make sure that our customers' online video business is successful and meeting their audiences' needs. We've been focused on allowing non-media companies to have the same powerful tool set as our media company customers. If you're an institution, the government, or a corporation with a message you want to deliver to your audience, you can use the exact same things that one of the top five channels in the U.S. would have been able to use in the past.
>
> We have focused on trying to make the system as simple as possible. Literally, if you have video content and you can encode it digitally, you can upload, launch, and create a video player experience in less than thirty minutes, skin it, brand it, put in on your Web site, and it's all done instantaneously. That is our design mantra.

The Brightcove platform
images courtesy of Brightcove

Much of the Brightcove offering is transparent to the end user. They have developed software that allows the user to find video on a Web page and play it without adjusting settings or waiting for buffering. The software automatically recognizes the available bandwidth and adjusts to it: If it sees a high-speed connection, it delivers a high-quality version of the video. If it recognizes an overloaded wireless connection, it automatically degrades the quality of the video to avoid stuttering or long buffering times. The system infrastructure is also designed to accommodate lots of individual variability, cause by sudden peaks of traffic generated by special events like weather, sports or politics. One customer's spike in usage is another's trough, so collectively no single customer needs to over-provision hardware when they have temporary spikes. Bob has attempted to optimize the balance between automated solutions and allowing human judgment to play a part:

> When we start thinking about how you want to promote different videos—why is this video important to associate with this other video—there can be metadata matching and some algorithmic things that allow things to be connected together, but in many circumstances, there's an innate sense of understanding who your audience is, what content you have available, what's occurring during the day today, and what the news is. Trying to tie all those different things together really requires someone who has an intimate knowledge of their audience, and giving them some manual controls is really important.

Brightcove is a software service business, with all revenues coming from license fees. Price structures vary depending on the size of the customer's organization, the complexity of the business needs, and the number of videos that people are watching. Free tools and services for video delivery work adequately for consumers and prosumers, but there are many levels of demand from businesses and organizations where people are willing to spend thousands, even tens of thousands of dollars, a month to have a very robust and reliable system, with relationships that encompasses strategic vision, account management, and sophisticated customer support. Bob talks about the positioning of his offering in comparison to the free services:

> What is interesting about YouTube is the question of what's good enough. We spend hours on end watching a high production value on television or going to the movies, but there is an equal amount of interest and engagement around stuff that is lower quality and valuable in a different way. That is

what YouTube proved out in the marketplace. Though the video quality experience is mixed in YouTube, the total user experience allows people to get very engaged in a different type of environment.

You see other content-oriented sites, like Hulu, delivering high-quality content and a very rich user experience. People really resonate with that, whereas they are looking to YouTube to provide a different type of experience. Each company has their own challenges. Obviously Hulu would love to have the audience that YouTube has, but for YouTube it's more difficult to monetize. From our perspective, our content partners are really looking to be able to communicate directly to their audience. YouTube, Hulu, and all these other video platforms are important as part of their distribution strategy, but fundamentally they want to have a relationship directly with their audience. That's where a platform like Brightcove really provides a lot of value.

At the time of this interview, in 2008, high-definition (HD) video was still not very widespread. It had reached farther into television distribution than online, helped by satellite and cable, but it was not prevalent online. The limitations came first from bandwidth, with countries like Korea making the infrastructure investments to allow distribution, but the United States still lagging far behind. Screens with 1,920 by 1,080 pixels to deliver full HD were also limited and expensive, but the signs of change were already there, so what are the implications?

I think the investments that the phone and cable companies are making to improve bandwidth in North America will facilitate a reduction in the differentiation between what is online video versus what is more traditional broadcast media. I think you'll start to see fluid connections between your PC experience, your mobile experience, and your television experience. That will be particularly exciting over the next five to ten years.

In many circumstances the problems around online video delivery are going to increase in complexity over time, and having a strong technology platform and vendors to help people wade through that will allow them to focus purely on what they do best: create great content. In the early days of the Web, you had many companies that built their own content-management systems as well as their own ad-serving systems. The market eventually got to a state where you had very large successful companies that addressed and tackled those particular areas. I think we are at a similar early stage of recognizing that trend in the video space and anticipating a broader platform investment that companies are going to need around rich media in general.

I think there'll be a lot of interesting things that happen from a technology perspective—increased usage of HD; fluid access of content from mobile devices to PCs, to televisions—but I think what will be most interesting is just the breadth of stories that will be able to be told. You'll start seeing content produced by companies that you would not normally think of as a traditional media company or a video company, but they are going to be broadcasters in this space, and they'll have equal rights to be able to reach and build their own audiences.

DESIGNING THE INTERACTIONS

When Bob and Jeremy started the company in 2005, they created a design based on a linear workflow, with tabs separating each major step. First was a Dashboard tab, with tutorials and explanations of the terms used to structure the interface. The Assets tab enabled uploading of images and video, which could then be packaged into video Titles, consisting of a package of metadata and media that could be displayed to an end user. The Lineups tab allowed choices about organization of the material, from full manual control to completely automatic using self-organizing algorithms. Under the Players tab, templates allowed the speedy creation of video experiences without

Brightcove player styling and player menu
images courtesy Brightcove

writing a single line of code by adding branding treatments and
selecting the desired appearance elements.

By the fall of 2008 they had completed a redesign based on a better
understanding of the behavior and needs of their customers. They
launched a new product called Brightcove 3, replacing the tabs with
three main workflow modules: one for managing media, a second
for publishing video, and the third for controlling advertising. In
the Media module, a unified interface offered the ability to manage
what had previously been separated into the Assets, Titles, and
Lineups tabs, with simple drag-and-drop actions. Playlists could be
published with the aid of dialog boxes, choosing between manual
control and Smart Playlists, with search-and-sort choices. Once the
content was organized, it could be easily programmed into different
video players. In the Publishing module, templates were provided for
creating players with unique appearances, drawing from libraries of
navigation tools, fonts, and colors. The results were instantly available
and updated in real time. The Advertising module offered control for
the person interested in revenue generation. The video library and
players could be set up to manage campaigns by adding advertising
"Key Value Pairs," turning ads on or off for different videos, or setting
up the ad policies for the players, for example, pre-roll, mid-roll, or
post-roll ads.

Jeremy Merle is a user-interface designer focused on understanding
the people who will use the product. The research that his team
conducted identified three main stakeholders: media producers,
design integrators, and business developers. The media producers
programmed content, assigning all of the attributes, grouping,

Examples of Brightcove's media organization
image courtesy of Brightcove

uploading and ingesting the content, and then programming it into the appropriate video player. They asked questions like, What's the name of that video? What description of it should appear on the Web site? and What related links might there be and where that should they go? The design integrators were focused on the look and feel of the players and how the branding integrated into the Web sites that they were developing. The business developers were more focused on revenue, advertising, and advertising policies—which ad should play and when, and how the revenue generating mechanisms should be programmed into the content.

> **Jeremy:** As part of the new design, we looked at breaking Brightcove down into separate modules that are focused on a separate user experience—but which are also consistent throughout the whole product. There is a place where producers can group their content, organizing it into Playlists,

and then grouping those Playlists and programming them into video players. There is another part to focus on creating the video player and choosing a template or layout to put on the Web site, and organizing the look and feel of the player experience—selecting the color and fonts to match the company's brand.

Some of our customers spend all their time working with a single module, but there are also people who cross back and forth between all of the modules. I think we've done a nice job to add the consistency not only with the visual design but also with the interaction metaphors, so that if someone is using the video player in the Publishing module and then they switch over to the Media module to organize content, the behaviors and gestures are exactly the same. They are essentially familiar with the application without using it. In the future I think we will continue to move toward seamless integration, focusing on how users are interacting.

IN THE NEXT INTERVIEW WE STEP ASIDE from the world of online video to learn more about the most minimal of—and perhaps most surprising—new connections. How and why has Twitter become so pervasive? Why is a real-time message of less than 140 characters so attractive? Ev Williams reveals the secrets.

EV WILLIAMS

Interviewed December 2, 2008

EV WILLIAMS

Ev is very entrepreneurial and likes to create products and companies. He enjoyed programming at high school in Nebraska but dropped out of college to found Plexus, a CD-ROM development company. He came to San Francisco to be closer to the Internet boom, worked for O'Reilly Media for a short time, and then cofounded Pyra Labs with Meg Hourihan to make project-management software. A note-taking feature spun off as Blogger, one of the first Web applications for creating and managing blogs. Google acquired Pyra Labs in early 2003, but Ev was not comfortable in a larger organization, so he left Google in October 2004 to cofound Odeo, with the idea of combining streaming audio with blogging. While there, he experimented with real-time short messages, leading to the start of Twitter. In late 2006 he created a new company to combine Odeo and Twitter. He then sold the Odeo part of the enterprise and focused his energies on developing Twitter with his cofounder Jack Dorsey and the design team that they had by that time assembled.

⟵ Ev Williams
photos by author

The Twitter offices, with their generous paned windows and large advertising billboards on the roof, are located on a handsome office block in San Francisco. Ev Williams sat on a couch as we recorded the interview, with a series of rooms behind him giving on to the main corridor and light streaming through from the outside windows. It was around lunchtime. The kitchen was the first room, so we saw people coming in to pick up a cup of coffee and a snack or returning from a trip out via the elevators. It felt like a friendly community of cheerful young people enjoying their opportunity to develop new software together.

A SERIAL ENTREPRENEUR

Ev Williams was young when he started hacking around, trying to figure out how to build things. He stumbled on the Internet and knew intuitively that it would be the next big thing, so he set about teaching himself HTML, graphic design, and Web application development skills. He started a family business in Nebraska with his brother and some money from his dad during the early years of the Internet boom. They created a couple of CD-ROMs and tried many different projects to build software and media products, learning as they went along, spending sixteen hours a day for several years gradually acquiring expertise. After a while Ev became frustrated with the lack of money and ability to create the types of products he wanted to design, so he headed for California. He got a job with O'Reilly Media, the book and Web publisher, to develop Web and server software.

> I actually didn't survive too long as an employee, even though it was a great company and later was very useful for me in terms of connections and support. But I didn't like being an employee, so I left there after a few months and started working as a contractor doing Web and Web application development. This was mid-boom time, in 1998. After a year or year and a half my confidence was bolstered enough to take on another entrepreneurial venture.

Tweeting
photo by Nicolas Zurcher

Ev cofounded Pyra Labs with Meg Hourihan to develop Web-based tools for project management and team collaboration. He had lot of theories about personal information manager (PIM) software, as he was always trying to get his own head more organized. When the Web came along, and he was working with other people in teams, it seemed obvious that the tools should be online and support collaboration. At that time Microsoft Outlook was dominant, but he felt that the design of their PIM/email task management offering was stilted. He had a lot of innovative ideas about linking email to tasks and making events and messages task-related.

> Blogger came shortly after the PIMs for a very similar reason. Weblogs were just becoming a thing in early '99, at least the thing people talked about, and I and a couple other people on my team read Weblogs, plus I'd always had a personal Web site which I turned into a blog. I had written a script just to allow me to publish to it; just a tool that I used myself. I've always been very selfish in designing, when using something it occurs to me how it could be better or what I want it to do. So that's where I always start.
>
> My script meant that when I had a thought I could put it on the Web, and I found that really changed the dynamic of having a personal site. It was pretty exciting and tapped into the whole idea of blogs, and more importantly automated the process of publishing. That was the initial spark for the product, and then there was a lot of theorizing about whether it was worthwhile to build and if we should build it, but as it was so simple and we could do it quickly, so why not just throw it out there? And that worked!

Jorn Barger, the editor of RobotWisdom.com, coined the term *Weblog* in 1997. The short form *blog* was coined by a friend of Ev, Peter Merholz, who jokingly broke the word *Weblog* into the phrase *we blog* in the sidebar of his own blog in 1999. Ev soon adopted *blog* as both a noun and a verb and devised the term *blogger* as a brand name for the tool that he was developing, leading to the widespread use of *blog* and *blogger*.

> We always said we were creating a tool for Web geeks, and we considered ourselves to be part of that group. That was a great idea at first, but I think it kept us a little bit out of the mainstream that we could have gotten to faster. It was always just, "What do we want in this tool?"
>
> We made odd choices because we thought we were going to build a tool that lets you publish to your existing Web site, so Blogger would transfer files from our server to your server, assuming that everyone had their own server and they knew how to set up FTP. At first we didn't offer any predesigned

Publishing a blog post
screen capture

templates, because we assumed you would want to create your own design. Obviously a much more mainstream audience has neither of those things. They didn't have a hosting provider, and they wanted to choose a pretty template. That allowed us to create something very simple at first that did attract people like us who had followings already and had some influence. Eventually we enabled a wider audience to tap into the same desire by making it easier and easier.

You can't invent something new by going and asking people what they want because they don't know, but I think you can invent something new by imagining yourself what you may want and then being more free thinking. Once that exists, in order to make it better you've got to start listening to people. That's what happened with Blogger.

For a long time we were listening to our early adopters, who were always our core customers and important to us, but their needs weren't the same as a more mainstream user's needs in the long term. We focused a lot on building more power features when we could have been working on the ease of use and the more mainstream stuff. That was a really tough choice. I think it comes up with a lot of Web apps and other software. We had to make a choice and we weren't very disciplined about making it at first. Eventually Blogger found its place, to become a mainstream blog publishing tool that is easy to use, but without the most features.

Ev did the initial design of the site himself, but when he was pushing for a more consumer-facing design, he asked for help from an accomplished Web designer, Derek Powazek, who created the orange Blogger logo and helped to make the site seem fresh and accessible.

Pyra Labs launched Blogger in 1999, and Ev raised half a million dollars to expand the company and put a team in place, growing to a peak of seven people in 2000. Then the dot-com bubble burst and resources suddenly dried up, so that by the beginning of 2001 Ev was the only employee, running the service from soup to nuts. This limitation on resources forced him to keep the design simple, as he couldn't write code for sophisticated new features at the same time as keeping the service afloat. He was always trying to grow, always trying to reach the mainstream audience, but he was paying the bills with a subscription service aimed at the more serious niche audience. He persisted and gradually expanded the service, increasing the server capacity and keeping the quality of the experience rewarding for the ever-increasing number of people who were taking advantage of the site to start blogs.

In 2003 Google offered to purchase Pyra Labs, but only if it became clear that Blogger would be focused as a mainstream product, so once they joined Google, they dropped the subscription service. Ev knew that he would learn a lot at Google and be able to work with amazing people. He wanted to get the most out of that and also to get Blogger to a point where it would do well within the Google structure. Once both of those things were accomplished, he felt it was time to leave, as he wasn't attuned to working in such a big company. He actually stayed a year and eight months, longer than the year he had expected.

TWITTER

I was anxious to do something next! I had some ideas, but my plan was just to take some time off. I actually stumbled into the next thing much sooner than I expected, because a friend of mine was working on it. I was advising and investing, and then found myself being the CEO. That was a company called Odeo, founded by Noah Glass. He had a service called Audio Blogger, which allowed people to post audio to their blogs. We had done a deal with them when I was running Blogger. And it was a neat little feature to let people call up a phone number from any phone and leave a voice mail that would be posted as an MP3 to their blog.

This was before the idea of podcasting was known. In talking with Noah, Biz Stone, who is one of the cofounders of Twitter, and I stumbled on this idea. What if you would download these MP3s to your iPod and subscribe to things? Shortly thereafter we heard other people were having the same idea, as is often the case, and it got labeled *podcasting*. It seemed like an opportunity that was interesting.

That was the idea. It was to be a podcasting company, which at the time meant too many things, but really in my mind it was about democratizing audio, mostly spoken-word audio, not music necessarily. There have been a lot of advances in music, but spoken-word audio was a medium that hadn't really seen the effects of the Internet yet. It was still very limited in terms of consumer choice and very difficult to put out there as a creator. I was always a fan of books on tape and lectures on tape, and it seemed like there was tons of material from conferences, or just things that people could create that had interesting aspects. People could listen to it during the thousands of hours a year they spend in the car. You can consume audio in times when you can't consume any other type of media, and yet it's really limited in how you get it, and how you pay for it, and how you create it and distribute it. That was the idea: to enable that.

They worked on the design for six months, running to get ahead of the competition as podcasting began to get a lot of hype, but there was nothing available with a simple and easy user experience. Just before they were ready to launch, Apple announced a solution that connected iPods and iTunes with podcasting software, putting the solution onto 10 million desktops overnight, so the podcasting idea had to be scrapped for Odeo. Another difficulty they encountered was the basic challenge of creating good audio.

To create listenable audio I think actually takes more skill than creating a watchable video, but we didn't understand that at the time. I think it's a medium where there'll be a flatter tail. There's still an opportunity there. There's still stuff people will listen to, but it just had different dynamics than we were expecting. Why couldn't anyone be the next Ira

Glass? Everybody has stories. Millions of people have stories and people could go collect the stories, go tell the stories. It could be great.

I think the opportunity will be much more along the lines of a marketing and distribution-focused company than a content creator-focused company, which was more in our DNA, having come from blogging.

The first ideas for Twitter came from Jack Dorsey, an engineer at Odeo, who had been thinking about something similar for a number of years. He had come from the world of dispatch and courier software, which has the concept of "status," where the couriers report their status and messages are sent to them. Jack had the idea of creating a social status broadcast system a long time before. The Odeo team was toying with some new ideas in brainstorm mode, searching for something to focus on instead of the podcasting product, so Jack's concept became a side project, working with Biz Stone, who became a cofounder and creative director for Twitter. Ev was interested in bringing audio to people on the move.

I thought that audio podcasts needed to get to where they would be the most compelling form of media, but that's not in front of a computer. When you're out and about, when you're walking down the street or in your car, getting fresh content to the iPod is difficult, but getting it to the phone may be easier. For that reason we were looking into SMS, and Jack put two and two together and said SMS could be a transport mechanism for this idea of status, and we could tie the audio message into that. Then we said, "What if we throw the audio part out?" Then we'll have something that doesn't relate to Odeo at all, but it's kind of interesting. So Jack and Biz built a prototype, we started using it and found it instantly pretty compelling.

We were using it through our phones and text messages, keeping it very, very simple. It was novel. At the time I hadn't personally used text messages a lot, but I soon became a fan of SMS because it's elegant and instantaneous and mobile. To get these messages was just fun! It was that human

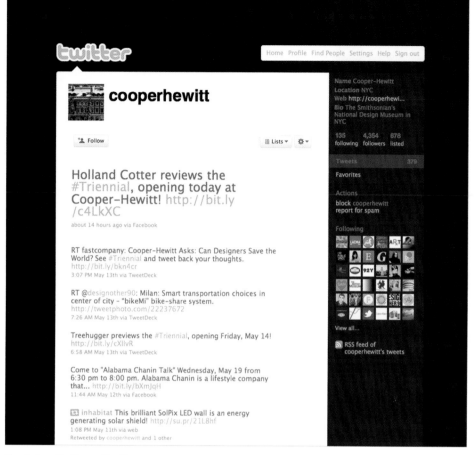

Tweets from the Cooper-Hewitt
screen capture

connection, fun, lightweight, the endorphin rush that drives a lot of the social activities on the Web and everywhere else, and it happened with this very simple mechanism.

SMS informed the design of everything about Twitter at the start, always combined with the Web, so you could log onto the Web site and see the status of each friend and turn SMS on or off. The messages on Twitter are limited to 140 characters, based on the 160 characters in SMS, with room for a user name of 15 characters, a colon, and a space. As SMS has a single field, it reads like a command line, but in more recent versions you can add other things on the Web, like a picture, title, or emoticon.

Jack Dorsey was a minimalist with a very pure vision, and his adherence to the constraints of SMS kept Twitter simple. The text-only limitation made it very easy to integrate into anything else, and the simplicity has

What are you doing?
photo by Keiyac/Creative Commons

helped to attract application developers, with people building all kinds of clients and services that work with Twitter.

> It also has allowed flexibility. Even though we framed Twitter around the question, "What are you doing?" people use it in all kinds of different ways. I think that's partially because it's like a blank canvas. It's a small canvas but that allows you to think up new, creative uses. Jack was the main driver of it philosophically. There are a lot of people here who feel very strongly about maintaining the elegance of Twitter and

the simplicity. When there are obvious things to add, and our users want them, and we want them, then we come back to "How do we do that without making it more complicated?"

One of the other important aspects of Twitter is that it's real-time. Our challenge is to get information to people faster than any other medium. It's not interesting to hear from a friend that they had lunch last week at a restaurant that you've been to, but in the moment it creates a sense of connection that isn't otherwise possible. We are always looking for other things that we can enable through this real-time aspect, as that's unique to Twitter.

Twitter partnered with Current TV *(see the interview with Joel Hyatt in chapter 4)*, the participatory news and information service, to report on the 2008 U.S. presidential election. When the debates were going on, everyone was gathered around their television set, with the real-time comments from Twitter included as part of the Current TV broadcast. Current took a slice of the content based on keywords and presented it along with the main TV feed from the debates. The partnership offered an information feed with two components, without forcing Twitter to make their own service more complicated.

Some things are goofy, like we'll take all the Twitters that contain cuss words and put them up on a page and you can watch that, or lots of interesting visualizations, where people present the data in interesting ways. Twittervision plots tweets on a global Google map and shows them in real time. You can see all over the world what people are saying. Google used that during the election cycle Super Tuesday, where they took election-related tweets and plotted them on a map as they were coming in during the day, giving a unique view on what real people were saying about the election while it was happening all over the country.

By the beginning of 2008 it had become obvious that a search function would be advantageous to the main Twitter site. At that time the team only had nine engineers who were developing code, so Ev thought he would need to go outside to develop search. He started talking to some major Internet companies about the task, but a small company called Summize had built a search engine based on Twitter, and it looked like they had done a great job. He ended up buying Summize and incorporating their engine into the product, while at the same time adding five engineers to his staff. Search allowed you to immediately see what people were saying about any topic under the sun. It might be a television show that you're watching, or a new product that just came out, or anything. It gave a view into the value of Twitter that wasn't otherwise obvious.

In 2009 Twitter concentrated on introducing the concept to a wider audience, and then guiding people through the experience. They also added capabilities, but they tried to do so without losing simplicity, so that the software would be context sensitive, recognizing the desire of the user as they enter text.

> People are starting to get now that there's a whole world within Twitter, but at first it seemed like the most ludicrous idea ever. It's like we'll take blogging, we'll take out all these features and we'll limit the size of the post and that will be a whole thing. It's just very nonintuitive. I'm really attracted to the idea that you can have something that seems really small but it actually is like a molecule that is everywhere. I think that speaks to the trend of infinite diversification that I see continuing forever. As many people have said, media never die, just new ones are born.

> Someone wrote me recently from *The Economist* and asked me to comment on the hypothesis that blogging is dead. You could see how they reached that conclusion by saying, "Well, things like Twitter and Facebook and these other applications are where people who would have been blogging are spending their time." I answer that in two ways. First of all, blogs are still growing themselves. They are becoming richer and entire media empires unto themselves. The other thing is that Facebook, Twitter, and blogging are really the same motivation. It's in a different package, but it's about people sharing things on a one-to-many basis and putting things out there. There's been a bunch of social media applications over the years that I think are just the same concept in different permutations and often just more focused rather than all one big thing.

Up to 2009 Twitter was focused on design and content development without worrying about the business side. Ev believes that the value in Twitter is going to be dictated by the size of the network and the ability of people to communicate, and that there will be many ways to generate revenue. There is already a lot of commercial activity happening on Twitter, so once the value is recognized, companies will be willing to pay for it.

> Whatever we do, we want it to add value to the product, as when Google had the insight, "Well, what if the ads were actually helping solve what the user is trying to do?" I think we have similar opportunities that we're excited about but we're not focusing on right now.
>
> Very few highly successful Web products have died because they haven't found a way to monetize. There were some during the first dot-com bust, but "popular" then was a fraction of what "popular" is today. The built-in economics of the Web are much better today. Now it's more about the strength of your business model, with Google at one end with the best business model ever and banner ads on their own at the other end being the worst business model ever. Even though we're making zero money today, there are ways that in a very short period of time we could make money. We just want to do it in a way that doesn't hurt the user experience at all and optimizes the business.

TWITTER OFFERS SOCIAL NETWORKING at a minimal scale, leveraging the real-time opportunities that come with the nimbleness of messages that are short and quickly created and received. For the final interview in this chapter, we talk with Mark Zuckerberg, the founder and CEO of Facebook, who has developed a richer form of social networking with a design approach that looks for empathy and openness.

MARK ZUCKERBERG

Interviewed November 20, 2009

MARK ZUCKERBERG

Mark was born in 1984, so he was only twenty-five at the time of this interview and twenty when he founded Facebook. At the end of 2009, Facebook had 350 million users and more than 1,000 employees, with headquarters in Palo Alto, California, and nine branches around the United States as well as seven international offices. Three rounds of venture capital amounting to $40 million had funded the company. In 2007 Facebook sold a 1.6 percent stake to Microsoft for $240 million, rejecting a competing offer from Google. This would indicate that Facebook had a market value of $15 billion at the time of the sale. All this growth and potential value amounts to an amazing achievement for someone so young. It may have only been possible because Mark was a prolific software designer from the age of ten and wrote programs to solve the problems that he encountered in high school and college. He founded Facebook while he was at Harvard studying psychology and computer science; he later moved the company to Palo Alto. He is both the founder and CEO, responsible for setting the overall direction and product strategy for the company. He leads the design of Facebook's services and development of its core technology and infrastructure.

←···· **Mark Zuckerberg**
photos by author

The interview with Mark Zuckerberg was the last for this book, not because it was a late idea, but because it was so difficult to pin him down. At IDEO we know Facebook well, as their headquarters is close to ours and we connect socially. I tried to arrange a meeting without success for more than a year. Mark is notoriously shy of interviews, particularly with video recording, so it was no great surprise that when we arrived to set up the cameras, we were told that our one-hour slot was reduced to twenty minutes. He used that short time to communicate some interesting ideas. The light in the room where we were shooting was perfect for video, thanks to the high windows and north-facing skylights. The building (designed by Studio O+A) is open and full of light, with internal structures glowing in bright colors. As we were leaving after the interview, I thought to myself that I had seen a lot of people in the reception area and open spaces, none of whom were more than half my age!

invite friends | click anywhere to drag | mouse wheel to zoom at mouse pointer | double-click nodes to visit profile pages   zoom − +

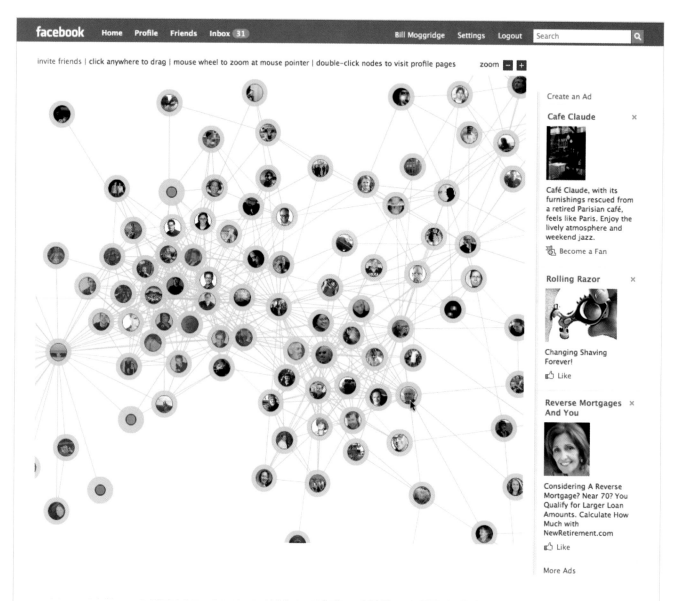

THE JOY OF DESIGNING CODE

Mark got his first computer in fifth grade and within months was thinking about how to build things for it and customize it more. He reveled in developing games and new programs to solve the problems around him. At high school he was always writing programs, including one to help the workers in his father's office communicate and a version of Risk as a single-player game.

In his senior year Mark teamed up with a friend for a music project called Synapse. They built MP3 player software and an artificial intelligence system that learned listening habits and compared one listener to others in order to offer recommendations. Microsoft and AOL were both impressed enough with the design to offer to purchase the program and recruit Mark, but he decided to go to Harvard instead.

> When I was growing up, this was the thing I really loved doing. I'd go to school and class, and then come home and think, "I have five whole hours just to sit and play on my computer and write software." And then Friday afternoon would come along and it would be like, "OK, now I have two whole days to sit and write software. This is amazing!" To sit down and write software or design something is like sculpting: You sit down, you craft something, you build it, and then you're done. You walk away and you have something that you've built that you can share with other people.

← Facebook's Social Graph
image courtesy of author

This passion for designing software defines Mark's very existence, but he is interested in people as well as the structure of algorithms. He chose to study psychology and computer science at Harvard to learn more about what makes people tick. He was responsive to the environment that he found himself in, always looking for a new design opportunity to solve an information need or to provide a software-based service.

When Facebook came along, I wanted to have the ability to see what was going on with the people around me whom I cared about and stay connected with them. It's impossible to build an application that lets you do that unless other people are also using the application, so that was among the first set of things that I built that were for other people as well as myself.

When I was in college, I played with a lot of different ideas around seeing certain pieces of information that would reveal what was going on around you. One of the first was an application called Coursematch. I downloaded the Harvard course catalog. People could fill out what courses they were exploring during the shopping period before they chose which courses they were going to take. The interface allowed you to click on any course and see all of the people at Harvard who had also said that they were thinking about taking that course. It was the first graph application that I built. Showing the connections between people and the classes that they were taking has the same properties of a graph that Facebook and the Social Graph have now. I was playing with the data set, the Harvard course catalog. It was online for a little while during the shopping period and then my computer crashed and I had no backup of it, so I don't have anything like that any more.

During my sophomore year at school I built a lot of things like that. Another one allowed you to look through the archives of the *Harvard Crimson*, type in any two people's names, and see which articles they were connected through. These were just experiments with interesting types of software, but by the time that I got around to thinking about Facebook and making something that could give you a lot of context for the people who are around you, I had built a lot of the specific pieces already, whether it was the courses people were taking or the news articles that they were in, so I was able to put Facebook together very quickly, in a couple of weeks.

The speed with which the first version of Facebook was designed has entered the annals of software development lore, so it is interesting to hear Mark trying to gently explain it away as something that emerged naturally as an extension of his other programs. The first version was very simple, and it evolved slowly through an iterative process of development, responding to the needs and desires of the community of people who were participating in the experiment. Mark explains his own insights about the process:

> I think that two elements make it work. There's got to be some kind of big-picture thing that you're moving toward in the future that reflects the ideology behind what you are doing—for example, that we think social networks should be platforms, that we think the world should be generally more open and transparent, and that people should be willing to share more stuff. There has also got to be a very tactical use case that drives what people, your users, are going to be doing on a day-to-day basis. Unless you have that use case yourself, you probably don't have enough empathy for what people who have that use case are feeling.

> I was shopping for classes myself when I built Coursematch. I wanted to see what courses I should take. I designed a pretty simple application, as it was something I was able to build quickly, both in terms of figuring out what was important and in deciding the list of things that I could triage out and didn't have to worry about in order to design it in two days.

CONNECTING PEOPLE

This combination of long-term vision and pragmatic evolution is common to many examples of successful design development. Perhaps Mark is partly boy genius in that he was able to write such effective programs at such a young age, but the insight about combining vision with iterative development transcends time. The example of vision that he gives is based on the promise of connectivity offered by the growth of the Internet.

> The world is on a trajectory to become more open. I have this picture of people in college in the 1960s or '70s spending a lot of time sitting around talking about civil rights and the big social issues of the decade. Similarly, I spent a lot of time talking to my friends who studied computer science, math,

and psychology, and the things that we talked about were how the Internet was changing society so profoundly, because now there was so much more information available.

Going back to the time when the first browsers were available, it seemed like the amount of information that was available was increasing exponentially. You can plot out a trajectory that this will continue to happen into the future with technology that's imminently on the horizon. Almost everyone is going to have a mobile phone, and they are going to keep on getting better and better. There's going to be more access to information, and that's going to make it so that people have a better understanding of what's going on around them, and that's good, right? It makes people more efficient at what they do, more understanding, more tolerant.

In talking to my friends, it just seemed like this was it for our generation—that this was probably the most transformative thing that was going to happen. At the same time, none of this tied in with any of the applications we were building then. We just had this philosophy in the back of our minds, so it's not really a coincidence that Facebook is an application that pushes toward connecting people to each other and to information.

It is interesting to compare the vision and philosophy behind Facebook with that of Google. In the interview for *Designing Interactions* with Larry Page and Sergey Brin in 2002, well before there was talk about going public, they were talking about the ideology that lay behind their approach, with a mission to "organize the world's information and make it universally accessible and useful," while at the same time keeping their focus on search. This has provided the seed for a company culture that values the development of clever algorithms in the service of the people who use them. Mark compares the culture of Google with that of Facebook:

I think Google is a great company! Their founders have such good focus, very deep in the discipline of computer science, giving the company that academic type of feel to it. Facebook is a bit different. The background of a lot of the people here is more connected to the interface between

Screens of the original Facebook
images courtesy of Facebook

computing and society, and how the social norms of people relate to technology.

Google's focus seems to be primarily on algorithmically sorting what's there, whereas our focus has always been on making it so that people share more information and have the tools that they need to share the things that they want, and connect with the people that they want, and control their privacy in the way that they want.

Search is basically just indexing all the information that's out there and making it easily available to the public, but there is a huge amount of information that people don't want to share with everyone. If you give people a way to share some information with just their school community—or just their work community, or their family or their friends—then you actually enable a huge amount more sharing than they would otherwise want.

Facebook 2007 screen shots, profile and news feed
images courtesy of Facebook

DESIGNING FOR SHARING

Social networking should be designed to help people connect without feeling that a layer of technology stands in the way. The challenges are very similar to service design, where the human touch makes the solution sympathetic, but most of the enabling technology needs to be hidden from or transparent to the users. Mark strives to balance human qualities with successful algorithms, while always learning from an iterative process of trying out designs and then improving them in a new version.

> We've found that things that are very human do better. Just seeing someone's face makes a very big difference in how a product feels and thus how it performs. Our brains are made up of different parts that process different things. We have parts that process math that are more analytical, but there are whole parts of the brain that are just for processing people's faces and understanding really small gestures, like how people shape their eyes, and how they convey different emotions. Faces are very powerful to humans! That's an example of

something that we've both realized empirically through seeing how people use the products but that also ties into our overall thinking and philosophy of design. There are other projects where the interface is relatively simple on the front end and most of the value is generated by optimizing an algorithm.

Facebook's news feed is a good example of the best of both the personal and the algorithmic design qualities. The activities of all your friends for the past eight hours are presented as a scroll, identified by faces and names, with plenty of photos and discussions. The design of the presentation is like a personalized newspaper that is updated in real time for every individual, with very human qualities. The goal is to know exactly who your friends are and what kind of content you care about and to offer it to you in real time. The challenge is to present the information very efficiently, grouping pieces of information together to give them context while picking the thirty items that you most want to see from all the thousands of possibilities. By offering this service, Facebook is competing with traditional local newspapers, but Mark thinks there are distinct differences.

> As people have a finite amount of time, if they're not looking at newspapers as much and they're spending more time on Facebook, then that's competing, but I think fundamentally we're doing pretty different things. They produce content; we don't. We are a social filter through which people can see what's going on and what the people around them care about. A big part of that is news, and we don't produce any of that content. The *New York Times* produces a lot of that. So I think we actually have the potential to generate a lot of traffic and help them out with a lot of what they are doing.
>
> I also think that the world moves pretty quickly, and that the state of these industries is probably always going to be somewhat in flux. I think that, going forward, these systems will just continue to evolve at a faster and faster rate, and you won't think about it as "this is the way it was" and "this is the way it is." It's just going to be in motion. Newspapers aren't

going away. They do something that is extremely valuable. Will their relative importance compared to everything else that exists in the world change? Yes. That's because the world keeps shifting over time. Some years they'll be more important than they were the year before, and some years they'll be less important than they were the year before. The relative importance of these different media shifts around over time as the world evolves.

Mark spends a lot of time thinking about new connections, about how things are becoming more open. Everyone has personal information that he or she wants to share, given the right context and security protections, so connecting to friends helps people get information about the people who are most important to them. Facebook has been designed and developed based on Mark's belief that this information about friends is the most important asset that the Internet can offer. He thinks that people will share more, more information will be accessible, and the world will become more open. He expects that mobile platforms will grow the fastest, as people will want to have devices with them to share information in real time, all the time.

COMMENTARY

Jorge Just is still young, but he has already made a lot of new connections. He connected with fans of OK Go by writing them personal notes. He developed a Web site that connected with journalists and advertisers professionally and with fans intimately. He connected with YouTube before any other band, musician, or record label had.

The members of OK Go came up with music videos with intricate dances, connecting boy band moves and cheerleading routines, and gave out DVDs while on tour. The contest to imaginatively re-create the band's dancing turned viral, with the derivative videos popping up everywhere.

The idea for using treadmills in the "Here It Goes Again" video also proved to have an irresistibly viral quality. The fan base for OK Go was there and ready, and the open competition had become popular, so the moment they put the new video out, it floated to the top of the YouTube ratings. The band went from obscurity to worldwide fame with the help of an ingenious connection to a new medium, combined with inspired performances that engaged and charmed people by their unselfconscious vitality.

I find it encouraging that OK Go achieved this incredible viral success by focusing on simple values, combining their music and amusing dance routines, connected through the new medium of YouTube. Who *hasn't* seen the treadmill video? The connections enabled by YouTube are amazingly powerful, but this story reminds us to stick to simple and strong emotional values for artistic content rather than going for slickness and hype.

Chad Hurley, the only designer at PayPal, learned about designing for the Web by direct experience, and he benefited financially when eBay acquired PayPal in 2002. He became part of an entrepreneurial development community and started out by designing something for himself and his friends. They noticed that Flickr was having success in connecting people through shared photos and saw a similar opportunity for video. Inexpensive video cameras and editing software were already available, but it was difficult to share video online because of varying formats, large file sizes, lack of standardized media players, and limited bandwidths. They thought this might be a huge opportunity to make new connections.

At first they tried to define a set of standards to allow an easy video file sharing experience based on a single type of content, but they soon realized that they would do better to create an open platform and avoid being defined by one specific type of video or site. They solved the file type challenge by reencoding everything into Flash; they built an underlying architecture that would scale at a reasonable cost; and they made the video portable so that anyone could embed a link to a YouTube video in HTML and put it on their own Web site or blog.

By 2004 the costs of bandwidth were plunging, so Chad was able to start with inexpensive hosting services, but he and his team started to build their own architecture to serve the data themselves, as they were determined to create a neutral platform. This decision continues to create engineering challenges, as traffic is increasing all the time.

Chad was careful to create a sympathetic design for the YouTube Web site, avoiding anything that was overproduced, slick, or corporate-looking. He used basic HTML code and a simple design because he wanted the brand to be playful but also trustworthy. As with the treadmill video from OK Go, there is a complete lack of self-consciousness in the design and presentation of the YouTube site. Chad succeeded in facilitating connections by carefully designing for simple functionality and presenting YouTube in a form that appears friendly and familiar.

Site navigation has emerged as a difficult challenge. The design tries to harness the power of the masses to curate the site and prioritize viewing, with the popularity of pages as a mechanism to bring items to the surface. This approach needs to be combined with the ability to search to find narrowcast content, so Chad and his team are continuously trying to improve their search functions. Users can search titles, keywords, or any of the metadata associated with the video, but they hope to discover more powerful solutions to unlock the entire tail of content, beyond the analysis of views and ratings.

From the start, YouTube planned a business model that relies on advertising revenue, which only becomes successful when a tipping point of scale is reached. This point came quickly for YouTube, as they established a leading position almost immediately, and the Google purchase for $1.65 billion secured their dominance.

Chad is making progress with the complicated problems of intellectual property for both video and music. As each video is uploaded, it is run through a content-identification system for music, allowing royalties to be paid where appropriate or for removal of the video if necessary. Revenues are also generated for independent video makers, through a partner program for ad placement.

Chad sees all of the different forms of moving-image media converging, and he foresees a future with people accessing video from the cloud, scaled for delivery to any device, and paid for by some rules around usage—perhaps a per-play rate, a service subscription, or advertising. I find this prediction convincing.

Alexandra Juhasz teaches media studies and is interested in the political and artistic uses of media. As a scholar and activist, she is instinctively repelled by the YouTube experience, believing that the communal building of knowledge can't happen in that medium and that the idea that the site is democratic is untrue.

Her analysis indicates that YouTube is organized by popularity, keeping what she calls "NicheTube" almost invisible, and she sees popularity as a limited and even juvenile way to organize life. She thinks that the design is structured to cause people to connect as quickly and unpredictably as possible from one thing to another, in order to maximize exposure to ads. She sees this as a viable business model but not a viable way to support democracy, culture, art, or community.

Alexandra also points out that although we've been raised in a culture surrounded by images, most of us are not fluent image makers. We are better equipped as writers because of the literate nature of our education, so the sudden access to the tools to make video has not been paired with access to education about media production. She sees a need for teachers and educators to raise the level of video creation skills, so that most people can become competent participants rather than just consumers.

Online video is expanding exponentially, fueled by inexpensive video cameras and video editing software combined with the arrival of adequate bandwidth for viewing on personal computers and handhelds. This means that video content of all types is becoming available online as well as in traditional media, so the door is open for new connections. Entrepreneurial offerings are springing up for a host of specialist applications that complement the dominant YouTube. Hulu delivers TV shows and movies. Vimeo allows people to publish videos for public consumption or just for friends and family. Apple is educating consumers on the benefits of watching video through iTunes Movie Rentals on iPhones, iPods, iPads, and Apple TV devices, and companies like Netflix have pioneered the movement from physical DVD rentals to downloading streamed versions on demand.

There are also opportunities for subscription services, offering business-to-business solutions for integrating video onto Web sites. An early innovator in this space is Brightcove, founded by Jeremy Allaire and Bob Mason. The service allows video content owners to publish, distribute and deliver video to their audiences. Bob is focused on making the system as simple as possible, so video can be encoded, uploaded, launched, and presented in a branded player on a Web site in less than thirty minutes. Much of the Brightcove offering is transparent to the end user, with the connections automatically adjusted by the software.

Bob predicts that coming bandwidth improvements will allow fluid connections of online video across platforms, with PC, mobile, and TV experiences accessing common source material. He expects there to be much more material being created for business purposes, so that content will be produced by companies that you would not think of as media or video companies.

Jeremy Merle leads the team of user interface designers at Brightcove. His first priority is to understand the people who will use the product. The research that his team conducted revealed three main stakeholders— media producers, design integrators, and business developers—and he has developed separate modules to satisfy each of these.

Ev Williams is a serial entrepreneur. After starting a family business to develop CD-ROMs in Nebraska during the early years of the Internet boom, he headed for California in search of opportunities. He cofounded Pyra Labs to develop Web-based collaboration tools for project and task management, with ideas about connecting email to tasks and making events and messages task-related.

Weblogs were being talked about in 1999, and Ev wrote a script to let him publish messages to his personal Web site. He found that it really changed the dynamic of having a personal site. Soon Blogger emerged as a brand name for the tool that he was developing. In 2003 Google offered to purchase Pyra Labs on the condition that Blogger would be focused as a mainstream product, so Ev spent the next twenty months at Google making that happen.

After Google, Ev was invited to run a company called Odeo. For six months they worked on a podcasting idea, but Apple beat them to the punch, and they needed something else to focus their attention on. The first ideas for Twitter came from Jack Dorsey, an engineer at Odeo. He had the idea of creating a social-status broadcast system. The Odeo team toyed with some new ideas and decided to build a prototype using SMS as a transport mechanism for real-time connections. They found their prototype surprisingly engaging—another example of an innovative design idea emerging from a group of creative people prototyping solutions for themselves! The Odeo team were rigorous about simplicity, so whenever a new feature was requested for Twitter they would only add it if it was possible to avoid complex interactions.

Ev has been surprised by the growth of Twitter and tweets—initially it struck him as odd to reduce the capability of blogging so drastically, but it seems that the very simple structure has been a remarkable asset. Ev sees Facebook, Twitter, and Blogger as all being about making connections on a one-to-many basis.

Mark Zuckerberg seems camera shy in the formal situation of a video interview, but I got the sense that an endless conversation with him in a relaxed environment would be very rewarding. Here is a summary of some of the points that interest me, taken from Wikipedia and other sources.

Mark invented Facemash in 2003 while attending Harvard as a sophomore. He hacked into the protected areas of Harvard's computer network and copied the ID images of the students, placing two next to each other at a time and asking users to choose the "hotter" person. He wrote in his personal blog, "Perhaps Harvard will squelch it [Facemash] for legal reasons without realizing its value as a venture that could possibly be expanded to other schools (maybe even ones with good-looking people …), but one thing is certain, and it's that I'm a jerk for making this site. Oh well. Someone had to do it eventually." The site was quickly forwarded to several campus-group list servers but was shut down a few days later by the Harvard administration. Mark was charged by the administration with breach of security and violating copyrights and individual privacy. He faced expulsion, but ultimately the charges were dropped.

In January 2004 Mark began writing code for a new Web site and launched "Thefacebook" in February. He told the *Harvard Crimson*, "Everyone's been talking a lot about a universal face book within Harvard. I think it's kind of silly that it would take the University a couple of years to get around to it. I can do it better than they can, and I can do it in a week." When Mark finished the site, the uptake was swift, and it spread to other universities. He incorporated the company in the summer and moved the headquarters to California.

I find it prescient that both the strength and the dilemmas of Facebook were already visible during these first experiments. People were fascinated by the chance to see themselves compared and connected to others online, with an interface that was more visual and welcoming than email or texting, but Mark's desire to open everything up was getting him in trouble right from the start, posing a dilemma that is still difficult and contentious to solve.

Mark emphasizes his interest in psychology as well as his passion for algorithms, revealing a strong philosophy that complements his pragmatic design approach. I particularly enjoyed his enthusiasm for the creative delights of writing code: "You craft something, you build it … and you have something … that you can share with other people."

Behind this pleasure in his craft is a combination of long-term vision and pragmatic evolution, attributes that you find in many examples of successful design development. He describes two necessary elements: First, a kind of big-picture thing that reflects the ideology behind what you are doing—for example, that the world should be generally more open and transparent. Second, a tactical use case that drives what people do on a day-to-day basis. He believes that the world is on a trajectory to become more open, that there will be more access to information, leading to a better understanding for people about of what is happening in the world. Mark is profoundly optimistic and believes that this openness will make people more efficient at what they do, more understanding, more tolerant. Let's hope he's right!

The opportunities for creating online communities have been slow to develop, but Facebook and other social-networking services show what is possible. Facebook is an application that pushes toward connecting people to one another and to information. The human-to-human connections in social networking are very personal and need to be designed to help people connect without an obtrusive technological interface. As Mark says, "Our focus has always been on making it so that people share more information and have the tools that they need to share the things that they want, and connect with the people that they want, and control their privacy in the way that they want. … We've found that things that are very human do better. Just seeing someone's face makes a very big difference in how a product feels and thus how it performs."

Mark is pushing Facebook to develop designs with a deep awareness of human perceptions as one of the elements to be synthesized in creating a solution. He wants the site to offer a social filter through which people can see what's going on and what the people around them care about. This mandate, to help people see more and be better connected, is difficult to balance with the desire for privacy. Social-networking sites like Facebook will probably always suffer from the implications of this paradox.

When it comes to the business success of Facebook and the value of the enterprise, the jury is still out, but the rumors and offers already received indicate a valuation that is counted in billions of dollars. So far, Mark has been careful to resist temptations to be purchased or to go public, but I wouldn't be surprised if that changes by the time you read this.

CHAPTER 4, "BOTH WORLDS," provides some examples of new connections linking to old ones, with combinations between traditional media and new media that enhance the output of both, even if they challenge the financial structures of the past. The first interview is with Joel Hyatt, cofounder and CEO of Current TV. During the 2008 U.S. presidential election, Current TV made a new connection to Twitter, using old-world broadcast television coverage combined with new-world Twitter participation in real time.

4 BOTH WORLDS

Interviews with Joel Hyatt, Bruce Nussbaum, Jessie Scanlon,
Jane Friedman, Martin Eberhard, and Rich Archuleta

During the 1970s, improvements in offset lithography led to a bloom of specialty magazines; no longer were there a dozen or two magazines on newsstands, but hundreds, most about only specific topics. Proliferations of, first, analog cable television systems during the 1980s, then digital ones during the late 1990s, increased the average American's number of accessible TV stations from four to hundreds, mostly specialty channels (Home & Garden TV, the Golf Channel, the Military Channel, etc.). Then the Internet became publicly accessible during the 1990s and the average individual quickly had access to millions of websites, most of those sites about very specific topics.

Chris Anderson, *The Long Tail*

THE EXPLOSION IN MEDIA CAPACITY that Chris Anderson describes can be likened to the big bang; it seems endlessly expansive with no prospect of reversing direction. All media organizations have had to deal with the challenges posed by this ever-increasing expansion. Most traditional media companies are steered by executives in their forties and fifties, for whom the increase in quantity and variety in the medium that they work in has been easier to grasp than the new unfamiliar versions being created on the Internet, which initially seemed irrelevant to many.

It would be convenient for decision makers if high-quality content were always equally successful across platforms. Then they could stop worrying about new media: a good film could play equally successfully on a big screen, a personal computer, and a mobile phone. If only a journalist could send in a story as audio and have it translate word-for-word into a newspaper report, or a blog, or perhaps even a tweet! Real life is not so easy for the people who generate original material—the nature of the content and the medium of delivery make a difference. The people at the source are most likely to succeed when they design the presentation to suit the medium, with different versions for the new world and the old. If the producers of traditional media transpose their content directly into Internet-based versions, the qualities that engage people are likely to get lost in the translation.

This chapter provides some examples of content creators having developed successful combinations of traditional media and new

←···· **Newsstand**
photo by Alberto Coto/Getty Images

media, designing versions that complement one another and enhance the output of both the old world and the new, even when the results challenge established financial structures.

Joel Hyatt, vice chairman of Current Media and subject of the first interview, saw a closed media industry that he wanted to help transform into something that could support a vibrant democratic society. The idea of building a new kind of media company that could help facilitate a global conversation was an inspiring challenge. With Al Gore as a founding partner, he set about creating a television production company that would have 40 percent of the output generated by the audience but also benefit from professional editorial control and curation. It would also leverage Internet-based content for influence, commentary and discussion.

The next interview is with Bruce Nussbaum, a managing editor for *BusinessWeek*. He wrote the editorial page throughout the nineties, expressing the magazine's point of view on all topics while becoming more engaged with emerging technology and design. In 2005 he started the Innovation and Design channel online and the NussbaumOnDesign blog for *BusinessWeek*. The content yielded its own unique style, which allowed Bruce to start a quarterly supplement for print called *IN: Inside Innovation*.

To develop the Innovation and Design channel Bruce pulled together a group of people who were able to work fluently in multiple media, confident that they could create material for print, online, video, and blog. To begin with, he brought Jessie Scanlon in to start the channel and lead the editing, as she thrived online and "was totally cool." In the next interview, Jessie talks about her experience in developing the design.

Jane Friedman has been marketing books for more than four decades, and from 1997 to 2008 she was president and CEO of HarperCollins Publishers. She believes in print and the longevity of books as a medium but has always sought the best of both worlds by combining electronic media with physical books. In her interview she tells how she invented the author tour, promoted by radio and television. She developed audio books in the eighties. She built a digital warehouse to improve online search access and revels in the ability to use the Web to reach potential readers. She sees social networking as a welcome extension of word of mouth and on-demand publishing and electronic books as opportunities to reduce publishing costs.

RocketBook and Softbook were launched in 1998 from two newstart Silicon Valley companies competing for the emerging market in electronic books. They were both a little ahead of their time, as electronic books needed some new technologies before they would start selling in viable quantities. Our next interview is with Martin Eberhard, the founder and CEO of NuvoMedia, the company that created the RocketBook. Amazon's Kindle and the Sony Reader have made electronic books a likely choice for road warriors who like to travel light but also need access to a stack of different titles for work or study. Electronic books are on the threshold of more general acceptance, as the enabling technologies mature and new designs emerge. QUE is an offering from Plastic Logic that was launched in January 2010, a few weeks before the announcement of the iPad from Apple. The iPad has a lot in common with the iPhone, and the historical precedent of the RocketBook. QUE uses a plastic substrate for E Ink to allow a generous display on a product with physical dimensions similar to a pad of paper, so the reading experience is more like the Kindle or the Sony Reader. Rich Archuleta is the CEO of Plastic Logic; he describes his ideas about e-readers and e-books in the last interview in this chapter.

JOEL HYATT

Interviewed November 25, 2008

JOEL HYATT

Joel served as national finance chair for the Democratic Party in the presidential election campaign of 2000, getting to know Al Gore in the process. After the election they decided to build a new, exciting, and different form of medium to democratize the creation of TV content. Before 2000 Joel had a distinguished legal and political career with a recurring theme of opening closed systems to enhance participation.

Joel and Al developed a concept to combine television broadcasting with participation by audience members, enabled by the Internet. In 2004 they purchased Newsworld International, a cable news channel programmed by the Canadian Broadcasting Corporation that aired news programming from around the world, and started to build a team in San Francisco. They relaunched the network as the Current TV platform on August 1, 2005, providing a news and information service that pioneered the concept of user-generated content on cable and satellite TV.

<--- **Joel Hyatt**
photos by author

Current TV is located in a beautiful old office building close to the water's edge on San Francisco Bay. When I arrived to set up cameras for the interview with Joel Hyatt, I admired the red-brick facade, which had a grid of metal-framed windows set into the front openings, glowing in a strong turquoise blue. I stepped inside and climbed a broad steel staircase to the reception desk, passing the TV studios full of recording equipment and people busy creating programming. Joel sat with me in his office, close to a large photo of Al Gore, and talked eloquently about his work and philosophy.

CURRENT TV

Joel Hyatt started the interview by describing the origins of Current TV and its focus on combining the best of the traditional world of television with the new possibilities of user-generated content.

Al Gore, my partner and cofounder of Current TV, and I decided we wanted to create an entirely new kind of media company, the core innovation of which would be to empower our young adult audience to contribute in significant ways to the creation of the content they consume. At the time that Al and I set out to build Current, no one had ever heard of user-generated content. YouTube had not been founded. The media industry was this oligopoly of a handful of companies that really controlled the dissemination of information and entertainment into all the homes in the U.S. and indeed, for that matter, much around the world. And we believed that with technology we could unleash the creativity of a young adult generation that knew how to use the digital tools of the modern world and then take the powerful media platforms that existed and share that power with them and in that way give voice to a whole generation whose voice was not being heard.

From the outset, the Internet was critical for our production infrastructure. It was how young people submitted content to us, into an online studio that we developed, a virtual production studio that allowed content creators to communicate with each other [and] to comment on, vet, and vote on content. And the very best would make it to television. We built out that production studio with training components and professional guidance, none of which existed before. First we wanted to have a training program that, no matter what your level of skills with video, we could help you improve your ability to create

←---- **Al Gore at the launch of the Italian branch of Current TV in Rome**
photo by Simone Brunozzi/Creative Commons

broadcast-quality TV. Someone could pick up a camera and come to us and learn, "How can I use this camera to tell my story and share my story with my generation?"

On the other hand, we knew that the stuff that would get to television had to be really high quality, so it was also a production studio for very skilled independent filmmakers and videographers who were looking to break out and get their work seen, so at the high end there was also a lot of guidance and help that we could give. We built a community of content creators around the content, working with each other in trying to improve it, and that online studio has became more robust but still exists today at Current.com. We were really pleased that while it was indeed teaching, it was really fun. We had talent and hosts to talk about how you do lighting, how you do sound. We had guests from Robert Redford to all kinds of famous editors, and actors, and storytellers, and so it was as much entertaining as it was educational.

As we continued to build Current, we launched our first destination Web site in October 2007. That now has about seven million monthly unique [visits]; it's one of the fastest growing social media sites on the Internet.

As a young man, Joel created a law firm to provide low-cost and convenient legal services to low-income families. He built a new kind of delivery system for legal services, believing that the promise of democracy is unfulfilled unless people have the ability to protect and enforce their legal rights. He went on to create Hyatt Legal Plans, making legal care a fringe benefit for employees, and sold the company to MetLife in 1997. He then taught entrepreneurship at Stanford Business School for five years, coming off the faculty to start Current with Al Gore.

Joel and Al noticed that the content on the Web combined top-down and bottom-up delivery. Traditional media organizations, which had embraced both the physical and the digital, were aggregating high-quality products from various places and delivering them in a top-down structure. Examples of this approach were the *New York Times* with NYTimes.com (*see the interview with Arthur Sulzberger Jr., chapter 5*) and CNN with CNN.com. They were also intrigued by bottom-up percolations like Digg.com, where people can discover and share content from anywhere

Current TV building
photo by BizStone/Creative Commons

on the Web, but noticed that they were limited almost exclusively to the technology-savvy community. They could find nothing that captured the middle ground, using the principles of bottom-up but also bringing the editorial and curation of the top-down. This could be a fertile opportunity for leveraging both worlds.

We thought that there was a very important value proposition in that middle ground. When you come to Current.com, you get the benefits of what a community thinks ought to be news, with the added value of a secret sauce of good editorial and curation, so that your take-away value is much higher. And we were really quite amazed that there was no one in the middle trying to provide a solid value proposition of allowing community involvement, engagement, and participation but providing really first-class editorial and curation.

Good democracies require good leadership. You know Winston Churchill's great statement about democracy, "It's the worst form of government except for everything else known to mankind." Our view is that we're building a democracy in the context of tremendous empowerment, engagement, participation, and feedback loops, but it won't be really good unless we can provide good leadership for it.

Someone challenged me early on. They said, "You know, this is a network, a media company and Web site properties that are all geared to eighteen- to thirty-four-year-olds (let's call them twenty-somethings). But it can't be what the parents of twenty-somethings would like twenty-somethings to be doing. It's gotta be what twenty-somethings want to be doing." I understood what was being said to me back then. It's been a challenge to make sure that the programming decisions that get made here are for those demographics.

Current TV is the only television network with programming that is heavily influenced by its audience. Viewers create about 40 percent of the output, and the audience influences all of it. The example created by Current TV and Current.com has influenced media giants with feet in both worlds. For example, CNN has added iReport.com to its Web presence, with the slogan, "Unedited. Unfiltered. News." and the request to "Send us in some cell phone footage."

Not only did none of that exist, but in fairness to us, that part of the so-called journalism profession was derisive about these developments. They really scoffed at the notion of what Current was setting out to do, but we proved very early on how powerful the format is and how compelling it can be, and there is not a news organization in the country today that doesn't copy something of what we started.

The business model for Current has two revenue streams: A license fee is paid by the systems that carry Current into people's homes, such as Direct TV, Comcast, and Time Warner Cable, with 58 million households in 2008. The second revenue stream is from advertising, which supports Current.com and contributes to the television channel. Joel Hyatt's long experience as an entrepreneur has helped him to exert financial discipline. In 2006, its first full year on the air, Current TV was already in the black, making a little bit more the next year. The company has benefited greatly by starting afresh, without being encumbered by legacy systems, technologies, or thinking. Current installed an entirely digital infrastructure and has benefited from recent reductions in cost and new productivity tools.

The presidential debates in the 2008 election were naturally of passionate interest to Joel and Al, but they didn't like the format. The limitations imposed by a broadcast event followed by commentaries from pundits had caused the debates to become predictable, so they wanted to replace punditry with perspectives from real people, both

Obama and tweets on Current TV
photo by Mykl Roventine/Creative Commons

in the coverage of the debates and in the coverage of the election itself. Collaboration with Twitter gave access to what people were thinking and saying through their tweets, and Current TV displayed them in real time during the debates. The experience was much more lively because you could watch and listen to the candidates at the same time as reading how people were reacting to what they said. For the election eve and day coverage, Current TV worked with both Twitter and Digg in developing a new way of talking about the election, with participation by people from all over the country.

The world would have been a different place if in the last eight years we had Al Gore instead of George Bush, and we will pay a price for that for a very long time. Having said that, Election

Day was not only extraordinarily significant in a historical context, but it was also such a moment of hope and renewal for our country and for the world. To see the spontaneous reaction all over the world to what was done here in the United States was just remarkable. And we have a chance to lead the world again, to reinstill that peculiarly American sense of optimism, justice, and fairness. It's a very exciting time!

You can already see in the success of the Obama campaign the role of the Internet in engaging people and empowering people. I think we'll continue to see that the Internet's going to play a big role in governance. I'm very encouraged by how new forms of technology that offer new ways of communicating can add strength, and vigor, and vibrancy to our underlying democracy.

At Current, we set out to build a global participatory and cross-platform media company, but truly we are just at the tip of the iceberg. I mean, we're really just starting. We are already in the United Kingdom, Ireland, and Italy, but there's a lot more of the world to expand to for our television platform. There's also a lot of expansion potential for our Web platform, with more innovation to enable people to participate. We want to get our content on mobile phones. We're excited about what we've accomplished so far, but we really think we're just getting started.

We're launching a new unified cross-platform programming strategy, with channels for communities on the Web. Whether the topics are music, technology, culture, news, movies, or careers, those communities will actually be involved in helping to create a companion TV program on the same subject. Some will be in collaboration with Internet brands like Rotten Tomatoes, the wonderful movie review site that ten million people use every month. Together with them, we're going to build a whole community at Current.com around movie reviews, leading to a weekly TV show.

THE NEXT INTERVIEW is with Bruce Nussbaum. He has managed to achieve success in both worlds, by stepping boldly into the digital realm in starting the Innovation and Design channel online and NussbaumOnDesign blog for *Business Week* and by bringing back the material from this new world to create a supplement for the print world with his quarterly *IN: Inside Innovation.*

BRUCE NUSSBAUM

Interviewed September 12, 2008

BRUCE NUSSBAUM

As a managing editor for *BusinessWeek*, Bruce has become a leading voice in design and innovation in the world of business. After more than a decade as a page editor, he launched the Innovation and Design channel online and the NussbaumOnDesign blog in 2005. The following year he founded *IN: Inside Innovation*. In the inaugural issue of *IN* he declared a goal of making a meaningful difference in the difficult journey toward building innovative business cultures, hoping to inspire, to provoke, to teach, and to be a trusted advisor and guide. He also structured *IN* as a community, linking to the Innovation and Design site, with its blogs, columnists, metrics, and stories. Bruce has been a leader in bringing an online version of *BusinessWeek* into being, in parallel with the print version, and has a deep understanding of the comparative values of physical and virtual media. He is also an essayist and commentator on economic and social issues. In 2008 he was appointed as professor of Design and Innovation at Parsons The New School for Design in New York.

← **Bruce Nussbaum**
photos by author

Bruce and I went to the same design conference in the fall of 2008 at the Arizona Biltmore hotel, which is dubbed "The Jewel of the Desert" and resplendent with Frank Lloyd Wright-influenced architecture and beautiful grounds. I recorded an interview with him under a magnificent tree in one of the green enclosures in the garden. He seemed to relish being so removed from the hubbub of his everyday life in Manhattan.

BUSINESSWEEK, BOTH IN PRINT AND ONLINE

Bruce has had strong connections to the design community for two decades, writing cover stories about design for *BusinessWeek*. One was called "Smart Design" and another, more about the antithesis of smart, titled "I Can't Make that #*@§¶ Thing Work!" He encouraged connections between the magazine and the Industrial Designers Society of America (IDSA) and arranged for *BusinessWeek* to sponsor the organization's annual International Design Excellence Awards (IDEA) competition, bringing good design to the attention of business readers. His interest in design was triggered in 1990 when he was covering international finance for *BusinessWeek* and was on a plane coming back from a financial conference in Switzerland.

BusinessWeek
photo by Nicolas Zurcher

It was late. It was dark. I had my glasses off and was dozing, when all of a sudden something hits my face; liquid. I wake up and I'm looking around and I think, "Something's wrong with the plane!" As I put my glasses back on, I notice that people on both sides of the aisle keep popping up and doing the same thing, touching their face. Finally I focus and see this little figure. It was very bizarre. The figure turns around and starts coming back at me and I'm really frightened now. As she approaches I can see it's a little girl, and in her hand she had this donut-shaped milk bottle. She had her little hand around it, and she was squirting all the adults, torturing them gleefully, and feeding herself.

She went up and down the aisle, and she got me again! And I thought, my God, how marvelous! Had it been a regular milk bottle she never would have been able to do that. Someone had taken the time to look at how very tiny tots actually hold a bottle and how difficult it is for them to do it and made one just for them—but of course it had unintended consequences. Not only was this little girl able to feed herself, but she was also able to torture adults, which was perfect for her. It gave her a great deal of power. So I did a story and we got a great response from our audience.

The three major business magazines in the United States with a long tradition are *BusinessWeek*, *Forbes*, and *Fortune*. *Fortune* is aimed more at top management, with a reputation for thorough analysis and reporting. *BusinessWeek*, started in 1929, has always attempted to explain how the world works to middle and upper-middle managers. It began by explaining government policy, as regulations were developed to lift the economy out of the Great Depression.

Bruce Nussbaum was busy with the editorial page throughout the nineties and well in to the next decade, expressing the point of view of *BusinessWeek* on all of the issues that they were covering. He also enjoyed writing about design as digital technology became pervasive. When the Internet boom swept the world, the editorial staff at the magazine started talking about the implications. The business community at first focused on the opportunities for business-to-business sales, but gradually realized that it would soon be relevant for business-to-consumer.

BusinessWeek's involvement was very episodic, creating an online presence and then pulling back because of a recession or objections from the people running the print side. As with most print media, middle-aged men and women, who remained ambivalent about funding an Internet-based venture, were making the decisions. Eventually the control began to leave them, because the advertisers were following the audience onto the Web, shifting dramatically from print to online. This forced the magazine to take their Web presence seriously and caused Bruce to participate.

I got involved in the online version of the magazine in 2005 for two reasons: One was that by the turn of the century the business community had realized that design and design thinking were critical competencies that they had to have, and I thought that I could use our online presence to expand the

BusinessWeek, *Forbes*, and *Fortune*
photo by Nicolas Zurcher

coverage of the topic. This was a long journey. I began covering design in the early nineties, but it was still, even ten years later, considered something that a few artsy-fartsy folks did to pretty up a new technology or device, to be thrown at the marketplace.

It was a decade-long slog to change that mentality, and during that decade design itself changed—it became much more complex and sophisticated. The processes of design became more formalized, and it became much more of a methodology that business could see and understand, so its impact on industry and commerce grew. You can design business models now. You can also design new processes using the tools and methods of traditional design. There was a new focus on the consumer, the user, rather than simply the technology. All that came together to create an appetite in the business community to learn more about design. There was a huge demand by 2005 from the *BusinessWeek* audience for more stuff on design, design thinking, and innovation.

The second reason for me personally was that we got a new
guy in as the editor in chief of *BusinessWeek* who hated
the editorial page, which was what I was really doing for my
paycheck in the nineties. He came to me and said, "Bruce, I'm
killing the editorial page, now what are you gonna do?" I'd been
dying to try something new online, so at that point we launched
the new Innovation and Design channel.

This was the moment when Bruce became an innovative designer
himself, creating a unique approach to the channel that was different
from anything *BusinessWeek* had ever done in print or online.
In publications like *BusinessWeek* it is normal to use professional
journalists to create material. The magazine has its own editorial and
production staff, and staff journalists do the reporting. When the
Innovation and Design channel was launched, resources were scarce
due to a long recession, and Bruce wanted to try an open source
system, so he set about looking for partners.

The one person I hired was Jessie Scanlon, who had worked
at *Wired* for ten years. At that time she was in her early
thirties and totally cool! She had spent time online, from its
birth. Jessie and I, just the two of us, launched the entire
channel. The way we did it was to partner with people. Core77
was our first partner, our terrific partner. We partnered for
content, and we partnered for links, and in some cases we
even partnered for revenue.

Today the partnership model seems obvious, but at that time
it was a revolution for *BusinessWeek* to go outside the silo, to
actually have relationships and to bring in content from other
sources, not our own, and not our own journalists. That was a
complete revolution, and it worked. And that is the model we
use today. We've hired a couple of people to do some stories,
but basically it is still an open source model with partners, and
we even see our own journalists almost as partners now, in a
network of sources to provide content and revenue.

This was the beginning of the realization that you could provide
content to your readers by curating content and ideas that
don't necessarily have to originate inside your silo. Of course,
editors have always played that role. They're the ones who say,

> "We will tell you what is important in this sphere because we know you. You can trust us." We took this to a different level and called it curating. This idea has begun to influence the rest of *BusinessWeek* and mainstream journalism.

The next step was to bring back the curated material that was collected in the new online world for the benefit of the printed version of the magazine. Bruce launched a new magazine within *BusinessWeek* called *Inside Innovation (IN)*, using the data and stories harvested online and presenting them in print form for the benefit of the members of the business community, who still rely on print for a great deal of their analysis and information.

> We open-sourced a model for print within *BusinessWeek*— very interesting! At the very beginning, in our naive way, we thought going online meant taking print stories and simply putting them online. Everyone did that; the entire media did that, but very quickly we realized, especially from people like Jessie who grew up online, that people don't want that. People want engagement. They want a real community. They want to participate and have an active conversation with you. The kind of journalism you do online should be very different from the kind of journalism you do in print. Lots of people are still forgetting that, but for us it became apparent very quickly.

> Online journalism is interactive with dynamic engagement. The stories are always commented on, and then we comment on the comments, and the people who are doing the commenting will often comment to each other. Now we have videos to bring the conversations more alive. It is all much more direct than in print, which is a kind of conversation but much more static and flat. Those print journalists who are either young enough or open enough to the new, love it.

The conversational nature of online media is most obvious with blogging and Twittering *(see the interview with Ev Williams, chapter 3).* Bruce has always been adventurous experimenter, so when the new channel was up he was eager to try blogging. This led to the popular NussbaumOnDesign blog on BusinessWeek.com, which Bruce has thought of as his chance to learn how to thrive in the new medium, modestly claiming that he still has more to learn.

NussbaumOnDesign
screen capture

One of the things about blogging is that it's hugely labor-intensive. You are creating a community, and you have to participate in that community. It's less about content and it's more about linking and having a conversation. It's really hyperengagement. You have to do it early in the morning, because most people blog when they get to work (quiet, you know). You have to be right in that conversation.

It's hugely enriching, because you're creating and becoming part of a global conversation about certain subjects. I really love it. I use it as the first iteration of an idea. I don't edit myself a whole lot. I get it out there. I've become more fearless as I've gotten older, so I'm willing to try something out and have people come back to me and say, "Crazy, stupid," or "It's really this or that," and "Yeah, that's great!"

I actually use it as part of my thinking process. I've expanded my brain in some ways around the world to engage other brains, and so we have a borgy brain thing going on about innovation in design. A lot of things are harebrained—they're really stupid! And of course people on blogs will tell you that immediately, but that's part of the fun. I've gotten into great debates with people on several important issues.

> And now of course there's Twitter, which is micro-blogging and constant blogging. I've gotten deep into Twitter. I've created my own smart, social media algorithm that connects me to great news and analysis. And then there's Facebook. All these things are basically bloggy kinds of interactions with other people. You have to decide just how much interaction you want with people, because it can be a 24/7 kind of thing. It could eat up most of your creative juices. I find myself shutting it off every once in a while. I just say, "I'm stopping now! See you in a week." People get mad and angry and all the rest of it. But more and more bloggers are doing that because you need some quiet time to ponder some of these things and take your finger out of the socket—or at least I do.

As the Innovation and Design channel flourished, Bruce was able to expand the staff. He created a multigenerational team of people from a wide variety of backgrounds and nationalities. He was the oldest, with several people in their thirties and a couple in their twenties who gave a lot of jabs to the people in their thirties for not being *au courant* enough.

> Of all the things that I've designed, the team itself is the one that I'm most proud of. I think it's the most important. The team itself is full of energy because they are so polymath in so many different ways. At times I lead, but most of the time I'm following. Each person has their moments when they're leading and following. It's very dynamic. We're learning from each other all the time. I think the design of that culture is what really makes things happen. We put out the online Innovation and Design channel; we put out the *Inside Innovation* magazine; we also work for *BusinessWeek*, and it's the same team. That's the future!

The economics of print media publishing are increasingly challenging, as so much advertising is shifting from print to online, with advertisers attracted to the enhanced possibilities for targeting a specific audience and measuring the results. The luxurious forms of print, such as glossy fashion magazines, remain relatively unscathed, but the business press is hard hit. Online channels like Innovation and Design are attracting more advertisers than they can accommodate, but the space for ads is limited and the revenue is much less per ad, resulting in a drastic drop in total income for *Business Week*, even when both print and online worlds are combined.

> For every dollar of advertising that shifts from print to online, you're only getting about twenty cents online, because it's a very competitive market there. So even though the quantity of advertising online is surging, the amount of revenue you're getting is falling. The brand is suffering, and this is true for everyone, so it's a very difficult time.
>
> The newspapers are going through the same thing. The *New York Times* Web site is fantastic; it's one of the top eleven sites in the world. It's got a huge amount of traffic, it's really well designed, and they do wonderful video stuff, but the amount of revenue the brand is getting is falling rather dramatically because they're losing expensive print advertising and only gaining less expensive online advertising. That will continue until at some point we reach a new equilibrium, and of course that changes the business model, so you have to do journalism at a much lower cost. That's the harsh struggle that's going on now in the business. Lots of people are getting laid off.
>
> On my Innovation and Design team, we have six people who are able to do online journalism, print journalism, video, and blog. They do it all, they do it naturally, they do it at one price, and what they are getting paid is a lot less than senior print journalists make today. The business model for all mainstream media is changing rather dramatically.

It is much easier for new organizations and businesses to find the right balance between both worlds than it is for those with a long history of success in the traditional media. For many people who work at *Business Week*, the changes look like failure, as they rely on growth, or at least stability, to stay viable. Laying people off and cutting expenses to balance a shrinking revenue stream can have a demoralizing effect, so that even when new roles and opportunities are opening up to compensate, the culture of the community may be damaged.

Bruce has an admirable resilience, perhaps fueled by his endless curiosity, allowing him to embrace the new world and flourish in it without breaking ties with the old world. He enjoys the democratization

Whitewater
photo by Doug Rivers/Morgue File

of open source, the acquisition of design skills by ordinary people, and the increase in the availability of tools for creativity. He remains an optimist and believes that the changes can lead to great things, to a new burst of creativity from elements of societies around the world that have always been outside.

Wherever I go to talk these days, whether among my friends at cocktails, at the beach, in the city, or for a formal presentation, we're all talking about the same thing. We're talking about all our business models melting down, our careers completely morphing, and our lives changing dramatically. There is a mixture of fear, and anticipation, and excitement in all of this discussion. And right now my major line is, "We live life in beta."

This is a period of intense change for all kinds of reasons: technological, global, political, and economic. I've always wanted to lead an interesting life, and here it is on steroids! It's a little terrifying, but it's a great journey. It's as if you are going down a river on a raft, and then all of a sudden, whitewater. That's even better. Then all of a sudden it's really whitewater.

That's where we are now. We're just surging away and you have
a little control, but not a lot, and you're trying to navigate your
way through this life.

Bruce has managed to achieve success in both worlds, first by stepping
boldly into the digital realm when he started the online channel and
blog, and then bringing back the material from this new world to create a
supplement for the print world with *IN*. The challenge for *Business Week*
magazine, and many others in the magazine world, will be to adjust the
cost structures of the print world fast enough to avoid a demoralizing
effect on the staff. Even if the online version of the magazine grows
steadily, if the revenue generated is less than a fifth of the amount coming
from print, the adjustment to the business may be traumatic.

BRUCE TALKED ABOUT BRINGING JESSIE SCANLON aboard
to launch the Innovation and Design channel for *Business Week* online.
Next we meet Jessie in a 2009 interview to learn more about her
experiences both before and during the *Business Week* venture and to
understand her vision for designing for these changing times.

JESSIE SCANLON

Interviewed November 20, 2009

JESSIE SCANLON

← Jessie Scanlon
photos by Dan DeRuntz

Jessie writes about design and innovation. In 2005 she joined Bruce Nussbaum at BusinessWeek.com as the senior writer and editor for Innovation and Design. She wanted to create a strong new offering that would be truly innovative and well designed, but she found that the limitations of the preexisting website made it impossible to achieve many of her goals early on. The offering has gradually evolved to represent the initiative more successfully. Jessie decided to try journalism when her grandfather said, "You seem to like writing." She had been studying Latin American politics and history, so she headed for Chile to give it a try, landing her first job at the *South Pacific Mail* in Santiago. She next joined *Wired* magazine, first as an intern and eventually becoming a contributing editor. Later she became a freelance writer, reporting on design and technology for *ID*, *Popular Science*, the *New York Times,* and *Slate*. In 2004 she was a writing fellow in the Simplicity program at MIT Media Lab in Cambridge, Massachusetts. Jessie is also the coauthor of *Wired Style*, a guide to writing and editing in the digital age.

I had often heard about Jessie's work and writings before meeting her in person, so I was thrilled when she suggested that we record an interview for a *BusinessWeek* podcast to talk about my recently published book *Designing Interactions*. We met in Boston in December 2006 at a restaurant where we could enjoy a lunchtime conversation before finding a quiet corner to record the interview. I was very impressed by her depth of knowledge and perceptive questions as well as her graceful manner. It was my pleasure to ask her to be interviewed for *Designing Media*.

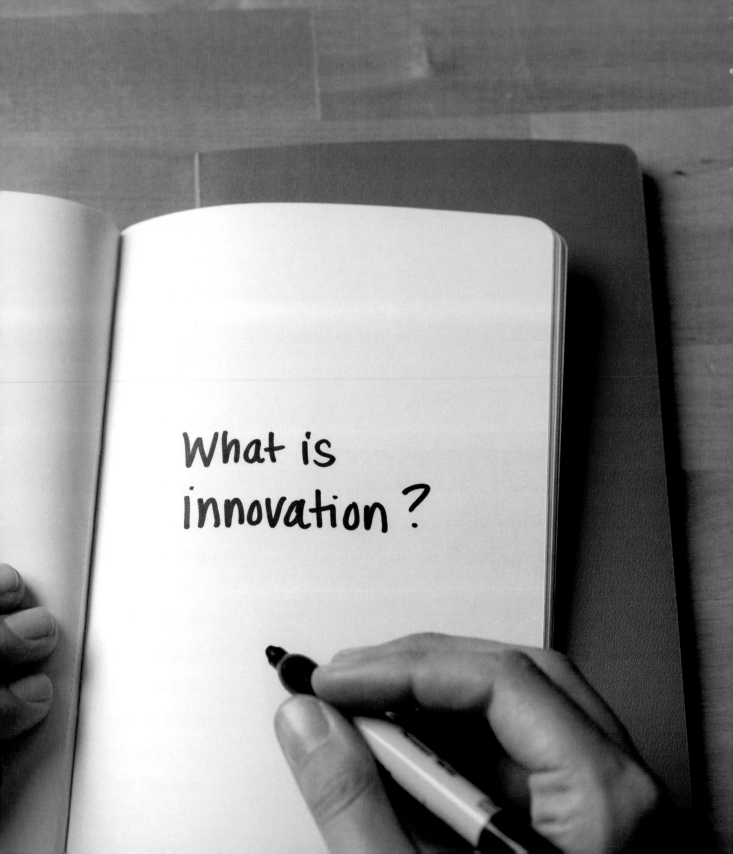

THE INNOVATION & DESIGN CHANNEL

Bruce Nussbaum had a clear vision for the Innovation and Design channel as a bridge between the design community and the business world. He wanted more interactive links than the traditional relationship, where the designer works to a brief provided by a business client or employer. The new channel was very close to launch when Jessie started, but the overworked staff of the design department had very little freedom because the design was dictated by the inflexible architecture of the rest of the BusinessWeek.com site.

Gianfranco Zaccai, the founder and president of the well-known design firm Design Continuum, sent in a list of critical comments right after the site launched, pointing out that it was cluttered, with unclear navigation systems and inconsistent labeling. Jessie remembers the frustration of launching an innovation and design site that was poorly designed and not so innovative.

⟵···· **What is innovation?**
photo by Nicolas Zurcher

I showed up on the first day and had the sense that as they had been putting this site together it had almost had a kind of grab bag feeling to it. I think they were getting very close to launch and they said, "Yikes, we need to bring somebody in." Because while Bruce was the visionary behind it, he didn't want to be involved in the day-to-day, as he travels a lot and he was still involved in the magazine. They needed someone to come in and handle the day-to-day aspects of actually running the Web site, which is an incredibly time-consuming job, as we were publishing daily. This was 2005. It was crazy! I took the job two weeks before my wedding, but I don't think I talked to friends for a year after that.

The Innovation and Design offering was structured as a main channel with a collection of subchannels, including architecture, cars, games, and branding. The grab bag feel came from the lack of a clear organization for the subchannels. There was a sense that a lot of things had been thrown in as experiments for *BusinessWeek* to see which would gain popularity, but without a clear organization built around an understanding of innovation and design.

They were kind of dipping their toe in. What happens if we start writing about games regularly? What happens if we have this brand channel? What happens if we write about cars? The topic of cars was actually enormously successful. It generated a lot of traffic and to some extent spun out into an actual car channel later.

While Bruce had a very clear sense of what it should be about, some of the people who were more involved with the day-to-day decisions didn't really have the same understanding of "What is design?" "What is innovation?" They would encourage us to do all kinds of stories which to my mind weren't necessarily the kinds we should be doing. For example, when we first launched, there was a link to JD Powers auto ratings. JD Powers is a sister company to *BusinessWeek*, owned by McGraw-Hill, but there was really no real connection to design or innovation. It was just, "Oh, hey, cars. Let's throw the JD Powers rating in there."

People seemed to have different ideas about what design is, misconceiving the role played by designers, what design does, and what is its impact. There was some tension in those early days, not between Bruce and I, but in relations with some of the other people. I reported to the editor in chief of *BusinessWeek* online, who is wonderful in many ways, but there was some tension. There was this sense that, "Oh, if we're covering architecture, we should do real estate as well."

Ultimately, even if the editor in chief was suggesting, "I think this would be a great story for you, I think you should really do it," I had a lot of autonomy. So it really was just up to me what I wanted to put up, what I wanted to publish, whether I wanted to publish it or not. I obviously took a hit in terms of

Designer Dwellings on the Cheap

These prefabricated modernist homes, created by respected architects, are a boon for those searching for stylish yet affordable options

Two years ago, *Dwell* magazine invited a select group of architects from around the globe to design a modernist home made from prefabricated materials. This fall, the publication is launching a mass-produced version of the winning entry -- designed by the New York-based firm Resolution: 4 Architecture -- along with two other sleek offerings. The residences, known as The Dwell Homes, are manufactured by Empyrean International (formerly known as Deck House), a Massachusetts-based homebuilder with a 57-year history.

The graceful forms and rich materials used in these homes defy the popular preconception of prefab housing as drab and primarily utilitarian. Since the components of the Dwell Homes and other modernist prefab houses are often less expensive because they're mass-produced, design becomes the priority.

Dwell's editor-in-chief, Allison Arieff, there's a reason why modernist prefab housing is timely now. "Apart from home design, every product on the market now is modern," says Arieff. "Most people have a high-tech phone, for example. There's a significant population of design-savvy consumers."

In addition, pricing is attractive: Prefab promises a budget-efficient option because of controlled costs. The Dwell Homes, for instance, are priced on average at $175 to $200 per square foot, based on a two-level, 2,500-square-foot home. Other modernist kit homes, like the LV by Rocio Romero and the Wee House by Alchemy Architects, can run as low as five figures.

"Prefab Chic" article and slideshow from BusinessWeek.com
screen capture

traffic if something was pushed on me and I said "no" and then it did very well elsewhere.

It was really hit-and-miss to a large extent, with lots of surprises. For example, we did a story on *Dwell* magazine's well-designed prefabs, with a slide show. It was so popular that we had six or seven million hits, actually shutting down the server of the company that was offering the prefab houses. Who knew? It was just so hard to predict at that point what story was going to do well.

It was challenging to create content that would appeal to people interested in design as well as those focused on innovation. At that time the overlap was not generally understood. People thought that innovation is driven by business and technology, while design emerges from a synthesis of human values, particularly subjective qualities, like aesthetics. Bruce and Jessie had the vision to see that innovation is most likely when technological feasibility and business viability are combined with the human values of usability and desirability, but that concept of overlapping interdisciplinary contributions was not widely accepted at the time.

With the benefit of hindsight, Jessie thinks that they could have done more to understand their target audience in advance. Over the years they have moved away from the idea of providing a bridge between design and innovation, seeing themselves as focused on talking to people in business who have a broad approach to innovation, including not just design-driven innovation but also process innovation, new business models, and so on.

It would have been much easier had we been working with a blank canvas. The *BusinessWeek* Web site already had a top news page, covering technology and investing. There were templates defining how every page had to look and how you could structure data, which made it very difficult to develop new designs that might have made more sense for our channel. Our audience had very different expectations from the readers of the Investing channel.

All Web designers struggle with the issue of templates. Khoi Vinh, former design director at NYTimes.com, and I know he's talked a lot about the systems that you need to be able to throw up so many stories every day. The *New York Times* couldn't have somebody designing every story page, so they need templates, but it takes away the chance to lay out a story with a unique design that make sense for that particular story.

If you look the design of Apple's iPhone apps, they've injected their graphic design, or interaction design DNA, into the tools that the software developers are using to create the apps. They are passing on some of their design skill and making it much harder for a software designer who doesn't have training in design to create an ugly app. Most of the tools and systems that underlie BusinessWeek.com or NYTimes.com were not developed by design-focused companies, so those tools didn't naturally lead to good-looking, well-designed experiences.

I hope that the situation will improve. I can imagine digital magazines with thin flexible screens that are almost like paper, feeling like paper as you're flipping through them. I can imagine a system where you could change layouts much more easily, where you could pull things around, or drop a photo in. It strikes me that the tools that designers have now are so crude, especially based on those early days at *BusinessWeek* online.

Roger Martin
photo by Jordan Fischer/Creative Commons

Tim Brown
photo by Nicolas Zurcher

After a year or so, they redesigned the pages, but that was a four- or six-month process. I wanted to be able to walk over to the art department and work with the designer to whip some things around on the computer screen, so that we could look at the layout and say, "Oh yeah, that works better!" You just couldn't do that. We didn't have that kind of flexibility. Especially for a site that was about innovation and design, that was very difficult.

The Innovation and Design channel has consistently been among the most popular five channels on Businessweek.com. Jessie has discovered that people love stories about big companies, but they don't want stories that claim, "Hey, this was a great innovation!" as much as descriptions about how the innovation was actually achieved, so she has shifted toward a case-study approach. The recession of 2008 caused budgets to be cut or trimmed, making people cautious about spending money on innovative projects. When they move forward, they want to be careful. This has increased the interest in how-to stories that hold the reader's hand and say, "Here's how this company did it, and it worked," so that they can then take it to their supervisor, their boss, or manager, and say, "Look, we can do something like this."

BusinessWeek was a pioneer among business magazines in writing about both design and innovation, with columnists such as Roger Martin from the Rotman School of Management and Tim Brown from IDEO. There is more competition now, with articles in *Fast Company*, *Forbes*, *Fortune*, and the *Harvard Business Review*, so the Innovation and Design channel has to be better, smarter, and faster to keep traffic levels up.

There are lots of innovation and design blogs, such as Design Observer. com, with contributions from a host of influential designers, or *Logic + Emotion*, where David Armano writes about branding and social media. A magazine like *BusinessWeek* tries to achieve an objective vantage point, aiming to be accurate and well reported, with information verified by fact checkers. Blogs are different, in that there is much more room for editorial voice and opinion, as the reader expects the content to be based on a stream of consciousness from the author. BusinessWeek.com positions itself between the magazine context and a blog, looking for a balance between traditional journalistic values and the opportunities to connect more directly to the audience and engage readers. For example, they have a regular feature called "The Reader Recommended Story," which aims to increase interaction and build a better connection between reporters and readers without becoming a social media site. They also have a feature called "Five Questions For," where they post an announcement that they will be interviewing somebody and use the questions that come in from readers in a video interview, which is then posted online. This gives readers a direct conduit to people they would not normally be able to ask questions of and interact with.

ONLINE VERSUS PRINT

Journal content works best when it is modified to suit the strengths and style of a particular medium. Print stories can be longer than their online equivalents because people have more patience to read longer pieces in print than they do online. That said, many people read a magazine online, and to them it's seamless. They have no sense that "this is an online piece" versus "this is a magazine piece." For a blog, you want more of a sense of the author, allowing their personality to come through. They can be more intimate and chattier, but they also need to get to the point right away. A two-paragraph lead on a blog post loses the audience.

Blogs, podcasts, and videos are more personal than traditional news reports or articles, so there is a trend for the brand of the reporter to become more important than the brand of the overall institution, with star journalists building a name across media. There are exceptions to this trend, such as *The Economist*, which speaks with one voice without star reporters. Jessie is not sure how this is going to end up.

I would have bet on the idea that reporters and writers are going to have increasingly strong brands working across media, but you certainly see *The Economist* being a counterbalance to that. At *BusinessWeek* Stephen Baker, who had been at the magazine for decades, led the magazine into blogs. He was one of the first magazine writers to be blogging very successfully, writing about Twitter. He's been very engaged in every new technology that comes along, linking it to his job and understanding how it changes his job, how it gives him new capabilities. All of a sudden you're blogging about the story you're writing and you're not just calling ten sources or twenty sources. You have this vast platform of people who are chirping up, offering their opinions, critiquing your work, and pointing you here and there. Chris Anderson wrote *The Long Tail* almost as he was blogging about it. He was blogging about the book, and getting advice, and getting pointers. John Battelle did a very similar thing with his book on Google—had a blog that was all about search.

It's obviously easier to blog with books than with magazine articles, because your competitors can be reading that blog and it's really easy to get scooped, but I think more and more reporters are deciding that that's probably a chance worth taking because it's strengthening their reporting skills, their reporting world. I think there's also a sense that blogs have a legitimacy, so once you have it up on your blog, even if someone beats you into print, you were still the one who broke the story. Blogs were not considered serious media initially. There was a period of thinking, "Oh, he's just a blogger." And I think that's really changed.

Not only are all of these technologies that underlie media changing, the business models are changing. They have to change. And readers are changing. As traditional magazines and newspapers have struggled financially in the last few years, it's become much more difficult for them to be so dismissive of the Internet because some of the most successful media operations are now blogs or Web sites.

I think it's really hard to know where we're going to end up, but I don't think it's going to be uniform. If you look historically at different media models, you had very expensive newsletter-type publications that sold for hundreds or thousands of dollars a year, most of them paid for by corporation's expense accounts. Advertising has supported most print media, with the purchase price hardly covering the mailing costs. Now we are seeing a steady shift of advertising dollars online, as advertisers see the benefits to them of knowing more about the behavior of their audiences.

The market for advertising was decimated during the recession of 2008 and 2009, both for print and online, but the shakeout set the advantages and disadvantages of each medium into sharper relief. In the early years of the growth of the Internet, companies and organizations were transferring their print materials to the screen with little regard for the design attributes of the interactive medium, so that readers were forced to browse endless pages of material that were not designed initially for screen resolutions and failed to take advantage of the interactive navigational attributes of the Internet. Gradually the opportunities to provide links, appropriate navigational structures, and interactive behaviors became more commonplace, so that now we see online materials presenting information in different formats than their printed equivalents, even when the text stream has the same words.

At last we are seeing clear differences between print and online versions, with print enjoying high-resolution images, voluptuous typography, and large well-composed pages, while online designs are rich with video, audio, blogs, and links to other material. People will continue to expect online material to be apparently free, supported only by advertising, while print materials will respond to the reduction in advertising revenues by being designed to command higher prices, using better materials and beautiful designs. Print media will tend to converge, so that it will be harder to say, "This is a magazine, but this is a newspaper," as they will be produced more intermittently. Daily newspapers are likely to become weekly special editions in print, with their online versions produced in a continuous real-time stream for news content. Jessie predicts increasing diversity.

Blogs are already an incredibly diverse universe. You have everything from individual bloggers writing about specific interests that they are passionate about, to groups of bloggers doing some original reporting and linking with each other and

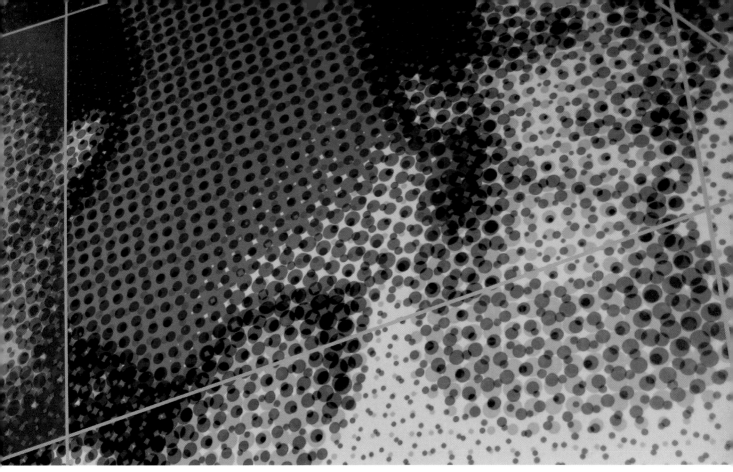

The beauty of print
photo by Katja Battarbee

other sources of information. I think we'll ultimately end up seeing micro payments, where you don't have to subscribe to an entire magazine or newspaper, but you automatically get charged a few cents every time you click on an article. It's going to be an evolution. The economy really needs to recover before we can even think about how it's going to settle down.

This year it's Twitter, but we don't know what's it's going to be next year. Not only is the technology changing, the business models need to change and adapt to the new technologies and to changing reader habits. My parents' media diet was not that different from that of their parents. My daughter is two, and her media habits are going to be completely different from the ones I grew up with. It's just going to take a while for that to really shake out, to figure out what works and what doesn't.

I was at a conference recently at MIT and someone from Facebook was there talking about a big redesign they had about a year ago. He talked about the role that design has played at Facebook and at MySpace. I don't know if you've gone to a MySpace page. It looks like a middle-school girl's locker. It is cluttered, messy, thrown up there. It's ugly. Facebook has very intentionally tried not to do that. It has tried to create a template that, while giving its users control, ensures that the result is visually pleasing. I think we ultimately will probably see more of that.

The contrast between a site like the HuffingtonPost.com and TheDailyBeast.com maybe tells you something about where we're headed. The *Huffington Post* emerged out of the blogging community, as Huffington wanted to create a place where people could have a platform, even if they didn't want to start their own blogs. *The Daily Beast* was started by Tina Brown. She came out of the magazine world—glossy, very high production values, and you see that, I think, when you go to their site. It's very beautifully designed, you know, templates, et cetera. It's online but it has a more polished design than the *Huffington Post*, which kind of reflects the blogosphere from which it emerged.

So back to my point about what is the place we're going to end up. We'll probably end up with both of those. You're going to end up with blogs that do have more of a polished, edited kind of feel—a professionally designed kind of feel. You'll have the personal blog, and you'll have the *Huffington Post*, which is a little rougher around the edges.

OUR NEXT INTERVIEW IS WITH JANE FRIEDMAN, who lives for books, authors, and book publishing. Throughout her marketing career at Random House, the world's largest English-language trade publisher, and as president and CEO of HarperCollins, she has harnessed the new world of electronic media in support of the traditional world of books. She describes her many achievements in both worlds but also warns of the financial instability inherent to book publishing in the United States as it is currently structured.

JANE FRIEDMAN

Interviewed November 13, 2008

JANE FRIEDMAN

Books and authors are part of Jane Friedman's DNA, and she is confident that there will always be books. At the same time, she sees the reading experience changing dramatically as electronic media mature. Throughout her career in book publishing, spanning four decades, she has led the way forward with innovations enabled by emerging technologies. She was executive vice president of Random House and of the Knopf Publishing Group, publisher of Vintage Books, and founder and president of Random House Audio Publishing. She is credited with inventing the author tour, making audio books successful, and leading the industry toward exploiting the Internet, saying, "I'm a marketer. The ability the Web gives you to reach thousands of people by pushing a button is a marketer's dream." From 1997 to 2008, she was the president and CEO of HarperCollins Publishers Worldwide, one of the world's leading English-language publishers. She expanded its international reach in China and in India. In 2009 she founded Open Road Integrated Media to publish the early works of big-name authors in electronic form.

I visited Jane Friedman in her Upper East Side apartment in New York to record the interview. At first she showed me into her living room, a sparse but carefully designed space with marble flooring and matching walls in a delicate texture. This seemed a little impersonal for the interview, so I asked her to show me around. We entered a library, the walls lined with books—the perfect backdrop for communicating her passion for books and publishing. I set up the cameras there. On a shelf by the window there was an architectural model of her beautiful house in the Hamptons, close enough to complement city life on most weekends. Next to the library was a small office containing her computer, where she admitted that she spends a great deal of her time, saying, "I'm an email fanatic!"

1 Tb minced shallot or
green onion
¼ cup port or Madeira
⅔ cup brown stock or
canned beef bouillon
2 Tb minced parsley

shallot or
pour in the w...
rapidly over hig...
Pour over the
serve.

Deglazing Sauce with Truffle

1 minced canned truffle and
the juice from its can

Ingredients for the preced-
ing brown deglazing
sauce minus the parsley

After saut...
ceding m...
and the
syrupy...

Suprêmes de Volaille à...
[Chicken Breasts Rolled i...

...ced in
...on the
...e burn-
...ffed to-
...er. Serve

...es with salt
...ake off ex.

BOOK PUBLISHING

Jane spent most of her energies in the first two decades of her career
supporting review coverage of books with off the book page coverage to
make them sell better and talking to her colleagues about words, books,
and literature, but she was always interested in the possibilities that were
opened up by new technologies.

I thought it would be appropriate to use the electronic media,
in those days radio and television, to promote the authors.
I am credited with inventing the author tour. I say I am credited with it because years before a very commercial author
called Jacqueline Susann went around America with books in
the trunk of her car; that was the original author tour. What
I did was take some quite literary authors and work with
television and radio talk shows and newspaper interviews in
various cities. That was the beginning of the author tour as
we know it today.

The actual launch was with Julia Child, the French chef. I like
to tell the story of going to Minneapolis and looking out of my
hotel window and seeing 1,000 women lined up (and they
were all women) outside the local department store at seven
in the morning, waiting to go upstairs to watch Julie Child
make mayonnaise. They had learned about this event from
a big story in the *Minneapolis Star Tribune* the day before,
and they had heard that Julia was going to be in Dayton's
department store because she appeared on radio and
television the day before as well. This was my first entrée
into the world of electronic media.

In 1985 I was asked if I wanted to start an audio books division
for Random House. I looked at the person who asked me and

Julia Child's *The Art of French Cooking*
photo by Nicolas Zurcher

said, "What is an audio books division?" He looked back at me and said, "I don't know. But we know that there is this small company in California called Books on Tape." (By the way, it is no longer small and actually has been acquired by Random House.) In those days it was more of a mom-and-pop shop that would license the audio rights to our books, hire little-known actors, and have the actors read the words of the author. All of the audiocassettes were sold through a catalog on a subscription basis, and we didn't see many royalties.

So I said, "Sure, I'll start this audio books division." I remember that Barnes and Noble thought I was out of my mind and gave us one shelf for the entire audio books business. Now, of course, audios have morphed from cassette, to CD, to downloadable, and the audio books business is a billion-dollar business. To me, it always seemed logical that it would succeed because I had read to my children, and I had been read to. I didn't understand why we had lost the art of hearing the words spoken. I found that fine actors were very willing to go into a studio to read wonderful words of literary writers for scale, so we had a business model that actually worked.

After almost thirty years at Random House/Knopf, Jane was invited by Rupert Murdoch to join HarperCollins as president and CEO, with a brief to revive the flagging fortunes of a company in trouble. It was a global organization with a wonderful history of almost two hundred years, but it had lost its way; so this was a perfect opportunity for Jane. Her first task was to improve the financial performance. She reveled in the responsibility and the fact that when you are in charge you can experiment as long as you deliver a profit for your owner. This led to looking into the digital world. She wanted to protect the rights of the authors and the copyrights, so she invested in a digital warehouse, where all of the digital files reside, with access given to search engines. HarperCollins would stay in control of the copyright and the copyrighted material.

During her tenure at HarperCollins, Jane achieved years of double-digit profitability, which is unusual in publishing. She focused on finding experts in cost containment and cost control and resisted chasing the best seller. She sees financial challenges facing the whole industry today.

The financial model of the book publishing industry is flawed and unworkable. The model of having books fully returnable comes from the Depression. What happened then was that publishers were not able to sell their books into bookstores so they said to booksellers, "Take them on consignment." And that has continued to this day. Well, it's a broken model. A publisher cannot take the risk of the cost of paper, printing, and binding, the overhead costs, the inventory that you hold, the inventory that you send to the bookstores, and the inventory that you ultimately take back. This is the way publishers have lived their lives.

The advances that publishers have been paid over the years have just gotten out of hand. I understand competition. I understand wanting to get the big book. But my way of publishing has always been to build up the "mid-list" author and really exploit the backlist, which is the backbone of a publishing company. And then, if you have one or two authors who are in that top-ten tier, okay, but most probably in the final analysis, you aren't going to make money on those titles anyway.

In my opinion, chasing the bestseller is something that just cannot continue. I believe all publishers today are looking at lowering advances, which might be able to be done if the entire community decides to do it. The agents can explain to the authors that it's not that the author's worth is diminished; it's just that the model doesn't work anymore. Publishers are not banks. So if the author wants to be published at a traditional publishing company, he has to get with the program.

The digital world is going to help us with the problems of inventory and returnability because a digital book does not require paper, print, bind, or huge stacks of copies. A digital world doesn't require actual foot traffic into a bookstore, which means that consumers don't have to fill up their gas tanks to get to the bookstore. I do not mean to say that there won't always be physical books. You're sitting in my library. I could not live without being surrounded by books. But the format of the book is changing. America is one of the only countries that still produces hardcover books. The profit and loss statement in

America is built on hardcover publishing as the first format and supposes a profit from that hardcover edition.

HarperCollins has long had a well-established international reach across the English-speaking world, but many of the satellite offices were no more than distributors of British and North American titles. Jane decided to build up local publishing, starting in Australia, Canada, and India. China was more intricate. She saw tremendous opportunity in bringing Chinese literature to the English-speaking world and in return publishing English books in China. She made good progress in spite of piracy being rampant and government censorship being paramount. She was a consultant to the part of the Chinese government that deals with culture and felt that she was really making headway.

> Just a lucky happenstance is that I was a CEO who read all my email. I am always looking for instant gratification. A manuscript came to me on email from a young woman. She said she was an eleven-year-old Chinese girl. I opened the file, started to read and thought, "This is really quite good." I immediately forwarded it to our Children's division. and they loved it. They also did some research and found out that yes, indeed, she was an eleven-year-old Chinese girl who lived in China and in America. The book is called *Swordbird*. It was published in English and Chinese. I went to China with the author and this became one of our first "crossing the bridge" moments. Nancy Yi Fan is a prodigy; there's no doubt about it. She writes, draws, and practices sword fighting. It was quite a positive experience to be with her in China. The Chinese government obviously liked this.

Surrounded by beautiful books
photo by Nicolas Zurcher

It was difficult to open an office in China, but News Corporation already had one there, so Jane was able to lease some space from her colleagues and share some of the expertise of those who had been there before HarperCollins.

> I think social networking is a good way to learn about things one is interested in. What is social networking but word of mouth? I've always said there is nothing new under the sun. However, the difference is that with word of mouth in the past, a potential customer had to walk into a bookstore to make

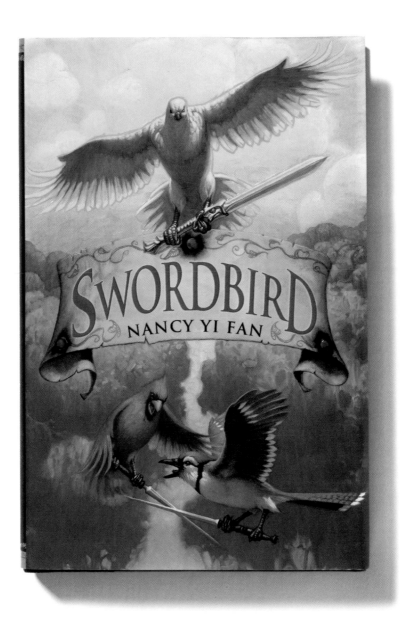

SWORDBIRD

NANCY YI FAN

a purchase. Social networking today requires only a click. That's the difference in a nutshell. I don't think the process is different. People talk to one another, saying, "Do you like these clothes? Do you like these books? Do you like these movies?" "I don't!" "Why don't you?" "I want to see you; I want to go out for a coffee, so maybe we can meet at the local bookstore." That's still going on. But for purchasing, social networking is making the product purchase one click away.

Amazon is brilliant. I've been a fan of Amazon from the beginning. Jeff Bezos came to Random House early on. I met with him and a few members of his team, and I believed in what he was trying to do. This was when people were afraid that their credit card numbers would get stolen and everybody would be bankrupt.

What I am concerned about, like all publishers, is whether Amazon will disintermediate the publishers. Will it eventually be where authors want to be published? At this point in time this is not a major problem, but depending on how the marketplace plays out, who knows?

So, am I a fan? Yes. Do I use it? Yes. Do I like its recommendations? Yes. Have I bought a book on a subject that they suggested? Yes. Their algorithms are smart! But I don't want them to be the only game in town.

Swordbird
photo by Nicolas Zurcher

We now know that the consumer really wants to be told what's available and how she can get that material, whether electronically or in physical form or over the phone lines. I do believe that marketing online will help defray a lot of marketing costs. I think one-to-one recommendations is very important, taking word of mouth to the nth degree. Print-on-demand technology is becoming more and more important in publishing. Publishers have to conquer the inventory problem, and I think print-on-demand is one way to do so. I believe that authors will start to communicate online directly with their fans, and that connection will become more and more

Oprah's Book Club seal
photo by Nicolas Zurcher

important. I think that this connection between the writer and the consumer is going to get very, very close.

I have heard that Oprah Winfrey is going to end her show in 2011 If that's a fact, publishers had better figure out what to do. She has been the single most effective salesperson for a book since I have been in the business—she gives her viewers permission to read, and then shares the experience with them. This an incomparable big deal.

Jane believes in books as a basic element of civilization. She thinks that people want home libraries because they want their children to see books in the house. Her ability to move fluently between the traditional world of books and the new world of digital technologies is illustrated by the way she welcomes the arrival of the electronic book. She thinks of the e-book as complementary to, rather than competing with, the paper book.

Physical books will not disappear, but the reading experience will change dramatically. I've tried Kindle, the Sony Reader and nook. My first experience with an electronic book was with a product called the Gemstar RocketBook. I remember going to Barcelona and bringing a stack of books with me, and my partner came with his reading material on the RocketBook. I was fascinated to watch him read.

And now Steve Jobs has brought us the iPad, a handheld device that is as aesthetically pleasing as the iPod. Perhaps the iPad will be the tipping point. Or perhaps something else that is more technologically attuned and less expensive is on the drawing board right now. All I know is that all these products will absolutely get better and better with time. And I am truly excited to see the future.

OUR NEXT INTERVIEW is with Martin Eberhard, who founded the company NuvoMedia to create the RocketBook. The rest of this chapter looks at several early and current examples of electronic books to understand more about how e-books will relate to and change the nature of traditional books.

E-BOOKS

Why would anyone want an electronic book? After all, a paper book is so wonderful! It's easy to carry around and very robust. The contrast ratio is excellent, and no batteries are needed. The resolution is 300 dots per inch in black and white or color, so that we can see images clearly and details of the fonts are crisp. It is a delight to browse through a book since you can flip the pages at any speed you like, stop at any point and open the spread, or turn one page at a time at a leisurely pace, reveling in the smooth and supple feel of the paper. You can enjoy a delicious moment as you open a new book and the smell of fresh ink and paper wafts around you. And all of this for such an amazingly small amount of money. Yes, this is a highly evolved medium!

The experience of reading an electronic book is not nearly as rich for sensual enjoyment, but it does offer unique and different advantages. Most often quoted is the example mentioned by Jane Friedman, of the traveler struggling with a pile of heavy books compared to the single e-book with all of the equivalent material loaded into it. There are other advantages for work or study. If you want to extract quotes to use in writing a paper or commentary, it's easy to copy them into a file format that can be transferred to your personal computer. You can add annotations without feeling guilty about defacing the pages, and you can use search functions to find the bit that you want to see again.

Electronic books are coming of age. The twenty-year hockey-stick curve of adoption that Paul Saffo (*see the interview with Paul Saffo, chapter 1*) talks about has not quite yet run its course, so the e-book may not be fully mature, but the promise of its viability is much more credible.

The e-book will never replace the printed book, but it will be used in parallel to offer those complementary advantages. We will soon find people who love books and have collections of them in their homes also owning an e-book or two for use on the road or for a specific work task. To begin with, we go back to an early version of an e-book in an interview with Martin Eberhard, the creator of the RocketBook, which was introduced in 1998.

MARTIN EBERHARD

Interviewed July 27, 2009

MARTIN EBERHARD

Martin was the CEO of NuvoMedia, which he cofounded with Marc Tarpenning in 1996 to develop an electronic book, believing that the emerging technologies at that time would make a successful design possible. Martin had started his career at Wyse Technology as an electrical engineer developing a character-based computer terminal. He went on to become chief engineer and a member of the founding team at Network Computing Devices (NCD), making X Window-based network terminals. After the RocketBook from NuvoMedia was successfully launched, Gemstar acquired the company in 2000. Martin then decided to focus on green technology, cofounding Tesla Motors to develop an all-electric sports car, taking the role of CEO, with Marc Tarpenning looking after the operations. The Tesla Roadster was launched in 2008, with a range of 240 miles on a single charge, dramatic acceleration of zero to sixty miles per hour in 3.9 seconds, and the equivalent energy cost of 120 miles per gallon. The largest investor, Elon Musk, ousted Martin in 2007 and proceeded to defame his reputation, causing Martin to fight back with a blog and sue. The lawsuit was settled in August 2009, and Martin has moved on to help VW Audi with its approach to greentech.

I have lots of personal connections to Martin Eberhard, so it was easy for me to ask him for an interview. He lives two doors away from me in the hills above Silicon Valley, and I often see him driving his Tesla Roadster (VIN #2) along our precipitous access road. I worked with him closely in the early start-up phase of Tesla Motors as a member of his advisory board, with a remit to establish a design brief and find the best people for the design work on the Roadster. Before we became friends, I also knew him as an entrepreneur for his work on the RocketBook and at NCD. Jim Sacherman created the industrial design for both those ventures. I had taught Jim when he was in the design program at Stanford, and he had worked with me when he graduated. It's a small world!

THE ROCKETBOOK

In 1996, after they had left NCD, Martin Eberhard and Mark Tarpenning were doing some consulting work for Silicon Valley companies, but they were bored. They spent a fair bit of time hanging around coffee shops, drinking caffeinated beverages and thinking about what they would like to do next, knowing that they wanted to start a company. As they brainstormed for ideas, the theme of mobile technology kept recurring. It was just becoming possible to get some real computing power into a handheld, together with enough batteries to make a device that could be used for long enough without recharging. They were both early adopters of the Palm Pilot and café users of laptop computers. Sitting around with this collection of electronics on the table in front them triggered the e-book concept.

> The new possibilities with this new technology made us consider electronic books. We both traveled a lot and we were both big readers. As we were sitting in the cafés, enjoying our cappuccinos and doing our email and whatnot on laptop computers, we were increasingly aware of what was possible to put in a handheld piece of electronics. The computing power was now at the threshold where you could actually run some real software. Batteries were good enough that electronic gear would run for a usable amount of time. The Palm Pilot was a useful enough PDA to be successful. One of the questions we had was, "Would people really read for any significant amount of time on a screen?" In the end, it came down to the screen. As we were thinking about the idea of electronic books, we decided that was the main problem to solve.

Electronics at a café in the mid-1990s
photo by Ken Usami/Getty Images

In their spare time they surveyed the manufacturers of screens in all the available technologies, to see what was real and what was actually readable. They found a lot of technologies that were either too immature, like electronic paper, or were difficult to read, like most LCD screens and all color screens at that time, as the color separation on the pixels took away the crispness of the type. They settled on a screen technology from Sharp that was called DMTN, a diode-matrix LCD display with excellent contrast ratio, no flicker, and an acceptable price. It also worked with the backlight both on and off, so that you could read it in bright light with low power consumption, and turn on the backlight to use it in dark surroundings. This was the key to their decision to start NuvoMedia to develop an electronic book.

How do you deliver a book from a bookstore into an electronic reader? That was the most challenging business problem, not just about the technology behind delivery, but also about protecting against theft of the intellectual property. At that time people in the publishing industry were absolutely paranoid about losing revenue—they had recently seen what happened to the music industry with Napster, the free online music file-sharing service created by Shawn Fanning in 1999. The Internet provided the communications infrastructure, but Martin and Marc became very serious about cryptography, both to stop people from downloading books without paying, and to convince publishers to release their front-list books in electronic form for the first time in history.

They developed a solution that allowed owners of the RocketBook to browse online bookstores from their personal computers, choosing from a library of books available in RocketBook format. When they clicked on the Buy button, a typical book would take about two minutes to download to the computer in encrypted form. All of the titles on their computer remained encrypted, only becoming readable when they were selected from the specific RocketBook that was paired with that computer. The computer provided storage and Internet connectivity, and the RocketBook would hold up to thirty titles at a time for portable use, transferring quickly when docked, and syncing any markups back onto the computer to save them for next time.

Martin enjoyed leading the development of the physical design of the RocketBook itself.

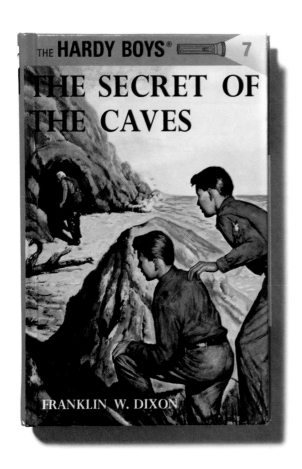

The size of a Hardy Boys book
photo by Nicolas Zurcher

My idea of the right size for the electronic book was that it should be the same size as a typical hardback, like a Hardy Boys book. Early on, as I was thinking about what an electronic book ought to look like, I went to a bookstore and bought a book of that size. I took my table saw to it and put in a fake screen, so that from the outside it looked like a book, but when you opened it you could see the screen. That was my first prototype of what the thing should look like.

I brought that to my designer friend, Jim Sacherman, as a thought experiment, saying, "Imagine that this is electronic,

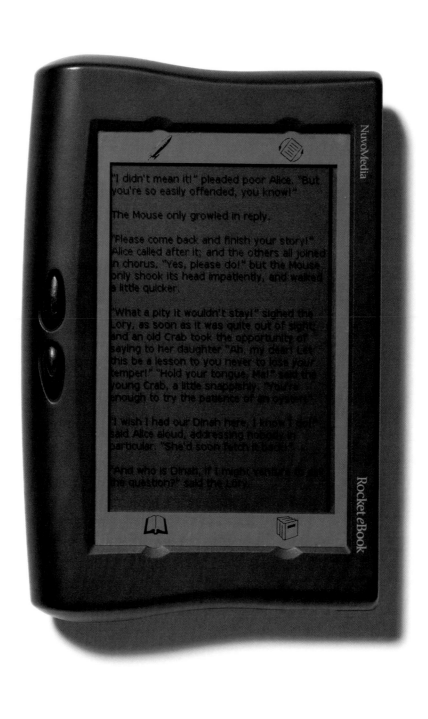

that you can read any book on it." He said that it's really tempting to make a new device look like the thing it's replacing, the cover and all that stuff, but you need to think about where it's going to eventually end up and try to express the device, the new thing, in its own way. So the RocketBook lost its cover and instead was optimized for being comfortable in the hand, balanced correctly, operable with one hand, and focused on the user interface and the readability. That first idea of cutting up a book was interesting because the size of the screen that I cut out was only half or three-quarters of an inch larger than the size of the DMTN screen we were able to get from Sharp.

It was a little heavier than I wanted, but not bad: it came in at about one pound. The battery life was great, lasting more than twenty hours with the backlight on. It was a little too heavy because we had four nickel–metal hydride batteries in order to get the battery life. Second-generation products had lithium-ion batteries.

More than a decade later, Martin still sees the quality and behavior of the display as the most important attribute for a successful design. Of course the electronics are smaller, faster, lighter, and less expensive, and wireless technology makes the connectivity much easier, but the question of display technology is still open. Electronic paper is becoming popular, as it offers high-contrast display on a surface that looks and feels much more like paper as well as very low power consumption, but it loses that surface quality with a touch screen in front of it. Then there is the need to refresh the image completely to change it.

← RocketBook
photo by Nicolas Zurcher

You have to flash the screen every time you change the page to make electronic paper work. You cancel the image by putting up a negative before you go to the next page. During our early usability studies with the RocketBook, we experimented with different graphical effects that could happen during page change—for example, peeling one page off to reveal the next. We tried maybe a dozen different ideas. Much to the chagrin of our user-interface people, the one that readers liked the best was where you just painted to the next screen as quickly as you could. We also instrumented the RocketBook to measure how fast people were reading, and then we'd give them a test to measure comprehension as well. We tried different technologies of page turning to see what worked and what didn't work. The minimum amount of interruption was the right answer, for sure!

In the original version of the RocketBook, the frame around the screen had our logo in the middle at the top. It said "Rocket eBook" up there in white letters on the dark background of the bezel. People found themselves noticing it every time they turned the page and it irritated them. It actually affected reading comprehension: if we got rid of the logo, they read faster. We wound up taking it off, turning it sideways on the side of the screen and making it a much lower contrast. Your brain is all in tuned to reading, so it reads every piece of text it finds.

NuvoMedia managed to persuade a growing number of publishers to allow front-list titles to be viewed in electronic form, so that by the time they sold the company to Gemstar International in 2000, they had 50 percent of the best sellers available in RocketBook form in any given week.

Martin's general advice when designing an electronic book is to avoid thinking that it's going to replace all books, because people who buy e-books are also likely to have hundreds of books in their house. He suggests that the designer or entrepreneur should think of ways to extend or improve the reading experience when the owner is away from their comfy chair in the living room. Perhaps they want to read during a commute or on an airplane or refer to information in a business meeting.

One of the big hits for the RocketBook was reading in bed. You could read in bed with the light off and your spouse could sleep. It was hugely popular to do that! It's the same thing on an airplane. When you're on that cross-country flight, or around the world flight, there is a period when they turn the lights off and everybody's trying to sleep. And when you turn your reading light on, you feel like a boor for doing so. Having an electronic book that gives off just enough light to read doesn't have the same effect; it's just great.

The funny thing is that there isn't one single compelling reason to have an electronic book that applies to everyone. For some people it's access to books while they're traveling. For others it's the ability to carry a bunch of books with them. For a different group it's instant access to large print for any title they want. For another group it's reading in marginal light situations. One unexpected group we identified was nursing mothers, because they can hold the book in one hand while they are nursing and read with no hassle. If you saw a pie chart of why people buy electronic books there isn't one big wedge; it's lots of small wedges. To be successful in this arena I think you need to understand all those wedges and make sure you're not losing too many of them due to your design choices.

THE QUE PROREADER FROM PLASTIC LOGIC was announced at the Consumer Electronics Show in Las Vegas in January 2010, using E Ink on a plastic backplane in a form factor that is similar to a pad of paper. Rich Archuleta joined Plastic Logic as CEO in 2007 to guide the QUE to market, coming from a stellar career at Hewlett-Packard. In the next interview he tells us why he believes that e-readers have come of age.

RICH ARCHULETA

Interviewed September 3, 2009

RICH ARCHULETA

Rich Archuleta, commonly known as Arch, thinks that electronic books and readers will gain widespread acceptance when three attributes come together—namely, consensus about the standards for electronic reading material, wireless communication technology, and new display technologies that are competitive with paper. Believing that this convergence is mature made him decide to leave his post as a senior vice president and general manager at Hewlett-Packard in order to become CEO of Plastic Logic in 2007. Arch joined HP in 1980, straight from the master's program in electrical engineering at Stanford University. He soon gained a reputation for excellent work in defining new products and business innovation and was quickly promoted to project management and then business leadership. In three years he transformed HP's Notebook PC business from twenty-seventh ranking into the top five. He became responsible for the standard Intel Architecture Server business and the Worldwide Volume Direct business, led planning for the merger integration of the HP and Compaq PC businesses, and was *Mobile Computing Magazine*'s "Mobile Industry Person of the Year."

IDEO had the opportunity to help with the QUE proReader (it was responsible for the industrial and interaction design of the final version announced at CES), so I was aware of the design approach as it neared completion. I thought it would be an interesting contrast to the early RocketBook, as it has new solutions to many of the challenges identified by Martin Eberhard. Gene Celso and I took our video cameras to Rich Archuleta's home for the interview. I was charmed by his friendly manner and impressed by his straightforward and clear articulation of the issues.

3 Notifications

Recent Activity ▾

24 Friday
September
2010

9 AM
Phase 2 Briefing

11:30 AM
Budget Review 📎 12

12 PM
Lunch with Steve Callahan

3 PM
Interview Kirsten 📎 1

3:30 PM
Meeting with Scott H.

2 more appointments...

Last Update: 09/24/10 at 8:03 AM

Recently Added ⇕ View More

new THE WALL STREET JOURNAL

Wall Street Journal

new Sporting News Today

The Huffington Post

Viral Loop: From
Facebook to Twitter, ...

Detroit Free Press

Workshop.doc

Financial Times

Market Report:
Electronic Readers 2...

Popular Science
Monthly

QUE Store Shop

You are
holding over
a million
titles in
your hand

Favorites Personalize

new USA Today

New York Trip
Itinerary

Phase 2 report

QUE

THREE GOOD REASONS

Plastic Logic has been developing core technology in flexible displays since a group of researchers from the Cavendish Laboratory at Cambridge University in the UK founded the company in 2000. They created a flexible backplane made out of plastics, which has embedded transistors capable of energizing electronic ink on the surface to appear black or white. This backplane allows them to make a large display that is very thin and light but avoids the fragility of silicon-processing technologies protected by glass.

E Ink is a development of E Ink Corporation, founded in 1997 by a group of researchers from MIT Media Lab. It consists of millions of tiny microcapsules, about the diameter of a human hair, with black and white particles suspended in a fluid. The white particles collect at the top of the capsules when a negative electric field is applied while at the same time an opposite electric field pulls the black particles to the bottom where they are hidden. By reversing this process, the black particles appear at the top of the capsule, making the surface appear dark. E Ink is used on most of the e-readers on the market.

Rich Archuleta looked carefully into the e-reader business when he was approached by the members of the board of Plastic Logic in 2006 and concluded that three attributes needed to come together for success.

The QUE proReader
photo by Plastic Logic

One of them was the evolution of standards, so that you could get electronic material to these things in a standard way. If you go back about ten years, there were twenty-plus different standards just for electronic books, let alone all of the different formats for the other material you might want to display on an electronic reading device. In the last couple of years we have started to see a consolidation of the standards, and it is clear that there are going to be a handful that will emerge. The standards space is coming together and that is one of the keys.

Another key is the wireless technology. Having a reading device that always needs to be tethered to another computer or intelligent device has some applicability but wouldn't foster huge growth. We see wireless standards, both Wi-Fi and especially the cellular networks with 3G, now able to handle reasonable amounts of data in a pretty efficient manner, and they are becoming much more global. That was the second piece for me.

The third piece was the display, because if you are building a reader it's all about the reading experience. E Ink technology, for the top layer of electrophoretic material, has done a good job of giving us a nice reading experience, but you were still putting it on a back plane that was essentially an active matrix display, which was using silicon and glass technology, so it would be hard to build something relatively large, like an 8½-by-11-inch piece of paper. I felt that the display technology from Plastic Logic could do something that for a user would feel like a very natural and comfortable reading experience.

THE READING EXPERIENCE

Liquid crystal displays (LCDs) are ubiquitous, found in laptops, smart phones, personal computers, and modern televisions. They are built in very large volume, using a mature technology that is reliable, robust, and low cost, offering a very rich experience with excellent color and full-motion video. Why then is LCD not ideal to use for reading? Arch gives two reasons.

I don't think that it's a very comfortable reading experience for long periods of time. The liquid crystals need backlight, so you're always shooting photons into people's eyes, and studies have shown that causes eyestrain. Secondly, the backlight is not bright enough for natural lighting conditions. If you take it outdoors, you can't read it.

Over the years, a number of companies have tried different technologies that can hold an image and create an experience that's almost like reading ink on paper, with ambient light reflecting off the image. At the same time they have looked for something to hold the image stable, without flickering or any other artifacts that detract from the long-term reading experience. The E Ink technology that we use for QUE is very stable. We've had displays that we've energized two years ago and we pulled them out of our labs and the same image is there.

There are other companies that have technologies in their labs that will do similar things to E Ink, but they are not in commercial manufacturing yet. There are a lot of different approaches to do this, and we're working with several.

E Ink is also excellent from a power conservation standpoint. When you are reading things you are usually maintaining an image for long enough to read the page, probably from ten seconds to a few minutes, whereas the LCD screen is refreshing the crystals at video speeds and the backlight is always on.

Reading is easier when the white background is bright and the contrast to the black ink is high. The development team at Plastic Logic has made extensive measurements of these attributes in order to compare the various technologies and implementations that are available. The current levels for E Ink are already better than standard newsprint, but not yet up to the quality of this book or a glossy magazine. Another threshold for the acceptability of the reading experience will be passed when the technology improves enough for the white state to be as bright as the best quality paper, with the blacks as dark as good ink. Arch sees those developments as evolutionary, with the next major inflection point associated with color and full-motion video.

There will be continuous improvements in the white state and contrast, with better readability than today, but those are minor improvements. I don't think they will cause a big knee in the curve growth. The next big piece is once you get rich color with full-motion video, in a product that still allows you to have black and white reading capability that's similar to today. A lot of the technologies that are coming for color make a trade-off between color and black and white, so if you have a really nice color display, the black and white text is not as readable.

By the time we have something that gives you great black and white text at the same time as really good quality color, we will have already seen a high level of adoption for black and white materials and people will be craving the color. I think color is important, especially when you get to magazines. For all the published material, the one piece that I think will take the longest to move over into electronic readers is the magazine format. The magazine experience relies on rich color and high-quality photographs, and that is going to take a while to replicate. The technology in 2010 will allow you to reach a newspaper cartoon–level color, and maybe even with a little animation. It may be good for some types of animated books, but it won't be able to match the rich color you have in a magazine. That will take a few years.

Arch expects to see a drastic shift toward electronic publication, with traditional media moving away from paper at an accelerating pace. He thinks that books and newspapers will be affected most initially, with a dramatic decline in readership for the paper versions. Newspapers are already seeing advertising revenues moving quickly to the online versions of their content, and as the advertising rates are so much less online, this is causing severe stress to the overall businesses. He sees books reducing in quantity more gradually, as the e-readers get better and people rely more on the connectivity that allows searching and sharing with others in their social networks. He sees the magazine industry as the last to be affected, as the experience of reading a magazine relies so much on the quality of color photography, both for editorial and for advertising.

I think we will see less printed matter and more things being delivered electronically. And I think you will see it on portable devices like we're building at Plastic Logic. Our device has been designed from the ground up to support large-format reading, to include things that are normally delivered to you in 8½-by-11 or even slightly larger format for magazines and newspapers. We've been working on the industrial design of the product, how it feels in your hand, how it is to hold it under different conditions. If I'm sitting on an airplane or a train, or reading things sitting at a desk or sitting on the sofa, I can easily hold it and read it very naturally. There's been a lot of thought and care that has gone into the form factor of the device, which I think is incredibly compelling.

The QUE proReader ----}
photo courtesy of Plastic Logic

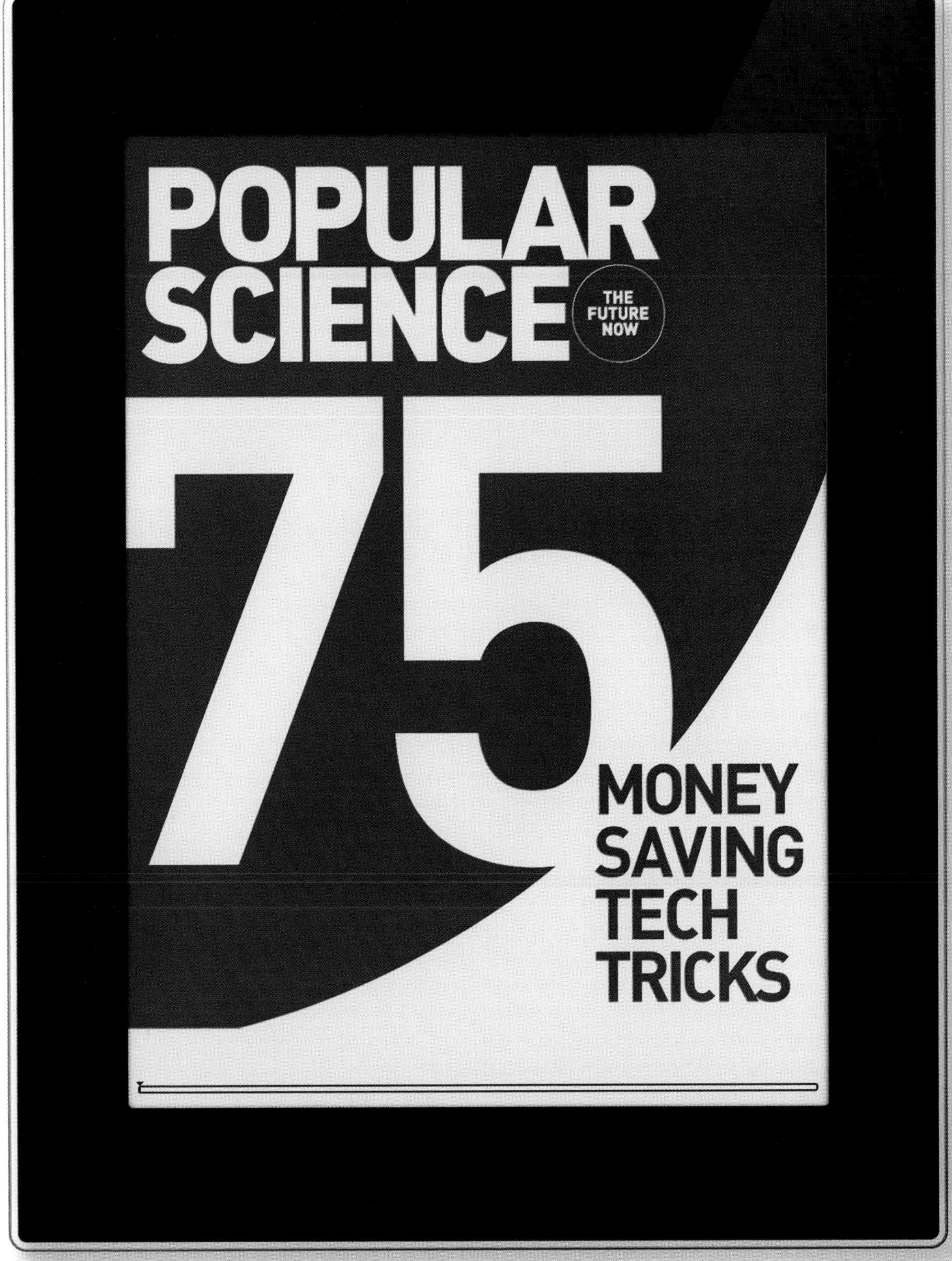
POPULAR SCIENCE
THE FUTURE NOW
75
MONEY SAVING TECH TRICKS

INTERACTION DESIGN

When Arch joined Plastic Logic in 2007, most of the people in the company were working at their headquarters in the UK and a lot of conceptual work had already been done. They had started out experimenting with things on their own, worked with outside experts for ethnographic studies, and brought in the celebrated industrial design firm Seymour Powell to develop design concepts. Arch also worked with consultants in Silicon Valley to try out ideas and test user interfaces, so there were a lot of people involved in exploring different paths and discovering what worked. When they got to the point where they needed to make decisions on bringing it all together, Arch looked for a design firm to help them synthesize the best ideas that had emerged from everything that had been done and to try to create an innovative new solution. He chose IDEO because it offered all of the resources that would be needed and has a reputation for successful collaboration.

The physical form of the QUE, dubbed a "Paperless Briefcase," is the same as an American letter-sized pad of paper, but it's only a third of an inch thick. The designer (Caroline Flagiello of IDEO, working with Plastic Logic as acting creative director) kept the form almost monolithic in its simplicity in order to celebrate black and white print, with textures and transparency used to make it look like a glass container for the E Ink. The weight of less than a pound was possible due to the plastic substrate, which is much lighter than glass. Research with potential users supported the idea of comparison with a magazine, as nobody complains that magazines are too heavy to hold or read.

When Arch joined the company, he helped to drive the decision to base the product design on a touch screen, based on how people read and the interactions that would enhance the experience.

> It's very natural for people to use gestures, and mark up or annotate things, or turn the edges of a piece of paper, or switch pages—it's just a very natural experience if you can touch it. It always seemed a little unnatural to us if somebody had to use buttons to move things around or to navigate.

> Now the downside of touch technologies is that when you have a reflective display and you put another layer between

The "Paperless Briefcase"
photo courtesy of Plastic Logic

your eye and the image, you do reduce the amount of light, and so it can potentially change the image. If you look at some of the early readers that have tried to use touch technology and put them side by side with readers that don't have touch, you can see a difference. One of the main areas that we've been working on over the last couple years is a touch technology that will allow a lot of the light to go through with very little light loss, so the image clarity remains very, very high. That's been a big thing for us, and we believe that will be a big differentiator in our product.

When I think about the evolution of readers, because we're still in the very early stages of this technology, I think about where we will be in ten years. I think all of these potential issues you see with touch today will all go away. I think we will find solutions where everything will be based on being able to touch the screen and interact with your material that way.

We've been thinking about not just book reading, but newspapers, magazines, user-generated material like emails, Microsoft Word documents, and PDFs for things like reference manuals or any type of document. How do you want to interact with that on an electronic device that is mobile and that you can have with you all the time and enjoy in different experiences? How do you build a user interface that some people refer to it as "sit-back reading," where you're really going to immerse yourself into the material and read for a long period of time, versus "lean-forward reading," where you want to review things and switch between documents and maybe add some annotation and be able to use that in a collaborative work manner with others.

Barnes and Noble is providing the back-end server and e-commerce infrastructure for Plastic Logic, with the online store in front carrying the QUE brand. Amazon has so far been the leader in electronic book content, but Arch believes that Barnes and Noble will compete head-to-head with Amazon and may well pull ahead.

Plastic Logic started as a group of researchers dedicated to developing plastic electronics technology. Now it's producing displays at its own factory in Dresden, Germany. It's also attempting to develop a new business model, to create the right system with all of the content coming together: the relationship with the publishers on content presentation, solutions to technical problems for the plastic electronics and display technology, collaborations with people on new front plane materials for the future of electronic books—all in a device that just yields a good user interface.

We have a stunning user interface! By "stunning" I don't mean that it's in your face. It's stunning from the designer's standpoint, but from a user's standpoint it's in the background, because what we're trying to create is something that removes the technology from the equation from the user's mind—

that things just happen the way that they expect them to with all these different types of content.

It seems that about every ten years you see a whole industry start to transform, and it's fun to be a part of. Publishers are struggling today. Profit margins have been eroded even in a segment like book publishing. You've seen the big guys gobble a lot of small independents and the profit margins are eroding for everyone. They are under pressure. For newspapers it's even worse! The whole publishing industry is going through this transformation because new technologies are enabling new ways to get information. We've seen it with the Internet, but now I think it's the turn of portable devices, where people can have a great experience that competes with traditional media. It's all coming together in a very short period of time, and it's pretty exciting!

COMMENTARY

The people in interviewed in this chapter thrive by operating in two worlds and combining the attributes of emerging media with those of traditional media. Joel Hyatt has added user-generated content and Twitter feeds to Current Media's television platform. Bruce Nussbaum and Jessie Scanlon have created an online channel to complement *BusinessWeek* magazine, bringing some of the material generated online back to print as a quarterly supplement. Jane Friedman expanded the reach of book publishing by adding the author tour, promoted by television and radio. She also started an audio book division at Random House. She has embraced digital publishing, electronic books, and social networking. Electronic books and readers exist in both worlds by delivering traditional books, newspapers, and magazines through an electronic medium. They are advancing rapidly as new technologies improve the chance to design for a better reading experience. We can see the progress by comparing Martin Eberhard's 1998 RocketBook with the 2010 QUE proReader.

These stories imply that content can belong happily in both traditional and virtual worlds, although the material must be presented appropriately to highlight the attributes of each medium. An article written for the printed page of a newspaper will be presented with a different tone and style for an online blog and adjusted again for a Twitter feed. Good communication design comes from a synthesis of all of the attributes of the media as well as the content. Magazine designers know by experience how best to lay out an attractive page, combining rich high-resolution images with easy-to-read typography for articles and salient type for headlines, pullouts, quotes, and sidebars. When translating the same story to the Web, the images need to be smaller, the text shorter, and the pagination structure different, but you have the chance to add a new dimension by including links, animated diagrams, podcasts, and videos. Similar design differences apply to other media.

The story of the development of the Innovation and Design channel for BusinessWeek demonstrates this design difference. Bruce Nussbaum and Jessie Scanlon developed a dynamic and interactive approach to the online offering, with a conversational design style that promoted dialogue through comments and blogging and leveraged partnerships with other organizations outside the *BusinessWeek* fold. I like Bruce's description of blogging as a "borgy brain thing," which I take as akin to "dancing with a lot of random people at the bar"; this contrasts starkly with his work as a commentator when he was a page editor for the magazine.

Bruce evolved his approach to designing online quickly and effectively, bringing in expertise in the person of Jessie and adding a versatile team as they moved forward. I am struck by the fact that he is more proud of designing his team than anything else in his career. He was able to put together a group of people who were multigenerational, interdisciplinary, and creatively fluent across media, moving easily from online, to print, video, podcasts, and blogs. As he says, they are "full of energy because they are so polymath in so many different ways!"

Lightweight teams like this may be needed to respond successfully to the new economic challenges facing organizations that want to occupy both worlds. Income shrinks dramatically as advertising revenue migrates toward the online versions, so the journalists and designers need to be much more productive and versatile to make ends meet. This is very difficult for entrenched organizations that have evolved to produce magazines like *BusinessWeek*, but the economics will eventually find a new equilibrium. Perhaps online outlets will be staffed by more teams like Bruce's. And as with the quarterly version of *Innovation and Design*, print material will be brought back from the online world.

Jessie points to a classic design lesson about understanding customers. She thinks that *BusinessWeek* should have done more thorough research in advance of designing the online offering, as the vision was initially to connect designers and businesspeople, helping them to interact more productively. As time went by and they heard back from readers, they discovered that more and more businesspeople are interested in learning about design, as they see innovation and design operating together. The audience evolved to become mostly businesspeople who want to use design processes to help them solve difficult problems in new ways. I wonder whether a design research effort at the beginning would have revealed this or whether it was necessary to dive in with an experiment and "live life in beta." Design is usually most successful when the process includes an iterative cycle of understanding people and trying a prototype solution, so perhaps the combination could have been productive.

The need for well-designed templates also comes out of Jessie's interview. The optimal balance between control and freedom is essential. Control is needed to give consistent visual identity and navigational behavior, but creative freedom is also necessary to make the design come alive and be responsive to the mood of individual content. The graphic designers, typographers, and art directors of print magazines have evolved a sophisticated balance between these priorities, but the early online equivalents tend to be mired down by their algorithmic controls, limiting creativity and flair. Jessie points to the design of the iPhone as a success story, with the tool kits provided to application developers giving the right balance between consistency and freedom, yielding good results even when the application developer has very little empathy for the design guidelines.

Current TV inhabits more than both worlds, as there is a political world of idealistic intention driving the thinking of both Joel Hyatt and Al Gore. This drives them to want to "give voice to a whole generation whose voice was not being heard." They need to strike a balance between the well-intentioned paternalism of their TV programming and the community participation of user-generated content. Joel wants to design an approach that will be popular for an audience ranging in age from eighteen to thirty-two, giving them what they really want, which is not always what an older generation of management thinks they should want. He believes in listening to and learning from the audience, while using the wisdom of experience to avoid the lowest common denominator. I hope that this idealistic version of both worlds can flourish in competition with more commercially motivated offerings.

Jane Friedman cannot live without her library and believes that books will always be highly valued. Her business acumen is fueled by a desire to get more books in the hands of more people, so she welcomes any new opportunity to reach an audience by stepping into a new world. She harnessed radio and television to sell books at a time when books were usually only promoted on the book pages of newspapers. She is open to any new design or technology that can help more people have access to books and welcomes Internet and electronic editions.

I said earlier that content should be adjusted to fit its medium: at least the presentation of the material needs to be designed to fit the attributes of each medium. Electronic books challenge this idea, as the design of the technology is trying to let you read the book in something close to its printed format. As Martin Eberhard points out, people are motivated to use e-books for lots of different reasons. I like his idea of reading in bed with the light off without disturbing your partner. Electronic readers also give tired eyes instant access to large print. And there are countless niche users too, like the nursing mother who wants to hold a book in one hand while feeding her baby. A successful design will provide a solution that satisfies as many needs and desires as possible, while accepting that the same people who are motivated to by en e-book are also likely to have lots of paper books and magazines, possibly even take a printed newspaper.

I have a personal connection to the design of electronic readers. In recent years I have been close to Martin Eberhard as a friend and neighbor, and I was a design advisor for his Tesla Roadster. When he was working on the RocketBook, though, I thought of him more as a competitor since IDEO was working on the design of the SoftBook, which was launched at almost the same time. The two versions came together in the next iteration as Gemstar purchased both NuvoMedia and the SoftBook Press, launching a new design that combined the best of both products.

The original SoftBook was larger than the RocketBook, with a screen that could display the page of a typical book at slightly larger than actual size to compensate somewhat for the low resolution of liquid crystal displays at that time. The shape was elegant, winning several awards for the industrial design (*BusinessWeek*'s IDEA Gold and *ID* magazine's Design Distinction awards), with a leather flap protecting the screen that was held in place by a magnetic latch. The IDEO team created the industrial design, interaction design, and engineering, so they were able to integrate the design solutions across disciplines.

This is how Duane Bray, a partner at IDEO, where he heads the firm's global Software Experiences Practice, described the interaction design in an interview in 2003:

> There were two areas where we tried to connect the screen experience to unique physical controls. One was with a hardware control for changing pages that we wanted to make as simple as skimming through pages in a book. You simply turn a rocker, and the page just flips, one to the next. You hold it down, and it begins to accelerate as if you were flipping through a book. The other control was a physical menu button, which avoided having the control interface on the screen while you were reading. The button was located above the screen, and when you pressed it a menu dropped down over the screen, giving the sense that pressing the button actually pushed a menu down over the book. The menu allowed you to change the size of the type, search for something, close the book, and open a different one, and so on.

Several aspects of the technology in SoftBook were not ready for the consumer market. At $599, the price was high. The display seemed a bit gray due to the low contrast ratio. Finally, the telephone download speeds were tedious: this was a barrier, as the unit did not attach to a computer, and you had to rely on a personal bookshelf at the server maintained by SoftBook Press. The RocketBook and SoftBook together sold less than 50,000 units by the time the companies were acquired by Gemstar in 2000.

I agree with Rich Archuleta's conclusions that three attributes are needed to come together for the e-book industry segment to succeed: evolution of standards, fast wireless technology, and a satisfying display. As Arch says, "It's all about the reading experience."

As I write this in early 2010, the jury is still out about the best display technology. The Amazon Kindle has been on the market since November 2007, launched with an E Ink display that I find almost as pleasant to read as paper, even if the unit is small and without the contrast ratio of ink on paper. Amazon also had an enormous array of over 88,000 titles available right from the start and used wireless for easy downloads. I didn't like the physical controls, with the irritating Select Wheel and a "Chiclet" keyboard that reminded me of the early home computers. The Kindle 2 and DX have done a lot to improve on the design. The DX was launched in June 2009, by which time the Amazon library had grown to more than 400,000 titles. I wonder if Martin Eberhard is right that people will dislike the flash as the screen refreshes enough to prefer a display that is more like a computer screen. That question will probably be answered by the time you read this, as the Apple iPad will have been on the market long enough to test the value of a full-color display with video capabilities and a touch interface. Perhaps Arch will be proved right about the drawbacks of LCD displays.

My guess is that the main battle for domination will be between Amazon and Apple, not so much because of their designs as because of the attributes of their business systems. Amazon can offer the best library of titles, whereas Apple can offer the connection to the iTunes store and the iPhone app store. Perhaps there will also be room in this expanding segment for innovative designs like the QUE. I feel confident that there will continue to be print versions of books, magazines, and newspapers sold, but they may need to be well-designed to survive.

IN THE NEXT CHAPTER WE MEET PEOPLE who believe that it's the content that matters most and that the role of design should be to adjust the presentation of the content to suit the medium. Arthur Sulzberger Jr. and Alice Rawsthorn talk about news journalism, Ira Glass discusses the differences between radio and television, and Colin Callender speaks about producing content for television and film.

5 CONTENT IS KING

Interviews with Arthur Sulzberger Jr., Alice Rawsthorn, Ira Glass, and Colin Callender

People sort of take it for granted, but the more you see of the media world …
the more you appreciate a paper like the *New York Times*, where its family
continues to invest in editorial quality. I think it truly is the best paper
in the world.

David Talbot, American journalist, founder of Salon.com

Newspapers
photo by Jane M. Sawyer/Morgue File

THE PEOPLE INTERVIEWED for this chapter believe passionately
in the ability of their content to transcend the medium. You can tell
in the interview that follows that Arthur Sulzberger Jr. believes first in
high-quality journalism. Indeed, he feels that it is journalism's mission
to give people the information they need to keep democracy alive.
He is confident that the print version of the newspaper is here to stay.
At the same time he welcomes additional media that give opportunities
to tell stories in other ways, allowing the same content to reach more
people with video, audio, slide shows, and, as he puts it, "all of these
things that have become so wonderful" on the Web. While content may
be king, there is evidently a financial struggle in progress. As publisher
and chairman of the board of the New York Times Company, Sulzberger
faces falling advertising revenues, a deep recession, and overhead costs
that must be hard to reduce, as they consist of an excellent journalistic
and editorial staff in addition to an elegant headquarters building.

Alice Rawsthorn has a direct link to the *New York Times* as a columnist
for the magazine. She is also the design critic of the *International
Herald Tribune*. She has read the *New York Times* Web site every day
for more than ten years but no longer enjoys the print version, so she
communicates enthusiasm for the content in the new medium. As a
newspaper journalist based in London, she has lived through more
than one revolution in the industry. In her interview she describes
the changes that she has experienced and revels in the access to rich
content that is increasingly enabled by new technologies.

"The laws of narrative are still the laws of narrative, and what engages
us is simply what engages us. I feel like those things still apply in the
new digital world!" says Ira Glass, summarizing his belief that content

Newspapers
photo by Jane M. Sawyer/Morgue File

is king in the world of radio. He has been creating engaging radio for more than three decades and has hosted *This American Life* since it started in 1995. He thinks that the Web is more like radio than most media since the Internet and radio share a form of intimacy. He has recently experimented with a television version of *This American Life*, discovering that there are differences in the design approaches that work well for the two media, but he looks first for the stories about people that will be interesting anywhere.

Colin Callender has produced innovative films throughout his career. From 1987 to 2008 he served as executive producer of HBO Showcase. He believes that the best film and television does more than entertain: it illuminates, informs, and engages emotionally. "At its very best, as any great art does, it enables the person viewing to look at the world with slightly different eyes, with a different perspective, with a different point of view—and maybe have a new empathy for other people," he says. Colin is confident that people will continue to enjoy watching entertainment on screens in their homes and that the content will be what matters, whether the image is on a computer screen, a computer-television linkage, or something that is carried around, such as a laptop, tablet, or smart phone.

ARTHUR SULZBERGER JR.

Interviewed November 14, 2008

ARTHUR SULZBERGER JR.

Arthur Sulzberger Jr. became the publisher of the *New York Times* in 1992 and chairman of the board of its owner, the New York Times Company, in 1997, succeeding his father, Arthur Ochs Sulzberger. After studying at Tufts University, Arthur Jr. gained experience as a journalist in North Carolina and London before joining the *New York Times* in 1978 as a correspondent in its Washington bureau. He moved to New York as a metro reporter in 1981 and was appointed assistant metro editor later that year. During the eighties he gained experience in a wide range of departments of the organization, becoming deputy publisher in 1988, overseeing the news and business departments. Arthur played a central role in the development of the Times Square Business Improvement District, serving as the first chairman. He is at the head of one of the most influential newspapers in the world, as well as its holding company, which owns the *International Herald Tribune*, fifteen regional papers, approximately thirty-five Web sites, nine television stations, and two radio stations.

⟵ **Arthur Sulzberger Jr.**
photos by author

I interviewed David Liddle for *Designing Interactions* and heard that he serves on the board of the New York Times Company, so I asked if he could help me make a connection to Arthur Sulzberger Jr. With David's assistance and advice, my interview was soon arranged. Catherine Mathis, senior vice president of corporate communications, works very closely with Arthur, and I corresponded with her in advance, so that she could help him prepare. I arrived at his offices on a wet November morning, setting up my cameras in his airy office high above the streets of Manhattan. He was gracious and hospitable, talking openly about his philosophy and values, occasionally turning to Catherine for help in recalling names and dates.

THE *NEW YORK TIMES*

The Times Square area takes its name from the presence of the *New York Times* building between 1904 and 1913. It was a hub for theater and entertainment as well as the annual New Year's Eve ball drop, but it became a dangerous neighborhood after the Great Depression, known for decades as a seedy center for adult entertainment. Arthur Sulzberger Jr. was instrumental in planning improvements in the area, serving as chairman of the organization that resuscitated the neighborhood, and pioneering the construction of a new fifty-two-story tower that has housed the *New York Times* since its completion in 2007. The tower was elegantly designed by the Italian architect Renzo Piano.

Arthur sits in his beautifully appointed office looking out over Manhattan through windows on two sides, with light controlled by adjustable blinds with a hint of transparency. Framed copies of the paper adorn the walls, highlighting significant historical moments, including a spread bearing the news of Lincoln's assassination. On the low table in front of his chair are several copies of the paper from November 5, 2008, the morning after the election of President Obama. The front page has a large image of Obama and his family, with his name in huge type and a subhead saying, "RACIAL BARRIER FALLS IN DECISIVE VICTORY." This issue has become a collector's item, even though more than 200,000 extra copies were printed. Arthur picks it up and says,

I think the most powerful story in this paper was this, and I'd like to read you the first graph if I might. Ethan Bronner (who is our Middle East correspondent) writing out of Gaza, wrote this: "From far away this is how it looks. There is a country out there where tens of millions of white Christians, voting freely, select as their leader a black man of modest origins, the son of a Muslim. There is a place on earth, call it America, where such a thing happens!" That's pretty powerful. It brought tears to my eyes when I first read it.

Arthur believes that content is king! He asserts that the first principle for a newspaper is to aggregate a quality audience through quality journalism; the principles of journalism should be defined by honesty in reporting, thoroughness, acknowledgment of mistakes, and correction of those mistakes. He is optimistic about the future of the print version of the newspaper, in spite of the economic challenges. He tells the story of the Obama election issue.

> Within hours we knew we were selling out in critical parts of the city and around the country, and we went back on press, but we still had lines of people coming to this building, lines snaking down 40th Street wanting to buy a printed copy of the *New York Times*. It was a wonderful moment, and it reminds us that there is some real value to print. Print is not dead.

> On a more global scale, three and a half years ago we had 650,000 people who had subscribed to the *New York Times* for two years or more. All of our research shows that if you are a subscriber to the *New York Times* for two years, we've pretty much got you for life. That number is now 822,000. It's going up, not down. So yes, newspapers are under enormous pressures. Street sales are way down. But if you think just about the growth from 650,000 to 820,000, papers are going to be around for a long time. Indeed one of our best sources of home-delivery subscription is the ads on the *New York Times* Web site's home page.

> Radio was supposed to kill newspapers. Television was supposed to kill newspapesrs. The Internet was supposed to kill newspapers. And perhaps there will be a time where there is a kind of a reading device that gives you the freedom and flexibility that you have with the print in which case people will move to that and so will we.

The economic challenges for newspapers have nothing to do with the quality of the journalism, which translates without too much difficulty to other media; rather, it's a matter of the cost structures being so dramatically different, with advertisers continuously shifting their spending to online media. Arthur seeks solace from the other side of the equation, pointing out that the biggest costs associated with running a

The cover of the *New York Times* on the day after Obama's election
photo by author

newspaper are people, paper, production, and distribution, the last three of which are absent for Web delivery, so you don't have to make as much money to stay profitable. He realizes that the changes that are needed will be hard to implement, and it will be very difficult to make it through the transitional period.

The paper itself has been redesigned many times, as is easy to see when you compare an issue from 1912 or 1975 with today's. In the early seventies they moved from two sections to four sections, with a major redesign. Later the page size was narrowed, and more recently they integrated the Metro section into the A book, so it's international news first, then national news, followed by local news from New York, New Jersey, and Connecticut. Arthur tells a story from farther back.

> It was some time in the 1850s and a New York publisher, I think the owner of the *Tribune*, wrote in his own paper that he had just witnessed the death of newspapers. Literature, he said, would survive, but newspapers would inevitably fade away. He had just met the telegraph. Of course, it was the combination of that same telegraph, which gave you the immediacy of speed, and the horrible news from the Civil War, which was a

huge birth of newspapers in this country, because now people desperately wanted to know what was happening 2,000 miles away and could get that information the next day.

Newspapers have always been dealing with challenges. When radio started, it was perceived as a challenge. Television was supposed to kill newspapers. When we bought WQXR, which was the radio station of the *New York Times*, and a classical radio station, back in the 1930s or '40s, it was seen as a way of extending our reach by putting our news on the air so that people could hear it instead of reading it. That's basically been the thought all the way through. We have had a partnership with the Discovery Channel to see if we can translate our journalism into television, and most recently, of course, digital.

At the end of the day our job is to get the quality news and information that we provide to as many people as we possibly can. The Internet was the first technology that took us back to the written word. Radio took us away from it. Television took us away from it. But the Internet took us back. It was not much of a leap to realize that this was a critical element in fulfilling the mission of this enterprise, which is to create, collect, and distribute high-quality news and information.

There were always questions like, Are you going to be canni-balizing yourself? Will readers give up print? It was not a hard organizational challenge to say, "Yes, this is something we need to master!" There were many moments when we found ourselves facing critical choices. The first choice was, Do we want to create a site that is a New York site, the way that Boston.com, which is the *Boston Globe*'s Web site, is for Boston, to be more of a community site? For the *New York Times* we felt that our community was no longer defined, if it ever had been, by the New York part of its title. It was a national newspaper with international aspirations through the *International Herald Tribune*, which we own, and we felt that the brand promise of the *Times* was sufficient to make it a destination in and of itself.

NYTIMES.COM

Martin Nisenholtz was hired from outside the newspaper industry. He brought deep digital experience to develop Nytimes.com and helped to shape the design concept. He chose to make the site reflect the *New York Times* in its design elements, including the banner, nameplates, and navigational structure, so that as you go through the site the subchannels are divided in the same sections as the printed paper. The judgment about news is also common to Web site and print, so the most critical stories of the day are on the homepage. Arthur supports the value of these design decisions.

> We are saying to our users, "You have come to the *New York Times*. You are here because we believe you will get a great journalistic experience, perhaps the best possible. And now of course we're going to give it to you in a variety of ways that we could never have done in the printed pages." It's how we're interacting with our audiences that I think has been the biggest change.

The Web newsroom started in a separate location and with separate staff, but it was combined with the print newsroom when they moved into the beautiful new headquarters tower, where they could integrate the digital and print newsrooms and advertising. The goal was to make all of the journalists aware that they were filing content for the *New York Times* that would appear in a variety of different ways—on the Web, in the pages of the *International Herald Tribune* as well as the *New York Times*, in videos, audio, and slide shows. They were encouraged to embrace multiple media to reach as large an audience as possible, without controlling how the audience receives the journalism.

The economics of this multifaceted approach remains confused, as the financial models for new media are still in flux and the advertising revenue is migrating away from the traditional newspaper, challenging the viability of the current overhead structure. Initially the Web site was offered for free. There was a period where the op-ed page columnists Maureen Dowd and Frank Rich were put behind a paid wall, but they found that the wall inhibited growth, so they took it down. In the winter of 2010, the Web site moved back to a subscription model, showing that

The New York Times
Saturday, January 23, 2010

Times Topics

Search All NYTimes.com
[ ] Go

Want to know more? Take a look at a Times Topic page.

Each topic page collects all the news, reference and archival information, photos, graphics, audio and video files published on topics ranging from Madonna to Myanmar. This treasure trove is available without charge on articles going back to 1981.

Read More...

Most Popular Topics

1. Haiti Earthquake of 2010
2. Google
3. China
4. Haiti
5. Barack Obama
6. Afghanistan
7. Global Warming
8. Conan O'Brien
9. Same-Sex Marriage
10. Health Care Reform

Topics for Discussion

Grammar and Usage

Every Tuesday, read and comment on a weekly critique of grammar, style and usage in The Times. **Read the latest** *After Deadline* **post >>**

BROWSE ALL TOPICS

A   B   C   D   E   F   G   H   I   J   K   L   M   N   O   P

Q   R   S   T   U   V   W   X   Y   Z

FEATURED TOPIC: THE EARTHQUAKE IN HAITI

Carlos Barria/Reuters

Haiti is struggling to recover from a massive earthquake that leveled the country's capital on Jan. 12.

PEOPLE IN THE NEWS

Scott Brown | Conan O'Brien | Janet Napolitano | Anwar al-Awlaki

SUBJECTS IN THE NEWS

Internet Censorship in China | Same-Sex Marriage | Marijuana | Health Care Reform

✉ E-MAIL

Can children have strokes?

ALSO IN HEALTH »
· Recipe: shrimp risotto with peas
· Narrowing an eating disorder

nytimes.com   HEALTH

Home | World | U.S. | N.Y. / Region | Business | Technology | Science | Health | Sports | Opinion | Arts | Style | Travel | Jobs | Real Estate | Automobiles | Back to Top

Copyright 2010 The New York Times Company | Privacy Policy | Search | Corrections | 🔊 RSS | First Look | Help | Contact Us | Work for Us | Advertise with Us | Site Map

the right balance remains elusive. The *New York Times* has a lot of assets to keep it afloat, but it must be a painful process to adjust to the changing economic landscape.

JOURNALISM FIRST

Even as the financial challenges for the *New York Times* are visible to everyone, with a stock price of over $50 in 2002 falling to a low of $3.44 in 2009, Arthur remains optimistic about the future of the organization, and he has great faith in the *Times* culture and belief in its mission.

A number of years ago now, the American Society of Newspaper Editors did a survey to find out how the culture of the newsroom compares to other cultures out there. They came up with two that were similar, emergency rooms and the military, which was rather a shock to my colleagues in the newsroom. The thought is this: they are mission-driven, and the mission is a great one. The mission of emergency rooms is to save lives and the mission of the military, when appropriately used, is to protect society. The mission of journalists is to give people the information they need to keep democracy alive. That was why it was so easy for the newsroom to move from being a print-only organization to a Web and print organization, because they saw that it enhanced their ability to fulfill the mission.

I think it was in *The Making of a President* in 1960, Teddy White wrote that there was an assumption made from Boston to Washington that if you picked up a phone and called somebody in the other place that you'd both read that day's *New York Times*. It's a lovely thought and the heart of it is, you were connected by us. The Web allows you to be connected, but our challenge now is to connect our readers to each other in a much more cohesive and engaging way. A lot of the work we've done of late is designed to give our readers more opportunity to own the way they read the paper, and to own the choices that they make.

NYTimes.com Times Topics section
screen capture

We've created a variety of tools to give people more ability to tell their friends what they have read in today's *New York Times* and say, "Look, these are the stories I think you should read." In addition, we want to give our readers the ability to get material from outside the *Times* but inside the *Times* Web experience. We have stake in a company called Blogrunner [a news aggregator that monitors articles and blog posts] that we use to select other sources of information, so if you have an interest in photography, we'll port to you those stories we think are of particular interest that appeared elsewhere.

This idea of personalization should be easy to deliver through the Internet. There are a lot of online versions, particularly with portals, but on-demand publishing could enable the concept in print as well. The *New York Times* has a research and development arm to look at future possibilities like this, aiming to stay a few steps ahead of competitors to maintain their reputation as the best newspaper in the United States. For example, when the iPhone was unveiled, the NYTimes application was one of the first apps available because they had been thinking about it in advance.

Nytimes.com is very well designed, with thoughtful layout and navigation, a video tab, and a series of subchannels under a Times Topics tab. Design director Khoi Vihn leads a full design team to innovate the user experience while retaining a consistent brand. He also writes a blog, Subtraction.com, that communicates his preference for controlled and minimalist design. The *New York Times* graphics department as a whole has a reputation for transforming data into visual media, both in print and online, creating diagrams, interactive maps, and videos. Their work won a National Design Award in Communication Design from the Cooper-Hewitt National Design Museum in 2009.

THE NEW YORK TIMES COMPANY REACHES an international audience through its ownership of the *International Herald Tribune*, for which Alice Rawsthorn writes a weekly column on design. In the next interview, Alice describes the dramatic changes in the newspaper industry that she has observed in the UK, both in terms of production and design.

ALICE RAWSTHORN

Interviewed September 22, 2008

ALICE RAWSTHORN

Alice is the design critic of the *International Herald Tribune*.
In her weekly "Design" column, published every Monday,
Alice explores new directions in every area of design and
their impact on our lives. Her column is syndicated to
other newspapers and magazines worldwide. She also
writes the "Object Lesson" column for the *New York Times
Magazine*. Alice graduated in art and architectural history
from Cambridge University in the UK and became a journalist.
Her first job was at *Campaign*, a British magazine that covers
media. In 1986 she joined the *Financial Times* and pioneered
its coverage of the creative industries during a period of
dramatic change for newspapers and journalism. From 2001
to 2006 Alice was director of the Design Museum in London.
During her directorship, the number of visits to the museum
rose by 40 percent, participation in the education program
doubled, and the Design Museum Web site became the
world's most popular design site. She is also very involved with
the arts, as a trustee of Arts Council England, the Whitechapel
Gallery in London, and other arts organizations.

In the early nineties Alice became the Paris correspondent for the *Financial Times*. She had been based in London writing about the creative industries before that, so I wanted to keep in touch with her. I took advantage of a trip to Paris to track her down, and we met on the terrace outside the Café Marly at the Louvre. She remembers the occasion because I showed her some examples from the IDEO portfolio on my laptop, but she was much more interested in the laptop itself than the material that I showed her. We have kept in touch ever since, and it was a pleasure to interview her for this book in her London home. I recorded her in the conservatory, with a wall of ivy behind. She was wearing a spectacular jacket designed by Balenciaga.

PRINT AND WEB

Alice speaks about newspapers, journalism, and design with deep knowledge born of experience.

Personally, I really enjoy seeing that incredibly old-fashioned—although now beautifully finessed by Matthew Carter—*New York Times* masthead on the Web. I think they have managed to replicate something that stylistically looks very much like the offline paper, but to do so in a way that makes the site very easy to navigate. And the articles are very legible when you see them. The *New York Times* has really interrogated the Web and found ways of working well with it. But lots of other newspapers have stumbled along on the way and continue to stumble now.

I do think that the decision as to whether people read newspapers and magazines offline or online is currently broadly dictated by age, so I suspect that for anyone who's under the age of twenty-five now, they will not grow up to have the same obsessive relationship with printed newspapers and printed magazines as my generation has, but they may very well be reading exactly the same content on the Web sites of those newspapers and magazines.

I do know from my personal experience that preference really is formed by habit. For example, the printed newspaper that I read every day here in Britain is the *Guardian*. The online newspaper that I read everyday wherever I am anywhere in the world as well as the *International Herald Tribune* is the *New York Times*. In the olden days, before the Web site was launched, I would read the *New York Times* if I felt like treating myself, because it cost so much if you buy it here in London, or when I was in New York, where plowing though all those

1960s: Woman working at a mainframe computer
photo by Getty Images

endless sections seemed like the kind of "New Yorky" thing to do. But now when I go to New York, I actually find the printed *New York Times* really irritating. I've read the *New York Times* Web site every single day for about ten years now, so my relationship with that newspaper is a relationship with the Web site.

The positive review that Alice gives Nytimes.com is high praise, considering her strongly critical stance on most Web site design. New media fascinates her when the design rules are not yet established. For Web sites, there are already some simple conventions, like the search box belonging in the top right-hand corner, or the tabs for the table of contents being stretched horizontally along the top under a masthead, but most of the other rules have been inherited from print graphics.

I think readers feel very poorly equipped to judge whether Web sites are well designed or not. An apt parallel is the user-interface software on digital devices. It's very hard for the 99 percent of us who don't have PhDs in computer programming to judge whether user-interface software is well designed, because we don't feel confident enough to comment positively on the various qualities it may or may not have, but we do know when it's badly designed. If you're using an overcomplicated cell phone or a ridiculously, neurotically complex MP3 player, you pick up on the bad points very, very quickly. And I think it's exactly the same with Web site designs.

Everybody complains about the obvious problems—too much clutter that stops you [from] finding what you want, or the impossibility of printing anything that seems legible from a Web site. Web designers seem so engrossed by their screens that they may forget that a lot of the rest of us do still want to print things in the old-fashioned way, and so on and so forth. New media design really is an amazing Wild West at the moment, even though there are some fabulous Web sites around. I mean, just look at the success of Google Maps—such a simple concept, brilliantly executed and absolutely irresistible.

Confusion about values and design conventions often occurs with new technologies and big changes, and Alice has encountered dramatic changes over her career. She remembers her first experience of new technology as a kid in the sixties, when her father took her with him on a business trip to Belgium.

> He took me into what he called "The Computer Room," which was literally full of big metal cupboards, probably the size of my house, but with even less power than an iPod nano. And I had a very vivid memory of clanging going on within the cupboards. It was huge—absolutely massive—and probably not particularly powerful, but it seemed very mysterious, enigmatic, and alluring. My father, who's an engineer and obsessed by mechanics and technology, told me that computers were the future, so I formed a very positive view of technology at an early age.

In 1980, when she graduated from university, she went into journalism by getting a place on a graduate training scheme, a form of apprenticeship that included all of the most mundane tasks in the office. One of them was standing over a prototype fax machine, which was called an Infotec. It took forty-five minutes to transmit a single sheet of paper from the magazine's office in central London to the printers, who were about sixty miles away, but that was quicker than the time it took a motorcycle messenger to get there, so the technology was welcomed as a leap forward into the future.

THE FINANCIAL TIMES

Alice joined the *Financial Times* in 1986, just when Rupert Murdoch was taking on the print unions. He set up a computerized printing operation in the East End of London for the *Times*, the *Sunday Times*, the *Sun*, and the *News of the World*, sparking a technological revolution that would transform the finances of newspapers. The unions had been led to assume that Murdoch intended to launch a London evening newspaper from the new presses, but he secretly planned to relocate all of his papers there. A bitter dispute started upon the dismissal of 6,000 employees who had gone on strike. Many suspected that the Conservative government of Margaret Thatcher had colluded in the affair as a way of weakening the British trade union movement.

This revolution in productivity led to the transformation of the *Financial Times* from a national newspaper dealing with the City of London and British financial affairs to an international financial paper. It was a time when technology transformed not only the way that newspapers were printed and produced but also the way journalists worked.

> When I first joined the *Financial Times* in 1986, I worked as a journalist in the traditional way. You had a great big cast-iron typewriter on which you typed out your stories. You then picked up the pieces of paper, generally with Tipp-Ex dribbling down your arm through all the corrections you've made, and walked to the news desk, which was a fairly terrifying experience because we were all very, very frightened by the indomitable news editor, David Walker. You then distributed various carbon copies in the correct tray, still with the Tipp-Ex curdling on your arm.
>
> Alternatively, if you were on location on a tight deadline, you had to phone your copy in to the paper. Say there was an important court case and you needed to report on the verdict. You had to physically go to the court, listen to the verdict, run out, try and beat all your competitors from rival newspapers into the nearest public telephone box, and dictate your report through to the copy editor. You had adrenaline surging. You felt like this proper old-school film noir reporter when you were doing it, but it wasn't an efficient way of working as a journalist.
>
> The paper was printed on a separate floor of the same building as the newsroom. Newspaper headquarters in those days were vertically integrated industrial operations. The printers even had their own pub inside the building where they seemed to spend most of their time, so they were certainly rarely at the printing presses. What was then called Fleet Street, the nickname of the national newspaper industry in Britain, was really an old-fashioned, industrial oligopoly. There was an unspoken, rather corrupt and nepotistic agreement between the newspaper proprietors and the newspaper unions, both of whom were equally corrupt and both of whom were in cahoots to drive up the cost of producing national newspapers, which of course prevented anyone from coming in and setting up competitors.

It was a very entrenched establishment industry with very invidious, very traditional, hopelessly antiquated working practices and completely implacable unions, who were absolutely resistant to change. They saw progress as a real threat to their way of life and their very high wages.

Computerized printing slashed the cost of newspaper production, while the quality of the visual presentation was much better, so people had to start thinking much more seriously about newspaper design. The size of the newspaper, the typeface that was used, and the quality of photography became more and more important in making a really attractive and appealing product. The print quality of the old-fashioned analog printing presses had been so poor that any subtlety or sophistication of design was lost.

The reproduction of photographs was dreadful. I remember writing a feature for the *Financial Times* and the only portrait that we could find of the subject was one in which he'd actually been photographed with his eyes closed. I showed this disconsolately to the features editor and said, "I suppose we can't use this, what are we going to do?" And he said, "It really doesn't matter; once it's been printed it will be so fuzzy, no one will notice the closed eyes." And this was in fact the case. So, the visual side of newspapers was completely ignored.

Design was not taken seriously in national newspapers in Britain until David Hillman of Pentagram redesigned the *Guardian* in the 1988, introducing British readers to the innovations of mixed-font titles and a two-section daily paper, beautifully designed on a grid-based system. The newspaper industry had never been imaginative or creative from a visual perspective, but the combination of the new print quality and Hillman's design precedent changed the standards forever.

Purely practical issues like cost have dominated many of the decisions made by newspaper proprietors. For example, the move toward smaller formats was driven by the need to reduce the costs of paper and ink rather than by the desire to make the papers easier to handle and read. In the early 2000s, when both the *Times* and the *Independent* decided to adopt a compact format, all they did was shrink the layout of the old-fashioned broadsheet to fit. The *Guardian* was the first national

Continuing a new series in which top writers teach you their craft

Catherine Tate
How to write comedy

Tomorrow Plays & screenplays

£0.80
Monday 22.09.08
Published
in London and
Manchester
guardian.co.uk

9 770261 307217 39

Comedy

PLUS
Download
an exclusive,
free Bob
Dylan track
see page 2

theguardian

American beauty

Europe slide to defeat as US seal commanding Ryder Cup victory

Brown plans crackdown on world markets

- PM wants more regulation in US and Asia
- Darling will compare crisis to global terrorism

Patrick Wintour and Larry Elliott

Inside

Gordon Brown yesterday pinned hopes
of reviving his premiership on a package
of measures designed to tackle the economic crisis, including a drive for tighter
international controls of the global money
markets and a crackdown on the culture of

"ambulance-chasing" the global crisis, but
recognise that it is the single world event
that can play to Brown's political strengths
and allow them to mark out substantially
different territory by advancing the case
for a strong interventionist state, to which
the Tories do not subscribe.

Fending off continuing calls to quit
from within his own ranks at party con-

friend. A
Britons,
pital an
at a bak
conditi
Britons
The

newspaper to think about how many columns were needed and how wide each column should be to allow reading in a way that was easy on the eyes and facilitated comprehension.

CONTENT LIBERATED BY NEW TECHNOLOGIES

Another innovation in the *Guardian* was to leverage the amazing print quality that was available by the early 2000s by printing a photograph on a full two-page spread in the middle of the paper called "The picture of the day." A dramatic image was always chosen, and the quality was highlighted through a clever use of micro and macro scales. This communicated a message that the image would not have worked on the limited-resolution media of television or Internet.

It was in the 1990s that technology really started changing the way journalists worked. I remember being equipped with an early mobile phone at the *Financial Times*. You were given this bricklike instrument, which would weigh your hand down horribly when you held it, with only enough battery power to last for 45 minutes, but this was seen as a huge revolution in journalism technology. And of course as soon as mobiles or cell phones became lighter and more efficient with longer lasting batteries, it transformed journalism completely.

For me, technology has been completely liberating. With a Blackberry, a cell phone, and a laptop, the idea that I can work anywhere in the world and, thanks to the Internet, have access to an incredible research archive wherever I am in the world, is quite astonishing. That has made journalism much more accessible to a wider range of people, particularly now that with blogs they don't even need to use established media outlets to communicate and disseminate their work.

Those technologies have also had a dramatic impact on the form, virtual and otherwise, that media takes. The nineties was a fascinating period to be a journalist because it was a period of considerable turbulence. A lot of journalists and editors do

The Guardian
photo by Nicolas Zurcher

tend to be quite geeky, and certainly technophiles, so there's an enormous amount of excitement as our computers become more and more sophisticated.

The more intelligent publishers of newspapers realized early that the Internet would soon become an important new medium, so they invested in it heavily, but sometimes without the support of the editors and reporters. The *Financial Times* hired a separate team to run the Web site, but without giving the online staff the same training and resources as those who worked on the paper. There was also a lot of uncertainty about how to use the Internet as a source of revenue. The first approach was to replicate the traditional financial structure, hoping that people would pay to use the Web site, as they did for the *Wall Street Journal* for many years. If the quality of output had matched the standards of the paper, perhaps the *Financial Times* might also have succeeded with a subscription model, as the audience and qualities of the two papers are similar. The *Financial Times* offered its Web site for free at first and then started charging a subscription—an obvious mistake as people resent having to pay for something they've had for free at first. Web site usage dropped dramatically.

Newspapers are still struggling to come to terms with how they present themselves on the Web. Do they do a pastiche, a pixilated online pastiche of the offline printed paper; or do they produce something dramatically different? The *New York Times* has been successful because it refined its newsprint design rather sensitively and intelligently so it looks appealing and legible on the Web, but there are many more newspapers that have found it very difficult.

The great thing about the Internet is that it has made the media and the dissemination of information accessible very cheaply and relatively easily for absolutely everyone. For us as readers it's been incredibly liberating because it has blown open the media and the process of communication. If you want to express a point of view, you can launch a blog and you can find the six or seven million other people in the world who want to engage with you on that subject. It's been a fantastically liberating medium from a cultural and communication point of view.

This has had a dramatic effect on the old-school media industry. The sensible newspapers and magazines realize that the Internet was yet another form of distribution for them, one that probably will eventually squeeze out old-fashioned printing on paper. Hence, the really imaginative, sophisticated titles will embrace this with relish and have very vigorous, interesting, stimulating Web sites. And of course all sorts of other institutions have done this as well.

The more sophisticated newspapers don't see the printed newspaper and the online version as being entirely separate. They really do integrate the two. Increasingly you'll see those little sentences at the bottom of the printed article telling you to go to the Web site for more information. It can satisfy the crusty old columnists who want to write 3,000 words about something they think is very important, but actually there's only space for 800 in the newspaper, so they can inveigh at the length they wish on the Web site.

The Internet has transformed the relationship between the reader, the writer, and the editorial hierarchy of the media. In the olden days, the only way that readers would interact with writers and editors was by writing a letter to the editor or a letter to an individual journalist. It was time consuming and laborious to draft and write the letter, find a stamp, and post it.

Now everything you write as a columnist is immediately blogged. Whether it's simply a link to the column from blogs or other Web sites, it becomes instantly accessible all over the world on thousands of other Web sites, literally on the day it's published on the site. You get immediate response. Sometimes people Google you, or they go through Facebook, or MySpace, or your own Web site. They will email you, picking up on arcane points you may or may not have made in the column. Other times they either sing your praises or point out in horrifying detail the flaws in your argument on their own blogs or Web sites. So you're very aware there'll be an immediate debate about everything you write. And if there wasn't, you should probably start worrying, because it means that it's so bland and boring that really nobody's bothered to respond to it.

It's made the process much more democratic, much more interactive, and I think more fun. And for somebody like me, writing for a wonderful but rather expensive newspaper like the *International Herald Tribune*, it's lovely to think that students all over the world on design courses can log on to it every Monday for no money whatsoever and engage in a very vigorous discussion. The *International Herald Tribune* sells around 250,000 copies a day around the world, but the Web site has a readership of nearly five million people, which is fantastic.

WITH IRA GLASS, WE MOVE from print to radio. Ira explains how he has perfected the art of narrative, hooking the listeners with an idea and keeping them engaged by the flow of events.

IRA GLASS

Interviewed December 8, 2008

IRA GLASS

Ira started work as an intern at National Public Radio more than thirty years ago. He was a reporter and host on several NPR programs, including *Morning Edition*, *All Things Considered*, and *Talk of the Nation*. Since 1995, he has hosted and produced *This American Life*, from WBEZ. The show was nationally syndicated in June 1996 and is distributed by Public Radio International. It reaches over 1.7 million listeners on more than 500 stations weekly, with an average listening time of 48 minutes. Ira's work is original and influential in radio. For a long time *This American Life* was exclusively a radio show, but in 2007 Ira and his team started experimenting with a television version, developed separately to suit the medium. He continues to produce the weekly radio show, which is also available as a free podcast. The television show aired on the Showtime network for two seasons.

← Ira Glass
photos by author

Ira moved his base of operations from Chicago to New York in 2006, so I was able to interview him in the IDEO office in New York. I was lucky to reach him, as he is firmly focused on producing *This American Life* and faces weekly deadlines. I made contact through Larry Keeley, a friend and president of Chicago-based Innovation and Design firm Doblin Group Inc., who sits on the board of WBEZ. I could tell that Ira was a professional interviewer: when I offered him the radio microphone, he nimbly installed it in just the right position on his shirt so that it would be out of sight to the cameras. When we had finished recording, he spent another hour talking to the people in our office, asking probing questions, obviously interested in what we do.

INTIMACY

The structure of most radio news stories is like that of a legal argument, similar to the format of an eighth-grade paper, with a topic sentence starting each paragraph, followed by a collection of facts and a quote or two, before moving on to the next topic sentence, facts, quotes, and so forth. Ira wanted something different.

From cutting tape and listening to other people's work, I came to feel that I didn't want to structure a story like an argument. I wanted to structure it with narrative motion. Something would happen that would lead to another, and so on, so you have the forward momentum of things happening. Every now and then you'd leave the action to say something about it, to have some thought about it. So the structure is an anecdote, then a moment of reflection and then another anecdote.

When I give seminars to reporters, I play a story about a guy who worked in an office and somebody's twelve-year-old kid came to the office every now and then. She was a good kid, so he would joke around with her. One day he goes into the bathroom, and when he comes out of the bathroom with his glasses in his pocket, he sees her down the hall, so he starts clowning around, putting his hands like claws, and wandering down the hall towards the girl saying, "I didn't expect to see you here."

Then I stop and say to the reporters, "At that point, nobody turns off the radio, but if you think about it, it's an incredibly banal story; it's just a story about somebody coming out of a bathroom in their office. There's nothing to it as narrative. It has none of the stage props of a great story, but you'd be hard pressed to turn it off because you can feel that it has motion.

← Mixing
photo by George Barcos

You can tell this is a story with a destination. You can tell that the glasses in the pocket are the X-factor, so that when he gets down to the end of the hall it's not going to work out well for him. You can just feel through the motion of this that it's a train in a station heading out towards a destination."

Once I understood that, whenever I had tape of my interviews, I divided the material off in my head into the action part of the story and the thought part of the story. When I talk about stories with the rest of the staff, we say, "Is this working? What do you think of this part? There's too much action! You need another thought here. Now this has too many thoughts in a row. Get rid of this and this."

Ira has honed the art of narrative. In each of the segments in *This American Life* he hooks his audience into the dream of an idea at the beginning and then starts the action, with one thing happening, then another and another, and you're stuck. You're listening and you don't know why exactly. You can tell it's going to go somewhere, but by the time he reveals the direction, you're five or six minutes in, and you're emotionally involved, often rubbing your eyes to hold back tears. You have connected with the characters in the story and you have to find out what will happen to them. Radio allows you to be much more intimately connected to the story than you could be on television or in print.

Radio has a number of advantages over print and TV. One of them is that the intimacy is the default position. That's intimacy in both a quiet, emotional way and also somebody being funny. There are certain moments in the show where, because it's playing out in real time on tape, it just carries a feeling to it. If you were trying to do it in print, you would have to be an incredibly skilled A+ level writer to pull it off with as much feeling as my intern can do with a digital tape recorder and a nice mic. You get so much so easily!

LEARNING RADIO

The fluency that allows Ira to make intimate radio so easily has been perfected during a long career. He started at NPR when he was nineteen, and his first assignment was to be production assistant to Joe Frank, who made a dreamy hour-long show where he would tell wandering stories. You couldn't be sure why you were listening, but you couldn't turn it off. Ira was very attracted to the material, wanting to learn how it came to have that irresistible quality.

He also worked as an assistant to Keith Talbot and claims that he garnered more than half of everything he knows about making radio from the experience. Keith's ideas about how to make documentaries were way ahead of his time. He experimented with the structure, unrestrained by the conventional approach. Documentary is generally built around the narrator, but Keith would sometimes have characters from within the documentary narrate.

> One of my favorite shows he ever did was a show called *Ocean Hour*, where the narration took you from place to place; it was a series of stories about people living in the ocean and on the ocean. For example, one segment of the story was about a person who lived on the beach, completely separate from the economy of the world, getting everything he needed to live from things that washed up, plus hunting and fishing.

> What took you from place to place were two guys sitting on a pier. One guy is telling the other guy about this imaginary character that he'd made up when he was a little kid, and the imaginary character loved the ocean. He was talking very softly, and you could hear the sound of the pier and the music that was composed for this purpose, with incredible audio soundscape. It was really beautiful! Between each of the segments, instead of having the news announcer say, "And next we're going to go to … wherever," this guy would tell the other guy a little story that he'd made up when we was a little kid, and the other character would react. It was very pleasant, like listening to two buddies talking, and it moved you gently into the next segment. It was just very lovely!

Keith taught me the technique of having people give an interview in which they narrate an entire story themselves and you would edit the interviewer out. They would provide all the anecdotes. You would never have to hear a question, so it would sound like a person just talking. And then I learned from him how to use music—the power of using music and where to bring it in and bring it out, and using music the way you'd use a score in a movie.

After this apprenticeship, Ira moved to daily news shows, becoming a news producer and reporter for *All Things Considered* and *Morning Edition*. He brought his skills with him, trying to do stories with characters, scenes, funny bits, and emotional bits, even if it was just the breaking news. He had learned from Keith, and he was listening to other people's work, and eventually he realized that he had evolved a template of his own with a unique approach to radio production. Another contributing influence came from the musicals that he had seen as a child.

When I was a kid the predominant cultural object of my childhood wasn't rock music. I was born in 1959 and grew up in the suburbs of Baltimore, so it was the sixties when I was growing up. I really should have been into rock music, but I wasn't a baby boomer, so I didn't have that. Instead, because we were Jews growing up on the East Coast of the United States, the music in my house, the records that my parents had were all Broadway musicals. When a musical would come to Baltimore my mom would take us, and some of my earliest memories were going to these shows, and they made a really strong impression. We'd play the records over and over. I still know all the words to *Man of La Mancha*, *Fiddler on the Roof*, *A Funny Thing Happened on the Way to the Forum*, and *Camelot*.

There's an aesthetic to those shows that includes funny parts, but they're about something grand, and they go toward some sort of emotional thing. They are both funny and sad, and they're willfully trying to entertain you. They're not hard to get; they want you to get them. There came a point in my work where I realized that there is a kind of template for the work

Ira Glass
photo by Stuart Mullenberg

that I do, and that even while I was doing news stories, I was trying to make them have the feeling of those old musicals, which is almost the least cool thing you could possibly say about anything you would ever do!

Ira had been working in public radio for sixteen years when he started *This American Life*, so he was one of their most experienced producers and reporters. He understood how powerful radio is for news reporting, political commentary, and music, but felt that it was not being used for telling stories. Where was the feeling you used to get from radio dramas? Where was the storytelling that had made radio a successful new medium in the twenties and thirties? He wanted to make a radio show that would have this kind of feeling. He set about designing it from the creative impetus of the template that he had evolved in his head for anecdotes and reflective commentary. He asked himself, "What does it sound like? What should the narration be like? What kinds of stories are best? What will be engaging to me?" He wanted to make something that he would be thrilled by, with something really traditional about it, where the stories would shape the whole design.

The normal pattern in broadcast journalism is that every story you start on ends up on the air, because it's expensive. Ira decided to be much more selective, starting work on fifteen or twenty stories to end up with three or four. His team works very much as a group, with many different people contributing to each piece. Finding the stories is about half of what they do, as they start with a long list of ideas, working toward a theme that has the right balance between an abstract concept and the finding of real people to make the story come to life. They don't normally choose a story unless they have a sense that it may lead to some new thought, but in the best stories, the plan inevitably changes once things get going.

I thought I invented this structure of storytelling, learning from all the people whose work I liked. I felt like I was sitting in an editing room at NPR in Washington and invented this structure of some action, and then a moment of reflection, and some action, and so on.

And then I went home to Baltimore, where I'm from, for the Jewish High Holidays. I went to the services where there was the same rabbi as when I was a kid. That rabbi was a total entertainment package. That guy could really give a sermon! He was funny, and then he'd do a little story from the Bible. Next were scenes from movies he'd just seen, then he'd be reading from the scriptures. At the end he said, "Here's what we're going to do with these thoughts this week. Here's what we're going to carry with us when we walk out that door!" He was just an incredible performer. We were in Baltimore, but he was from New York, with a thick New York accent. We always felt like he sounded like a real Jew to us, because of the New York accent.

My radio show had been on the air for four or five years at that point, so as I listened to his sermon, I was taking apart the structure in my head, and I realized that it had the same structure as my radio show! Since then I've talked to people who have been to seminary, and they assure me that every sermon has the structure of the radio show. It turns out that I reinvented the oldest structure of storytelling, but I do try to use it in a way that maximizes what you can do on the radio.

TELEVISION

In 2007 Ira and his team launched a television version of *This American Life*, distributed on the Showtime network. Initially the network suggested a season of twelve shows, but Ira begged them to limit it to six because they were doing the radio show at the same time. They soon discovered big differences between what worked on radio and what would be needed for television. On the radio they could reconstruct stories from the past by finding the people who could recount events. Some of the best radio is made by finding people who have had something interesting happen to them and are also good talkers. If you interview them and they tell their stories well, that's about as good as gets. Interviews about the past on television are usually not very interesting because they fail to harness the full power of the medium. You want to see the action that is being described, so you either have to reenact the story that is being told or capture the action as it happens.

> The longer we did it, the looser we got, but also the more we understood what works on TV. At the beginning we really tried to do a lot of stories where the action happened in the past. We tried to find things we could film to cover those plot points that happened in the past, or we'd do cartoons, or find some way to have visuals on screen while somebody is telling the story that happened in the past. We came to understand the real laws of television broadcasting, that it's better if the camera is there when it's happening, whereas for radio, it doesn't matter. It's often better to let the people who were there tell you about it, because they'll bring more feeling to it that way.

> You can have intimacy in TV, but the apparatus that gets you there is completely different and a lot more difficult to make happen. You have to build a whole scaffolding to support the moment of intimacy. It works best if you have a lot of motion before, so the quiet can seem more quiet. On film there's something about seeing somebody's face that carries so much feeling to it. That's definitely an advantage of film and television, but you also get something from not seeing their face, from being able to imagine it.

This American Life

What I Learned From Television

TOUR 2007

New York • Boston • Minneapolis • Chicago • Seattle • Los Angeles

There are characters who have been on the radio show where I think we're better off that people didn't see them. I feel like it's easier to imagine being the person, easier to relate if you don't see them. In terms of controlling the storytelling, since the audience can't see them, I am in control of every bit of information that comes at you and the speed at which it comes at you. If you see them you're getting information that I can't control about how they look, and how they dress, and where they're sitting.

By the time they had finished their second television season, they were having a hard time finding stories that had the right kind of narrative arc, since they were looking for plots with characters experiencing change for really interesting reasons as well as an overarching idea that offered a commentary of some kind with universal values. That is hard to find for television, where you want to record the story in real time. It's much easier to edit a story that makes a complete narrative by assembling elements, as you can in radio.

Ira's friend Robert Krulwich went from public radio to television successfully, achieving acclaimed innovation in both media. He said that you get to a point in radio where the levers of it are so simple you can learn them all, and if you've learned your craft you can always make something work. He said that in TV there are so many factors in play that it is never predictably controllable. Even if you've set the whole thing up perfectly, the person will glance toward the camera or away from the camera at the key moment and will destroy your quote, or something will happen in the background in a subtle way, or you have not framed it right. There are so many subtle variables that can interfere with the moment that you're trying to create.

What I Learned from Television poster courtesy of *This American Life* from Chicago Public Radio

A documentarian like Michael Moore invents scenes to create an entertaining way to stage his narrative as film, for example trying to get the head of General Motors to talk to him. That's a good theatrical conceit, used to carry everything else he's trying to do. Morgan Spurlock used a similar approach for *Super Size Me*, setting it up so that he could be filmed in real time going through the process of eating only at McDonald's for thirty days. This kind of overt construct turns the output into a polemic, while *This American Life* is a report of life as it is observed, carefully chosen to deliver a higher level insight at the same time. That is much more difficult to deliver in television than it is in radio.

> I don't feel like I have a personal relationship with John Stewart [of the *Daily Show*], though I adore John Stewart and I watch him all the time, but I feel like he's talking to millions. Whereas with Howard Stern, I know he's talking to millions, but it's much more direct, it's much more personal, and I have a closer relationship. My feelings about Howard Stern and everybody on his show, Artie Lange and Robin [Quivers], are so much stronger. And it's the same thing with Terry Gross, and Garrison Keillor, and the other people on the radio that I like. It's much more one-to-one.

Some 600,000 people listen to the podcast of *This American Life*, a larger number than anything else from public radio, but Ira feels that he didn't need to do anything to make that happen. There was no need to design the output in a different way for the podcast version, because radio is particularly suited to the Internet when it's done with the kind of intimacy that Ira creates.

> The Web is more like radio than it is like most things, because you're sitting there alone and somehow it's close to you. I think the reason it works over the Internet is because there's something in the intimacy of it that's like the intimacy of Facebook. As a character on the radio I don't seem further away than your friend on Facebook. I don't seem like an official sort of announcer. I just seem like somebody who happened to get a radio show.

> The laws of narrative are the laws of narrative, and what engages us is simply what engages us. I feel like those things still apply in the new digital world. We don't democratize our show at all. We don't even let you comment on our Web site. You take the product that we give you!

IN THE NEXT INTERVIEW, COLIN CALLENDER explains how he safeguards the integrity of content in his role as a film and television producer. He believes that great producers create protected working environments in which talented people can do their most brilliant work, and that his job is to deliver onscreen the vision that has been articulated and agreed on by the people responsible for the content.

COLIN CALLENDER

Interviewed February 26, 2009

COLIN CALLENDER

As a founding member of HBO's Programming Group and the president of HBO Films, Colin played a central role in turning HBO into a pioneering programming powerhouse. He has helped transform the entertainment landscape, setting new benchmarks for quality film and television production. Under his auspices, such acclaimed projects as *If These Walls Could Talk* (1996), *61** (2001), *Elephant (Palme d'Or)* (2003), *Angels in America* (2003), *Maria Full of Grace* (2004), *John Adams* (2008), and *Recount* (2008) reached the screen. In October 2008 he announced his intention to leave HBO to set up his own company. Born and raised in England, Colin began his career as a stage manager with London's Royal Court Theatre before joining Granada Television as a trainee. In 1983 he formed The Callender Company and reached an international audience as producer of the nine-hour, Emmy-winning *The Life and Adventures of Nicholas Nickleby*. In 1987 he ventured into feature films, serving as producer of Peter Greenaway's *The Belly of an Architect*. That same year he joined Home Box Office as executive producer of HBO Showcase, which produced innovative films that brought together a mix of exciting new and established talent.

← **Colin Callender**
photos by author

I saw Colin speak at a panel about the future of media and was impressed by the clarity of his vision, so I asked him for an interview. He lives and works in an enormous Beverly Hills house perched on the edge of a cliff above a green ravine, with a view of the Los Angeles basin in the distance. When I arrived for the interview there was a landscaping crew, with six gardeners and two pickup trucks, hard at work. Colin showed me into his office and I set up to record him sitting in a comfortable old leather chair in front of a poster of *The Life and Adventures of Nicholas Nickleby*. At one point in our conversation we were interrupted by his young daughter, and his face lit up with delight when he she came through the door.

THE LIFE AND ADVENTURES OF NICHOLAS NICKLEBY

Colin fell in love with the theater as a student, and he wanted to be part of everything that went on behind the scenes, leading him to a career as a television and film producer. He started working as a stagehand in the early seventies but soon had the opportunity to join Granada Television as a trainee, in which role he was introduced to all aspects of TV and film production. Film production in the UK had all but vanished, and Colin detected that an independent production sector was about to emerge in British television. He moved to Hollywood, because it was the home of independent production and he wanted to understand how it worked. He spent a year learning the ropes and then returned to London to set up his own company in 1977.

> After I left university I went to see a man called Jeremy Isaacs, who at the time ran the documentary division of one of the television networks. He sat there and he said, "Why are you here?" And I said, "Well, I'm very interested in working in television." And he said, "You just left university. What do you know about anything? I mean, if you're going to make documentaries about the world and about issues, you've got to have lived. Come back to me when you've lived a bit!" Some years later, I did go back to him.

By the time he returned, Colin had had started his own company and acquired the rights from the Royal Shakespeare Company to do *The Life and Adventures of Nicholas Nickleby*. Jeremy Isaacs had just been appointed the chief executive of Channel 4, a new broadcast network in Britain that would be dedicated to commissioning independent productions to attract new audience segments. Colin arranged a meeting with Isaacs and said, "Look, you probably won't remember, but you told me ten years ago to come back to you, and I'm coming back to you now." The result of the conversation was an agreement to embark on the production of *Nicholas Nickleby*, an experience that proved to be formative for Colin.

As well as the rights to *Nicholas Nickleby*, Colin put the financing together from three sources, Channel 4 in Britain, Mobile Oil in the United States, and an international distributor from Germany, but he realized that each financier had different requirements for the production. Channel 4 wanted to play the eight-and-a-half-hour production as it had been on the stage, in two chunks of over four hours; Mobile Oil wanted four two-hour films, and the German distributor wanted nine episodes, each under an hour.

> I remember thinking, "I don't think I can make this work." I called a meeting at Brown's Hotel in London and assembled the stage directors of the Royal Shakespeare Company, the director for the television adaptation, the three financiers, and the writer. I sat everyone around a table and said, "Look, it's 9:00 on a Tuesday. We've booked this room till 6:00, and we've got to come out of this room all in agreement on the right way to make this project. There's only one way to do it. We can't do three different versions. It just simply is not going to work. There is no way we can be a horse, a camel, and a donkey all at the same time. If we can come to an agreement at the end of the day on what it is we're making, then I feel confident we can go out and do it, but if we can't come to an agreement, then we should all go our separate ways."

> In fairness to all the partners, we had a very interesting conversation, with everyone making their case for their needs. Trevor Nunn, who was the artistic director of the Royal Shakespeare Company, made an impassioned plea for what he thought it should be. At the end of the day I said, "I have to tell you that I initially told Trevor Nunn that I could see how to adapt his concept to the screen. He and I agreed on what it should be. You've now heard what Trevor thinks it should be, and that's why I as the producer signed on. My job as the producer is to deliver on the screen the vision that he articulated and that we agreed on, and to protect that along

THE

LIFE AND ADVENTURES

OF

NICHOLAS NICKLEBY.

BY CHARLES DICKENS.

WITH ILLUSTRATIONS BY PHIZ.

LONDON:
CHAPMAN AND HALL, 186, STRAND.

MDCCCXXXIX.

the journey that this project goes through. This is the only way we can do it!" And everybody signed on.

From then on, that focus and clarity informed every single decision, whether it was a financial decision, a logistics decision, or a question of who to hire. I think that the producer's role is to protect the vision of the project at every step of the way.

The production brought together people from the theater, film, and television, with the disciplines intermingled. Theater people did the theater production, the director for the television adaptation was a television director, and the cinematographer was a film cinematographer. It was shot with a single camera recording on video, with the sound recorded separately by a film sound recordist. The Old Vic Theatre was turned into a sound stage, using both the proscenium arch and the audience over a ten-week period. The mingling and mixing of the disciplines, with diverse talents and different creative points of view, enabled an original approach.

No one had ever done this before. In the past, theater had been brought to the camera by shooting it as if it were a football match: there were a bunch of cameras, the thing would play live, you'd shoot it a couple of times, you'd shoot some reverses of the audience, and that would be it. Alternatively, you'd put it on a sound stage, or you'd shoot it like a straight film. But *Nicholas Nickleby* had a unique theatrical component to it, so that was very important.

We had Ingmar Bergman's *[The] Magic Flute* in mind for inspiration, as we thought about how to do it for the screen. We had to keep that theatricality. On the stage *Nicholas Nickleby* had almost no set. I think they'd gone off to scrap yards and picked up pieces of wood, but early on people said, "This is going to be on film, on television, so we've got to build realistic sets." Trevor Nunn said something to me back then which I remember to this day. He said, "No, no, no. Let the audience fill in the blanks, exactly like radio." And what he was saying was, "Allow the audience to participate in the process."

I learned two things out of *Nickleby*: The idea of letting the audience participate in the process, in the journey—to take them on a journey with you where they actually have to work a bit to be there. The second thing I learned was that the process of making something, the way in which the people are brought together and the way they work together, impacts the result on the screen. Those were two crucial lessons.

DIRECTORS, PRODUCERS, AND EXECUTIVES

The term *producer* is used in lots of different ways, causing confusion. Colin was a producer for years before he became an executive, and having sat on both sides of the table, he feels that the producer has a crucial role during the whole creative process. As an executive at HBO looking at movies that he might want to commission, his first question was, Who's the producer? His second question was, Whom do we call when the movie isn't quite working?

There is a saying in the industry that film is the director's medium, that theater is the writer's medium, and television is the producer's medium. Colin thinks that there is some truth to that, but that every project has a different history and a different way of unfolding. Sometimes the original concept is the director's, sometimes a writer's, and sometimes a producer's. Creative partnerships are crucial to success, and it's not an accident that some of the greatest directors in the world have had long-term relationships with the producers as well as with film editors and composers.

A few years ago we did a wonderful film called *The First Hundred Years of Films*. It was a set of compilations and interviews with directors, and there was a sequence in which there were interviews with Robert Altman and Fred Zinnemann about their movie-making styles. Fred Zinnemann talked with great passion about knowing exactly what he wanted to do when he walked onto a set: every shot was planned and choreographed, including the framing, composition, lighting, and wardrobe. Robert Altman, by contrast, would talk about how he didn't know what he was going to shoot or where he was going to put the camera. He left everything to chance, and that's how he made his movies. Every filmmaker is different!

Part of the challenge for the producer is to understand what that director's process is, and to build a working environment that allows them to do their very best work. I'll give you a fine example of that. One of the last pieces I did at HBO was a big production based on David McCullough's book *John Adams*, and it was a recreation of the story of the Founding Fathers told through the second president, John Adams. Tom Hooper was the immensely talented director from Britain. Because it was a period drama, it involved a lot of CGI and special effects.

Well, Tom is a brilliant director, but not unlike Robert Altman, he wings it on the day. The production team were having terrible trouble wrangling him, and they came to me and said, "Colin, you've got to tell him to have a shot list; he's got to shoot in a certain sort of way; it's the only way we can get this done." I was looking at the dailies of the film, some of which were startlingly brilliant, with composition and camera angles that were beyond eccentric and yet vibrantly emotional.

This went on for a while and finally I said to my production guys at HBO, "If we do that, we'll kill this guy. We'll kill the very thing that's making this really special. Your job is not to try and fit him into your predetermined process. Your job is to understand what his process is and work around him. You can't fix this by putting him into a straightjacket, as that would destroy the intuitive creativity that's happening moment by moment on the set." And to their credit, that's what they did!

There's a shot at the end, in the last hour of *John Adams* in which Paul Giamatti as John Adams is walking through a field of corn reflecting on his life, and for a moment there's a shot of him upside down. Now to this day I don't know what led Tom Hooper to put that inverted shot in the sequence. By any logical standards it made no sense whatsoever. I'm not even sure if he did it intentionally, but I saw it there and it took my breath away. It's an extraordinary moment, immensely powerful.

Colin believes that great producers create protected working environments in which talented people can do their most brilliant work, but behind the scenes they are also responsible for the finances, finding sponsors, raising money, and developing terms for distribution. When he came back to Britain to start his own company, Colin worked with distributor Richard Price, who represented television companies in the UK and handled the sale of their programming around the world. The VHS cassette had just arrived and that facilitated sales of British programming internationally, since foreign buyers were able to look at material more easily than before. So Colin began to raise money internationally in advance for British productions, finding outside financing and bringing it to the British broadcasters for collaborative projects.

If an idea is strong enough, Colin has always been able to find a way to finance a project. By a strong idea, he means one that is both powerful and simple yet distinctive and different. That was core to his thinking as a producer as he began to evolve Home Box Office into a compelling brand. Once the idea has those attributes, the two most important components in making it work are getting the script right and skillful editing. You can have the finest director in the world, but if you've got a terrible script there's nothing you can do. Editing is a combination of a technical craft and sheer inspiration.

It's that intersection that's so exciting. It's a left brain/right brain intersection, not just for editors, but also for everyone involved. I do think it is literally a combination, because making a big movie or television series is a very complicated process. It's not like painting, which needs an artist, canvas, brushes, and paint. A film or a television production is an enormously collaborative process involving a whole horde of people. Part of it is inspiration, intuition, and the creativity

An engaged audience
photo by Pavel Losevsky

of the moment, and part of it is stepping back from that and keeping a sense of what the whole is, and understanding the sort of internal DNA that makes something work and working with that DNA, playing with that DNA.

ENGAGING WITH CONTENT

As the Internet has grown, along with accessible and inexpensive tools for creating content, the idea that audiences want to interact with their entertainment has taken hold. It's assumed that people no longer want to sit back and passively watch television at home: now they either want to create or actively participate. Colin doesn't believe that analysis is completely true; he thinks that people still do enjoy sitting back in a movie theater or at home to watch, but he thinks they also want to engage—in a more subtle way, though, than interacting with a computer or do-it-yourself videography. He believes that people want to use their imaginations to become engaged with the content and to embark on an emotional journey as they watch, feeling that they are participating in the experience.

The majority of mainstream film and television has not engaged the audience or invited watchers to go on a journey. It does not treat the audience with respect or understand the way in which people want to participate. Instead it tends to serve up predictable material with no demands or surprises. If you've seen the preview for an episode, all too often you've enjoyed the most engaging moments in advance.

I think this notion of the emotional connection between an audience and the content that they're engaged with is very, very central to how we need to look at the audience and the creator. For example, *Slumdog Millionaire* [directed by Danny Boyle and Loveleen Tandan] won the Oscar for best film. In the opening sequence the audience is taken on a camera's-eye view of a journey that they've never been on before. They don't quite know where they are going, but they know it's unfamiliar territory, and you're asking them to do that with you.

The emotional resonance of that movie is not just the function of a good story well told or the fact that it plays out a traditional "boy meets girl, boy loses girl, boy gets girl" love story narrative. It also invites the audience to come on a journey with the characters. It doesn't answer all the questions, nor does it feed you the answers before the questions are asked.

If you hear producers talk about network television dramas or comedies, they will tell you that for success they need to signal the audience in advance about what is going to happen. I think that's why the networks have lost their audience—because it's boring, it's predictable, you know where it's going and the audience is ahead of the storyteller. That is why certain shows like *Lost* and *24* have been so engaging, because they have turned that idea on its head.

The impact of *The Sopranos* was that it took the gangster movie genre and said to the audience, "We're not going to give you any clues. You just need to come on this journey with us. Some of it will be familiar, some of it won't be familiar, but stick with us and come on this journey. We're going to constantly surprise you. We're going to kill off characters. We're going to have the characters you love do terrible things." For example, one of the principal characters kills somebody while on a trip with his daughter to try and get her into a college, leaving her in a motel while he commits the murder.

Successful designs for popular media leave at least some of the form or content in a familiar format. If the audience is very interested in the content, you can play with form and bring the audience along a journey with you, or you could use a familiar form and play with the content, but if you play with form and content at the same time, it is very difficult to get a broad audience to accept it. Some of the most interesting art does play with the intersection of both form and content, but that limits the audience to a narrower segment. For popular culture, one has to carefully balance surprises that attract and familiarity that reassures. Colin gives an example of pushing that limit.

> We made a movie called *Elephant* with Gus Van Sant that won the Palme d'Or. Gus came in after the Columbine shootings [in Colorado] and said, "I want to do a docudrama about Columbine," and we had a very interesting conversation about it. I remember saying to him, "Gus, anybody can do a docudrama about Columbine. You're Gus Van Sant. We're not taking advantage of you as a filmmaker if you do it as a docudrama. If you want to try to explore the roots of violence in schools in America today, doing a docudrama about Columbine is almost reductive, because it's going to make it specifically about Columbine.

> I gave him a film called *Elephant* by a British director called Alan Clarke, which is about sectarian violence in Northern Ireland. The film was a series of scenes in which you watched events unfold without knowing who was Catholic and who was Protestant. You'd see a man standing at a urinal, then somebody in a coat walk in, pull out a gun and shoot the guys head off, and walk out. Fade to black. The next minute you'd see a teacher in a school sitting behind a desk marking some homework with the school lights being turned off by the janitor, and someone would walk into the classroom, shoot the teacher, and walk out again. Through the course of this drama you had no idea who was Catholic, who was Protestant, what the setup was, or why they were being killed, but by the time you finished

Filmmaking
courtesy of Vancouver Film School/Creative Commons

watching, it was an extraordinary statement about the futility of random violence that was tearing Northern Irish society apart.

The fact that the film that Gus made about Columbine was called *Elephant* was a tribute to Alan Clarke. That led Gus down another road altogether in terms of how he made the film. It plays with form in terms of time and place, in terms of the cinematography and the composition. It basically breaks every single traditional rule about storytelling, but because it's about Columbine and violence amongst children in schools, you go with it. It's an extraordinary film.

Consumers pay for HBO as a monthly subscription, often packaged with other programs, so the success or failure of any one show or film doesn't directly impact the bottom line. This allowed Colin to give the producers unusual freedom, as they were not driven by ratings, advertisers, or box office. He tried to address underserved audiences, sometimes taking big risks that turned into big successes. In the very early days of HBO a lot of the programming was geared toward men, because broadcast television was primarily addressing women, and they wanted to present something different from the mainstream. Later, Colin wanted to broaden the audience to include women, so he decided to try something with "risky" content in hopes of attracting a new female audience.

> We made a trilogy of films called *If These Walls Could Talk*, about abortion in America. One film was set in the fifties, another in the seventies, and the third in the nineties. We had Demi Moore, Sissy Spacek, and Cher in the stories, and they were very, very tough. In the first story you saw Demi Moore self-abort with a hanger. When we had preview screenings in New York we had people fainting in the aisles and had to call the EMS crews. It was unlike anything that anyone had seen before—very powerful, but it wasn't a polemic. It was an exploration of the decisions that women have to make.

> Well, it got the most extraordinary audience on HBO. It just went through the roof. And suddenly we all looked at each other and said, "You know, women want something else. They don't just want the disease of the week, or the soap opera drama that network television is giving them. They want real stories about themselves where you really explore in an intelligent, smart way the sort of emotional journeys that women go on." And *Sex in the City* was the direct descendent of that.

> I think part of the excitement, the fun, is being able to take those creative risks that end up challenging and changing the conventional wisdom about what's doable and what isn't doable.

WHAT'S NEXT?

Colin is interested in how the Internet and social networking are giving content creators a new paradigm for thinking about the audience. Traditional demographics divide the audience by characteristics such as gender, economic status, age, and geography. Madison Avenue has used this type of analysis to sell advertising, but the information harvested on the Internet is eroding that kind of demographic chunking. Now the advertiser knows who participates in a special-interest group or groups with passionate interests in specific areas. As those groups transcend traditional boundaries, Colin wants to look at the audience in a different way, defining new and innovative programming based on that more distributed but well-informed analysis. He is not very interested in the groundswell of user-generated content.

I think the best film and television certainly entertains, but it does more than entertain; it illuminates, informs, and engages emotionally. At its very best, as any great art does, it enables the person viewing to look at the world with slightly different eyes—with a different perspective and point of view, and maybe have a new empathy with other people.

Filmmaking and television aspire to those high artistic ideals, beyond just being moving wallpaper, so I believe that there's the role of an artist in the middle of that. Although I embrace the notion of user-generated content and the democratization of production, I'm not sure that it necessarily results in more illuminating work. This is not to be elitist about it, as I certainly wouldn't want to do without it, but I'm not sure that one replaces the other. I think the challenge and the interesting thing is how the two worlds can live side by side.

There are certain sorts of forms of expression that will presumably disappear. The eight-track cassette doesn't exist any more, but the pencil still does—a piece of wood with a piece of lead in the middle of it, side by side with the computer. What interests me is the way these parallel universes live side by side rather than replace the other. I think there's no difference at all between the way you create a drama for Hulu and for cable television. I do think that people's viewing habits have changed, but not the way they engage with the content. An audience today doesn't make any distinction between cable and television.

Certainly the entertainment landscape is beyond bewildering, but one thing we know is that in one form or another people will be at home watching entertainment on a screen. The screen may be a television monitor, a computer screen, a computer attached to a TV, or a TV attached to a computer. The content may be a download, a DVD, a broadband delivery, or whatever. They will be watching stuff at home in one form or another.

I think the need for societies to create stories to help people define themselves is central to the way societies hold themselves together, so that in the final analysis it's the content that matters!

COMMENTARY

Yes, content is king! Without good material, the arts of communication and presentation are hollow and meaningless. I admire the idealism with which Arthur Sulzberger Jr. links the mission of journalism and democracy, or Ira Glass extols the power of narrative, or Colin Callender believes that societies hold themselves together by creating stories to define themselves. But what does this imply for design? Is design merely the lackey who polishes the king's shoes, or instead the embodiment of the soul of content? I think it's worth taking a look at some examples from this chapter to examine the issues behind that question.

The Saturday edition of the *New York Times* newspaper is not so huge since most of the material is saved up for Sunday. Let's look at Saturday, January 23, 2010. There are three main sections, with section A covering international and national news and editorial comment, section B including business and sports, and section C about the arts, with weather on the back page. The glossy weekend magazine usually arrives on Sunday, but some carriers include it with the Saturday delivery.

On the same day the online version, Nytimes.com, has five main tabs on the home page: Today's Paper, Video, Most Popular, Times Topics, and Most Recent. The home page is the width of a single screen with several screens of height that you can scroll through to find news, blog links, and headlines from twenty-four subchannels. The Times Topics tab has a row of its own tabs giving access to most of these subchannels, but in not quite the same organization. The Most Recent tab offers access to real-time news with links via a list of headlines with single sentence explanations, plus a linked photomontage. The Most Popular tab aggregates traffic to display the most emailed, blogged, searched, and popular movies. The Video tab is a thing unto itself, closer in appearance to YouTube or Hulu than to the printed newspaper. The Today's Paper tab provides the strongest link between physical and digital, with thumbnails of the front pages of the *New York Times* and the *International Herald Tribune*, comparable headlines, and a long list of material referencing the pages in the physical paper.

This comparison of the structure reveals that the design of the physical newspaper and the online version are very different. Content is king in the sense that the journalistic expertise and structure are essential to harvest the information and opinion for both versions, but this king is very hands off, not attempting to control the nature of the delivery of that information and opinion. Alice Rawsthorn sums it up nicely when she says, "The *New York Times* has really interrogated the Web and found ways of working well with it." This has kept her visiting the site every day for over ten years. She points to the visual connection between the old-fashioned masthead on the paper and the finessed version online, encouraging the sense of a connected identity between the two. With the exception of the Today's Paper tab, this is where the overlap in the reading experience ends. The online version is highly evolved to take advantage of all of those attributes of connectivity that the Internet offers, while the newspaper remains surprisingly similar to its past, offering the traditional satisfaction of scale and handling but without taking strides to redesign the experience in the way that the *Guardian* or *USA Today* have done. Alice Rawsthorn explains the leap forward that David Hillman created when he redesigned the *Guardian* to take advantage of the new high-quality printing technology, with mixed-font titles, a carefully thought-out grid for the layout, and a huge two-page photo in the centerfold.

I don't believe in design as a lackey, providing a superficial surface to royal content. Rather, I see design as a synthesis of all the requirements that connect people to the experience that they have with something. This synthesis evolves through iterative efforts to improve the design, developing ways to present and communicate the content that is unique to each medium. You really can enjoy the news and opinion generated by the reporters and editors at the *New York Times* in different ways in the paper and online. On the same day you can discover different items and experience different rewards with the two. The content provides the basic material, but the design of its presentation in each medium separates it into versions. It's the content and the medium combined that can be designed to yield a good reading and navigating experience.

Ira Glass has evolved an approach to radio that combines content and medium as a narrative flow, with anecdotes interspersed with reflection. When you listen to *This American Life*, he hooks you in to the story by leaving each anecdote hanging during the reflective commentary, so you are waiting for the next episode. I like his example of the X-factor added to a banal story of a man coming out of the bathroom and seeing a kid down the hall. The X-factor is the mention that he has his glasses in his pocket, so you subconsciously realize that something strange of threatening is likely to happen soon. When radio is designed like this, it harnesses the imagination with a powerful emotional intimacy, comparable to that exerted by a great orator or preacher.

When Ira tried television, he found that the design needed to be different. In radio he had evolved an approach to presenting the content over a period of more than thirty years, so the design of the structure and presentation was highly evolved to fit perfectly with the characteristics of the medium. In television he found that intimacy is much harder to achieve, as every visual cue needs to support the audio to be convincing, and close-up shots of the face carry much of the emotional quality, but you lose the power of the listener's imagination to fill in gaps. Film and television are complex and expensive, and even when they're well coordinated and choreographed, you can only rarely get that emotional connection to the narrator that Ira achieves for every radio episode of *This American Life*. Film and TV need to be recorded in real time or reenacted to communicate successfully, whereas in radio you can ask people to reconstruct stories from the past. Good talkers can make excellent radio when they describe something interesting that happened to them.

Colin Callender explains the balance between intimacy and sit-back viewing for film and television. He points out that people want to have their emotions and imagination engaged when they are watching, and he derides much mainstream material for failing to invite the audience on a participatory journey. I like his example of the opening sequence in *Slumdog Millionaire*, where the audience is taken on a camera's-eye view of a hectic run through the slums. It is the start of an invitation to the audience to come on a journey with the characters that continues throughout the film. Here again, you might think that content is king, in that the people and the place drive the effect, but the experience is skillfully designed to make the best of the medium. The team of filmmakers connected to the real slums in Mumbai, India, but they also know their craft of cinematography.

The stories told by Colin Callender and Ira Glass make us understand how challenging and complex it is to make successful film or television and why it is so expensive and time-consuming. In order to achieve the goal of letting the content appear to be king, we need producers like Colin who believe that their job is to enable the directors, writers, and actors to deliver the artistic vision. When the vision is supported, the audience can fill in the blanks, feeling a sense of participation and engagement. Colin is also a realist about popular appeal, carefully balancing surprises that attract and familiarity that reassures.

IN THE NEXT CHAPTER, "LET THE TRUTH BE TOLD," we meet some people who care most about the integrity of content. They see their roles to be primarily political—to delve into the truth behind the stories to reveal causes and implications.

6 LET THE TRUTH BE TOLD

Interviews with David Fanning, Mark Gerzon, Shinichi Takemura, and Hans Rosling with Ola Rosling and Anna Rosling Rönnlund

All media exist to invest our lives with artificial perceptions and arbitrary values.

Marshall McLuhan

ALL OF THE PEOPLE INTERVIEWED for this chapter would disagree fiercely with McLuhan's assessment of media. All of them have dedicated their lives to revealing the truth and have harnessed the power of the media to help them. They welcome the new media of clouds and crowds and are convinced that the truth will be told by communities at large—in contrast to the traditional media, which were controlled by a few powerful and potentially information-distorting entities. To be fair, McLuhan was living at a time when the media was in the hands of the elite, and even with his philosophical vision, he may not have imagined the connectivity of the Internet and the power of user-generated content and reporting.

David Fanning has made investigative documentaries for public television since 1983. He is keenly aware that he works in a medium that is prone to manipulation, as the journey of discovery always produces enormous amounts of material. This causes a dilemma for the editor, who is both trying to create a dramatic narrative and honor-bound not to manipulate the truth in favor of the drama. It is tempting to allow political or personal bias to influence the output, or to be swept along by the story. The spread of the Internet allowed David to support his broadcasts by putting the evidence online, with documents, audio, and video (as soon as the bandwidth increased). This made the journalism transparent, with a new contract between viewer and maker to reveal a more complete version of the truth.

Mark Gerzon saw Ronald Reagan using the power of the media to tell stories that made Americans hate Russians and that dehumanized the people of the Soviet Union. At the same time he saw anticapitalist films coming out of Russia that were the mirror image of what was happening in Hollywood. This was just the kind of bias that McLuhan was referring to. To counter the propaganda, Mark put together the Entertainment Summit to bring filmmakers together across the Cold War divide. His efforts may have accelerated the thaw and helped Mikhail Gorbachev's policy of glasnost. Mark is encouraged by the changes caused by the presence of ubiquitous camera phones and Internet communications; he believes that in the future it will be much more difficult to manipulate the media unchallenged.

After years conducting field research as an anthropologist, Shinichi Takemura decided that he wanted to harness the media to communicate the reality of what is happening to our planet. He adopted a new career as a media producer and founded a nonprofit organization called the Earth Literacy Program as a base for his activities. His Tangible Earth project is a multimedia globe that allows people to understand the condition of the world using interactive technology, based on information provided by scientists from various fields. He wants to communicate the truth by designing a social infrastructure—a public sensory platform for the global age.

Hans Rosling spent two decades studying outbreaks of disease in remote rural areas across Africa. In 2005 he cofounded the Gapminder Foundation with his son and daughter-in-law, who had been helping him by designing animated presentations for his lectures that reveal surprising truths about social, economic, and environmental development all over the world. Ola Rosling and Anna Rosling Rönnlund were studying to become artists but taught themselves to design software to convert the statistics into emotionally compelling and enjoyable media presentations that have won awards by being "humorous yet deadly serious." Ola and Anna are now working at Google, supporting their Trendalyzer software, which Google acquired in 2007.

DAVID FANNING

Interviewed November 12, 2008

DAVID FANNING

A self-taught filmmaker from South Africa, David came to the United States in 1973 and began producing and directing local and national documentaries for KOCE, a public television station in California. In 1977 he joined WGBH Boston, America's most prolific public broadcasting organization, to start the international documentary series *World*. He has been executive producer of *Frontline* since its first season in 1983. In 2007, after 24 seasons and more than 485 films, *Frontline* remains America's only regularly scheduled investigative documentary series on television. The series has won all of the major awards for broadcast journalism, including the Gold Baton (the highest duPont-Columbia Award) in 1990, 1996, and 2002, for its "total contribution to the world of exceptional television." David is happiest thinking through how best to edit complex narratives, sketching diagrams of how information fits together. He revels in deeply involved reporting of difficult subjects, in trying to explain topics by taking his audiences on journeys and adventures, and in going out into the world with all his senses alert.

David Fanning lives in a house overlooking the ocean, not so far from Boston. I arrived there to interview him on a bright fall day, with the sun streaming into his living room through the generous windows and patio doors, with the sparkling sea just outside. Everything about the atmosphere was comfortable and friendly. David still speaks with a pronounced South African accent. He was dressed in blue jeans and a shirt worn as a jacket over a colorful T-shirt. The room was made cozy with wooden tables, a rich Persian rug, comfortably upholstered chairs, potted plants, and a gilded mirror.

FRONTLINE

David grew up without television. He became a journalist, finding himself drawn toward trying to tell stories about politics. One day he talked his way onto a film crew that was working in the South African countryside and was captivated by the mechanics of putting everything together. At the end of the film he was fired and told by the director that he had no future in the business, which made him really want to try it. He borrowed a camera and with a friend managed to get into Soweto, outside of Johannesburg, and made a small film about African churches. As he was making that film, inventing the grammar of what he was doing, he got pulled into the structures and syntax of documentary.

He made a second film that was seen by someone from the BBC, who invited him to go to London and reedit it, so he found himself in a real editing room, with professional editors at the BBC. As a teenager David had enjoyed some time in Newport Beach, California, through a high-school exchange program, and the memory of the sunshine pulled him away from rainy London. He went back to southern California as soon as his editing was finished, discovered a little public television station in Huntington Beach, charmed his way into the film department and got hired as a cinematographer and editor. His dream had come true! There he was with an editing table in his office, a cabinet outside with cameras in it and a fridge full of film. He made short pieces for the local television station and little documentaries for instructional television. Four years later he moved, already an accomplished documentarian, to join WGBH in Boston.

> I think that making a great documentary is in many ways tougher than making a great feature film, which stands or falls on its script. Of course, the director can take it to places that are much more profound, and actors can do the same thing. But a documentary is an investigation; a journey into the world

Regina Mundi, Soweto's largest Catholic Church
photo by Woodlouse/ Creative Commons

in which you grab fragments of the world and bring them back. Because of the accidents of what you happen to get, or because somebody in an interview tells you something that they probably shouldn't tell you, or tells you something really quite emotional and profound, or the accident of finding a piece of stock footage that shifts and changes the kind of sequence you might build out of it, you're faced finally in the editing room with an enormous array of options. And so you begin to manipulate those options towards a kind of shape, a narrative.

It is such a deeply manipulative medium, which is why as a journalist it has a kind of double bind on you. On the one hand you are trying very hard to respect the art of storytelling and to really make a dramatic narrative out of it, and on the other hand you are also bound by the fact that you don't want to manipulate the truth in favor of the drama. You are edging your way towards a combination of *dramaturgy*, with a beginning, middle, and end, and rigorous reporting of a difficult subject. You try to both steer through the conclusions you've drawn in your reporting and respect the opposing view, leaving the audience saying, "I have now gone to a place I have never been before, in a way I've never been before." You are bound by respecting and being true to the facts, and therefore how you manipulate them.

David started producing *Frontline* in its first season in 1983. For a dozen years his teams collected huge amounts of material, but much of it was wasted because the broadcast medium was so limited by time constraints. The films were long and complicated, taking many months to make, and on a Tuesday night they were beamed into the air to be watched by the viewing audience. All of the unused material—the rest of the interviews, all the documents—was dumped in boxes and ended up in the trash somewhere. That was suddenly changed by the arrival of the Web.

In 1995 we were making a film about the Branch Davidians in Waco. We had come across the tapes of the negotiations between the FBI and David Koresh and they were tremendously interesting. We used 45 seconds here and another 45 seconds there in the documentary, but afterwards I was sitting in the office saying, "It's too bad we can't use the rest of these

Waco inferno
photo courtesy of LIFE Magazine

"Waco: The Inside Story"
screen capture

materials. Could we make a radio program out of them?"
And somebody said, "You can put them on the Web!"

I said, "Well, if we can put them up as Real Audio, what else
can we put up? Can we put the rest of the interviews up?"
And the producer said, "Why would we want to do that? Those
are our outtakes. You know, we never show those to anybody."
And I said, "No, no. We'll publish them at length; we'll still edit
them for legal reasons and for repetition, perhaps, but we'll
publish them at length. And we'll put documents up as well."

And in that moment everything changed for us because now
we were able to publish all of these additional materials. In
that moment we made our journalism transparent. We were
able to say to anybody, "If you looked at the documentary and
have some question with it, go to these interviews and read
them yourself and see what conclusions you draw about them."
That was both a great act of connection to our audience, and
an editorial investment in the producers themselves, to be
that much more aware of what they were doing. It was a new
contract between the viewer and the maker.

That was a paradigm-shifting moment in documentary journalism.
The 1995 Web site was one of the earliest deep-content editorial sites in
history. The next week they did it again, and they kept doing it. Soon David
was asking how soon they could put film online, but they had to wait until
2000 before they were really streaming pieces of *Frontline* on the Web.

My first image of the Web, when I first got excited about it, was an enormous warehouse of information. I opened the door and I could run down long corridors and go to a filing cabinet way down in the back of the stacks and pull something out and say, "Look what I've got!" I got very excited about the idea of being able to move through material that way.

We were doing a film at the time called "Smoke in the Eye," which was about CBS and the tobacco story—about Jeffrey Wigand, the whistleblower. In the film was the story of the five thousand pages of Brown & Williamson documents that were dumped on a professor's doorstep in San Francisco in a FedEx box. UCSF had posted them online and had prevailed over Brown & Williamson lawyers. We mentioned the story in the course of the documentary, but I challenged a friend who designed for the Web and said, "Why don't you figure out how we can make a journey through those documents?" We decided to call it a "Webumentary."

The Webumentary was called *The Cigarette Papers: A Docu-Drama in Three Acts*. It was a simple click-through summary on the Web site, with each page offering a key point in the story, illustrated by images from the actual documents. Links on the pages gave access to the full documentation on the Galen II Web site. The first act recorded the evidence that the tobacco companies realized that cigarette smoking is dangerous in 1953, but by the end of the first act they had decided that they could deal with it through public relations. The second act was the Surgeon General's warning, and by the end of the second act it was, "call in the lawyers." Then the third act was the real battle for the future of the tobacco companies.

It was this journey through it all, a kind of Shakespearian tale, using just the documents, that gave the idea that you could fly through the information around the world. Instead of me picking up a camera, or you coming across the country to interview me, there is going to be a way for me to find you,

smoke **in the eye**

Why did CBS and ABC back off from exposés on the tobacco industry?

> A TALK WITH LOWELL BERGMAN

He worked on the cancelled "60 Minutes" report and is portrayed by Al Pacino in the movie "The Insider"

> ANATOMY OF A DECISION

A detailed chronology of events leading up to, and following, the CBS decision not to air the Wigand interview

> INTERVIEWS

Media analysts discuss networks' corporate interests vs. the integrity of their news divisions

> TRAIL OF THE B&W TOBACCO DOCUMENTS

Which media outlets got the secret tobacco industry letters and memos?

> WEBUMENTARY

A "Docu-Drama in Three Acts," on three decades of internal tobacco industry documents

> READINGS

Including "60 Minutes'" originally-shelved report and ABC's apology to Philip Morris

> JOIN THE DISCUSSION

> SYNOPSIS   > TAPES & TRANSCRIPTS   > LINKS

New Content   ©1999 PBS Online and WGBH/FRONTLINE
Photo Copyright ©1999 Photodisc All Rights Reserved

←⋯ "Smoke in the Eye"
screen capture

and to interview you long-distance, and be able to place you in the context of those documents and that journey that I'm on. I'm not quite sure how it will work or how we'll do it, but the technology keeps getting better and better, and it gets easier and easier for me to gather stuff from a distance.

We have a wonderful executive editor at *Frontline* who's been with me for many years called Louis Wiley. I call him Mr. Wiley and he always calls me Mr. Fanning. I always imagined in the early days that we'd actually have a little character called Mr. Wiley who would welcome you in and say, "Let me take you to places and show you things I found out." And I still have this dream that one day we'll do a *Frontline* Web site that has a little bespectacled gentleman called Mr. Wiley who will lead you through the information space.

David is frustrated by the two-dimensionality of Web sites. He thinks about navigating a three-dimensional world and taking advantage of his spatial memory. He imagines browsing an Internet that is represented as a warehouse or a rollercoaster ride, or arranging his information in small piles around a room, so that he can remember where things are. He would like to be able to explore by moving in a general direction toward an objective but stopping at will when unexpected treasures come to light.

FREEZE THE BROADCAST

In 1997 the Corporation for Public Broadcasting was asking for suggestions for new uses of media. David took a film about the Clintons from
the *Frontline* archives called "Once upon a Time in Arkansas" and shot
a little video of somebody watching television in the future. He had
experimented with Web markers embedded in documentaries before,
but this was a demonstration of the possible future connectivity between
television and online material. On a screen with the piece about the
Clintons airing, a Web marker came up saying, "www.pbs.org | More of
this interview," pointing to material about the Castle Grandé scheme,
which was the real Whitewater scheme. The person who was watching
had a PDA-based remote controller, allowing them to navigate a room
full of artifacts. There were piles of disks, videotapes, and documents
containing depositions from the Clintons, links to the Paula Jones
lawsuit, and transcripts of interviews. As the cursor rolled over items
in this three-dimensional room, selectable annotations and links
popped up. The viewer could follow the information path or continue
watching the documentary.

> I remember at the time everybody saying, "Well, how're you
> gonna do that? You can't freeze the broadcast! And I said, "I
> have no idea, but these guys will figure it out for us somehow or
> other." Now, as television and computers are converging, we're
> right on the brink of really being able to use a concept like
> that elegantly. It could be a very powerful way to allow people
> to browse through the material, a kind of cabinet of curiosities
> that we have found on your behalf.

> The challenge, I think, is that I've dedicated my life to long-
> form narrative journalism: literary journalism in the tradition
> of the *New Yorker*—the idea that you take a very complicated
> subject and spend some time to get deep enough into it to
> understand its subtleties. But the experience of people on
> the Web, with the opportunity to stop, to browse, breaks that
> narrative, so I wonder if we are building into this the seeds of
> our own destruction as a form?

David is pushing his producers to reevaluate the nature of storytelling for the Web. Experienced documentary makers realize that many parallel efforts are needed to make a good product, and this approach works well in the Web-enabled environment. You can edit, post, and publish stories as you go along. You can harvest crowd-sourced material as part of your process. You can embed tags and links into the main feature to indicate connections in the broadcast version but allow direct linking for the versions that reside on the Web, continuously time shifted to the viewers whim.

> We're doing a film that's a follow-up to "Growing Up Online," to keep exploring the world of the "digital natives." We've been in South Korea, which is as digital as can be. The story will get edited quite soon and will go up on the Web a good nine months before the film actually gets made. We'll start to post and hope that those stories are good enough, and smart enough, and interesting enough to go a little viral—to see if they can't go out into the world on their own and sail away.

> At the same time we will gather more material, get responses to it, and perhaps even get some connections to interest groups, in this case some particular classrooms in schools, and ask them to participate with us. We hope that this will begin to shape the final documentary, before we know what the final *dramaturgy* is going to be. We will be building a new kind of engaged narrative.

> There's a story that we played with a little while back that I think is a template for this. We have a series called *Frontline/World*,

Experiment in connecting television and online material
screen captures

an international newsmagazine. A journalist called Mark
Schapiro from the Center for Investigative Reporting came to
us and said, "I want to report a story about the exporting of
nuclear triggers to Pakistan via South Africa."

It was a difficult story to tell, and it was not going to be easy
to pay for doing it, so I said, "Well, I'm not sure we can afford
to do this story. Good luck." But he came back to us and
said, "Well, I'm going to go to Cape Town because I think I've
isolated three people who will talk to me about the middleman,
the South African who was arrested in Houston." So I said,
"I'll tell you what. I'll give you the cheapest cameraman I can
find in Cape Town to shoot those interviews. Bring them back
and we'll figure out what to do later."

So he goes off to Cape Town. He's got an assignment for
Mother Jones, and he comes back with the three interviews.
We decide to post his *Mother Jones* story and the three
interviews on our Web site. The result is that the Commerce
Department, which hasn't been prepared to talk to him
about all of this, sees it on the Web and calls him up, so
then he calls me back and says, "It looks like the Commerce
investigators are going to talk to me." And I say, "I'll give you
the cheapest cameraman I can find in Washington, D.C., and
for five hundred bucks, go and shoot those as well." So we
posted those interviews.

The result is that Humayun Khan, who was the end receiver
in Pakistan, was so exercised by all of this on the Web,
because he was named in the story, that he then called the
reporter who turned his recorder on and got the interview on
the telephone, and we posted that. At the same time the *L.A.
Times* was doing a story, which we could post and link to.

The result was that this thing grew organically over a period
of time. The investigation began to unfold on the Web and
the result was that *The News Hour with Jim Lehrer* came to
us and said, "Can't you cut a story out of this?" We made
a fifteen-minute story for the *NewsHour* called, "Nuclear
Underground: U.S. Uncovers Plot to Export Nuclear Weapons

they fired Karni when they caught him double-dealing.

📽 WATCH VIDEO GO ▶

CHAPTER 2 (length 4:08)

An anonymous tipster in South Africa alerted U.S. officials to Asher Karni's secret deals with Pakistani businessman Humayun Khan. In December 2003, a team of South African police raided Karni's home office, seizing his computer files. Karni's lawyer, Peter Kantor, tells Schapiro that if Karni was really selling nuclear components to Pakistan, "he was leading a fundamentally dishonest life."

📽 WATCH VIDEO GO ▶

CHAPTER 3 (length 5:53)

Asher Karni claimed that the "triggered spark gaps" he was importing from the U.S. were bound for Baragwanath Hospital in Soweto, South Africa. The spark gaps are a "dual-use" item -- they can be used to trigger an atomic weapon or in a medical procedure to break up kidney stones. But Dr. Lloyd Thompson of Baragwanath's urology department tells Schapiro that the hospital never placed the order with Karni.

"Nuclear Underground"
screen capture

Parts to Pakistan." It was broadcast in July 2005, with a parallel printed story in *Mother Jones* magazine.

Now that's a kind of prototype for what one could be doing. The idea that you could start to investigate a territory, post newsworthy pieces of a story that people will contribute to, you could have a fairly active engagement with experts who come to you, and then in the course of that actually develop a seminal film. That is perhaps some kind of new territory for us to travel.

Of course, you get a lot of whacky stuff coming at you that you have to filter. You've got to be very careful that you're being journalistically responsible in what you publish, so you remain an editor. This is not just an open door through which everybody throws stuff. I think there is a difference journalistically from a political blog or a message board. Ultimately we are editors.

WAR

On the fifth anniversary of the Iraq invasion, *Frontline* launched a
four-and-a-half-hour film called "Bush's War" as a two-part series.
The broadcast drew on footage from the more than forty films on Iraq
and the war on terror made by *Frontline* over the seven years since the
9/11 attacks, and more than four hundred underlying interviews. While
they were preparing the documentary, they built a unique interactive
timeline on their Web site, presenting segments from the films and
interviews with annotations and commentaries, so that anyone could
access the extraordinary depth of the research that backed up the main
features at any time and browse the content in an elegantly presented
interactive format. This is an amazingly rich historical source for students,
scholars, and anyone from the public. People who are obsessed about the
politics and history can spend years digging their way back through the
material. The documentary itself had already had more than 5 million
viewings on the Web site by 2008, and there were over 100,000 inquiries
deep into the annotated documents.

A week before the 2008 election, *Frontline* aired a piece called "The War
Briefing" to give viewers an inside look at the policy choices that the next
president would face in foreign policy. It started off as a film about Iraq
and ended up being about Afghanistan and Pakistan.

> It became a deeper film about Afghanistan because we got
> lucky. A terrific cameraman who works for us was embedded
> with a company in the Korengal Valley and filmed the
> extraordinary experience of young men under fire against
> the Taliban, showing the nature of that war right now. That
> became a sequence for the first third of the film. It was very
> experiential and powerful.
>
> It was followed by a larger contemplation of the surrounding
> people, the "ghosts" they call them, the Taliban coming over
> those mountains and their war against Afghanistan. But very
> quickly it then takes you up into the tribal areas to understand
> who they are, the Pashtun of the tribal areas, but then shifts
> and begins to show the emergence of the Pakistani Taliban
> and their attempts to move down towards Islamabad and

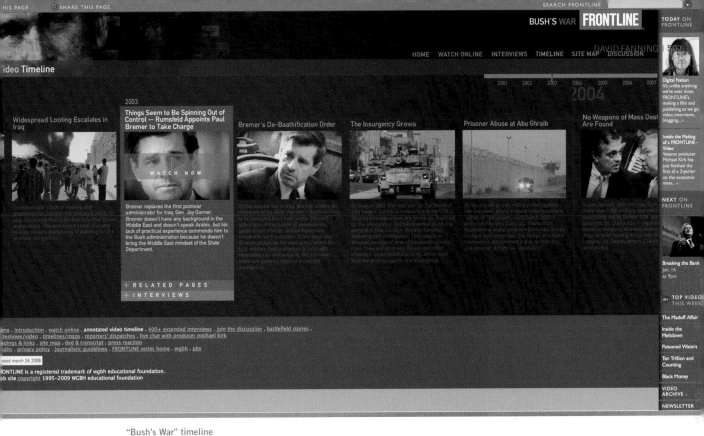

"Bush's War" timeline
screen capture

threaten Pakistan itself, a near failed state with fifty nuclear weapons. That's a pretty damned important story for people to understand!

The film of real action in the mountains could easily be its own short story in the world of new media, as sequences of what it's like to be under fire have a viral quality. The more complicated narrative of the Taliban and Pakistan is much harder to communicate if it is separated from the action context. Why would people care about a bomb in Lahore if they didn't understand what it was like for young soldiers under fire in the Korengal? Those two pieces are connected, and if the connection is broken, so is the audience's collective understanding of the world we live in.

New media is evolving to be delivered in ever-shorter chunks, endangering the journalist's ability to communicate the truth about complex issues, as it is the complicated narrative that gets cut first in

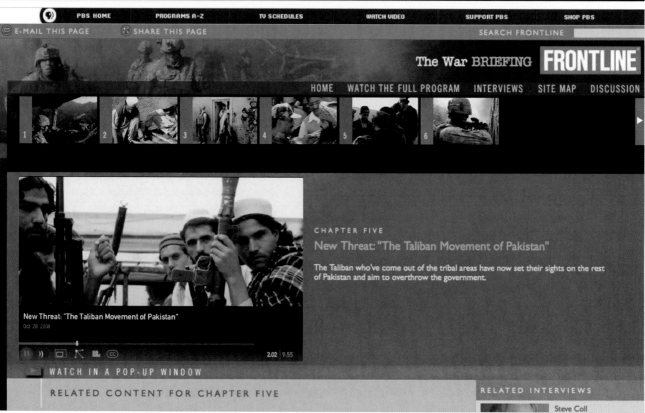

the editing. David has kept the conscience of American television alive for two and half decades. Let's hope that a new generation of journalists can master the balance between the impatience of the media-savvy public and the ability to explain our increasingly connected and complex world.

OUR NEXT SUBJECT, MARK GERZON, understood all too clearly the power that movies have to misinform and create propagandist effects. He tried to counter that by putting together the Entertainment Summit to bring filmmakers together across the Cold War divide. He sees evidence that camera phones and Internet communications will help to tell the truth in the future.

←⋯ **"The War Briefing"**
screen captures

MARK GERZON

Interviewed December 5, 2008

MARK GERZON

Transitioning from a career as a screenwriter and producer in Hollywood, Mark has been the president of Mediators Foundation for the past two decades as well as the founder and cochair of the Global Leadership Network. He teaches leaders and their organizations skills that are critical for dealing with conflict and collaborating across difficult social divides. He helps competing groups and splintered organizations find alignment around shared goals and values. He has directed and supported many projects with a goal of building a more just, peaceful, and sustainable world. His work in the film industries of the United States and the former Soviet Union helped to catalyze the end of the propaganda war between the two superpowers. He has designed bipartisan Congressional retreats, conducted leadership training, and lectured throughout the world. His most recent book is *Leading through Conflict: How Successful Leaders Transform Differences into Opportunities.*

I carry my video equipment in a shoulder bag (cameras) and a large cylindrical container (tripods and lights). On the day that I planned to interview Mark Gerzon in his apartment in Boulder, Colorado, my cylinder of gear failed to appear on the oversized-baggage claim carousel at the Denver airport. After tracking the claim tag and waiting an hour and a half, I was just about to cancel when the gear showed up, leaving me time to arrive at Mark's place at around four o'clock. The snow on the ground made the natural light beautiful, so I tried recording the interview by the window without artificial lighting, but the light started to fade fast as the looming Rocky Mountains obscured the setting sun, resulting in uneven lighting during the course of the conversation.

THE POWER OF STORIES

Even while he was still at Harvard, Mark wanted to eliminate the boundaries between disciplines. He couldn't understand why academia has separate departments for history, economics, political science, and philosophy, as it seemed obviously wrong to divide the world up that way. It was like asking which finger of which hand you want to use for the rest of your life. That desire to break down barriers and make connections between people has stayed with him and provided the belief structure for his career. After a start with a global newspaper and a series of other experiences, he moved to Hollywood to work as a screenwriter and producer, to learn more about the power of stories.

I went to Hollywood in the first place because of my concern about the stories that Americans were telling themselves about the world, making us behave in ways that I felt were disastrous. Ronald Reagan made the power of stories clear. He was a master storyteller, and he told stories that made you hate the Soviet Union, and want lots of nuclear weapons, and feel that you should be ready to use them at any moment. In Hollywood we told stories that dehumanized the Soviets, and if you dehumanize someone that's step one towards saying that killing them is okay.

I'm sensitive to the dehumanization that happens in the media, because the media can be used to humanize or dehumanize. I'm particularly sensitive to it because part of my family was killed in the concentration camps, so I'm very aware that dehumanization is not some abstraction. During the Reagan period we were becoming an extremely bellicose, warlike, aggressive power, threatening the evil empire with our nuclear weapons.

Nuclear explosion
photo by Kastehimself

Mark tried to make movies in Hollywood that took a different approach to the relationship between the United States and the Soviet Union, hoping to counterbalance the norm of aggressive *Rambo*-style films that portrayed Russians as evil barbarians. When he pitched concepts to the big studios in Hollywood, he was told, "You're not going to get these made! They may be good movies, but they're not going to get made because they don't fit the ideological paradigm that we want."

THE ENTERTAINMENT SUMMIT

He had started a for-profit company with investors who wanted movies that changed the way Americans think about the world and about politics, so they were supporting him to make movies that would challenge the anti-Communist status quo, and he had made several trips to Moscow to research the content. He decided to resist the pressure to write different scripts that would be easier to sell, and to take a stand.

> I said to myself, "I'm not going to accept this! I want this industry to wake up!" But then I thought, "How are we going to wake up?" I noticed that in the Soviet Union there was an anticapitalist grip on the film industry, the exact mirror image of what was happening in Hollywood. The Communist Party was running the film union, but Gorbachev was just coming in and they were just starting to change. And I thought, "Wait a minute, if they can break out of their anticapitalist trance and we can break out of our anti-Communist trance, we might make better movies." And that was my pitch to both sides. We ended up bringing the top Soviet filmmakers to Hollywood and the top Hollywood people to the Soviet Union, a series of exchanges we called the Entertainment Summit, or встреча на высшем уровне развлечения in Russian.

With the help of the American Film Institute, Mark assembled clips that revealed the stereotypes, from a century of Soviet filmmaking portraying capitalists and almost a century of American filmmaking of Communists. He condensed the collection down to two thirty-minute reels of clips, which they then showed to hundreds of people on both sides.

McCarthy hearings
photo by Bettman/Corbis

It was so powerful! It was just like being hit by a truck! I remember we showed it in Hollywood at the American Film Institute. Alan Pakula, the director of *All the President's Men*, said, "My friends, we have a problem!" That quote hit a nerve with the media and found its way onto the *CBS Evening News*, the front page of the *New York Times*, and was reported all over the world.

Reagan had originally worked in Hollywood, and when he saw what was happening there, he felt the shift. Combined with the shift that was happening in Moscow with Gorbachev, this created a different climate, largely due to the power of the media to reflect back to human consciousness a new reality,

Gorbachev and Reagan signing ceremony
photo courtesy of Google Images

a new level of awareness. If you had to say, "Mark, what
was the project you've done that had the most tangible and
immediate effect on history?" it's clearly that project, and it
was totally media-driven.

The full thirty-minute reels were only shown privately, but three-minute
excerpts of each were shown on all kinds of media, including entertainment and news programs, and at schools and universities. The widespread media coverage derived from the combination of the high-level
political message and the sensationalist imagery, as the clips were full
of violence and brutality. On the American side it ended the Cold War
on the big screen. If you look at the films before and after '86–'87, it's as
if the world changed. This was a case where politics and media imagery
were moving in exactly the same direction and reinforcing each other to
end the Cold War. You could suddenly talk to people in the Soviet Union.
An organization called the American Soviet Film Initiative was started
to make coproductions, an attractive proposition in Hollywood, partly
because they were less expensive to produce in Russia.

It was a reframing, and I got to experience that reframing up
close and personal. People in the White House told me that
this moved Reagan, because he was a product of that blacklist
McCarthy period. He was doing "evil empire" talk for the first
part of his administration, but in the last part he was reaching
out to Gorbachev, shaking his hand and saying, "Let's go to
Iceland. Let's ban nuclear weapons!"

I saw the late Sydney Pollack a couple of years later. He was
a great director who was active in the Entertainment Summit,
and I said, "Sydney, I still haven't made a movie and you've

made so many great movies." Sydney said to me, "Mark, you may not have made any movies, but you did something that I never did. You changed this town!"

THE IMPACT OF TERRORISM

The storyteller looks for protagonists and antagonists, in Hollywood usually the good Americans and the evil enemies. After 9/11 it became clear that Muslim Arabs are the new favorite enemies. There was a period of uncertainty in American filmmaking after the end of the Cold War, but even before 9/11 you could see Arabs as villains. The Middle East had become the new Soviet Union. Mark watched this happen and started to wonder if it would be valuable to try a second summit.

I said to myself, "Something needs to be done!" I tried to do it first in film and a number of people said, "But film isn't what's actually impacting people, it's television." I had no professional history in television, so it was more challenging than the first time. I had to try to organize a community that was not my professional community, and that's one reason why it hasn't quite worked yet. The other reason is that we're in a different arc in terms of the enemy. The Soviet Union was our enemy for sixty years before the thaw. Now we're in the ascendancy of a time when the Muslim Arab is seen as our enemy, so I don't think media is powerful enough to influence a change, either here or in the Middle East. In the Middle East the Western infidels are hated quite profoundly, and in the West there is a great fear of terrorism. You saw what happened to Barack Obama during the election campaign. "He's a Muslim!" was the worst thing you could say about him, even though it wasn't true. If you had said to me five years ago, "Mark, somebody with the middle name Hussein will be the president of the United States," I would have said, "What have you been smoking?"

We had a meeting in Dubai last year of television professionals from Al Arabiya, CNN, the BBC, and a number of other television enterprises, having a conversation about why they

put certain images on the screen. They all said the same thing. As they work in a commercial field, there is pressure to screen and repeat images that attract viewers. The Al Arabiya folks said, "It's a lot better for us to put on images of Western or Israeli aggression against poor and defenseless Muslims and Arabs, so when something happens that fits that model, we play it again and again." The Western news people said, "It plays better for our audiences to show a car that attacks Heathrow and starts to burn; when that happens, we'll play the image of the burning car again and again and again. We'll play 9/11 till Hell freezes over. Our audience wants to see those images."

The economics of the media drive a reinforcement of existing worldviews, and simplistic heroes and villains make good stories—people are always looking for easily identifiable targets. The optic nerve has a unique relationship to the brain: when someone with a certain attitude sees images repeated, it can imprint opinions. An example of that is the toppling of the Saddam Hussein statue in Baghdad.

After 9/11, one of the most widely seen images around the world was the toppling of the statue of Saddam Hussein in Firdos Square in downtown Baghdad, and then Iraqis stepping on the statue and dancing and hitting it with sledgehammers and celebrating, and some hitting it with their shoes. It was shown around the world, implying, "Look how glad the Iraqi people are, how jubilant they are to be finally free." The statue was actually toppled by a U.S. Army tank, and it was a psychological operations unit of the U.S. Army that brought a group of Iraqis in by bus to stomp on the statue.

(top left) **Civilian Casualties**
photo courtesy of Google Images

(top right) **Statue of Saddam**
photo courtesy of Google Images

(bottom) **9/11 Aftermath**
photo by Slagheap/Creative Commons

We have video on YouTube showing this second version, so you've got the official version that went around the world and you've got the alternative version. And that's the difference now compared to when I was a boy. Then I would only have seen the official version, because there wouldn't have been a second version. Now you see a second version, a third, and a fourth. Why? Because someone's there with a video camera, or somebody's there with a second camera. The human brain through the optic nerve is now being fed multiple stories, not one story. I believe that is one way that media is liberating our level of consciousness.

CAMERAS EVERYWHERE

A dramatic incident of reporting from a second camera occurred in downtown Rangoon in Myanmar in September 2007, when the army was breaking up a crowd of demonstrators. Kenji Nagai, a seasoned Japanese photojournalist, was on the edge of the panic-stricken crowd when he was pushed to the ground by a soldier and shot dead at point-blank range. Video of the incident was captured on a cell phone and smuggled out of the country. In the few seconds before he was killed, Nagai appeared to be filming the military as it faced down the crowd.

I got curious and tracked down the person who smuggled the images out of Myanmar. The story was very simple. A friend of his was standing on a rooftop in Myanmar watching the riot; he pulled out his cell phone and shot a video with it of the soldier killing the Japanese photographer. When he realized what was recorded, he sent it to his friend in Los Angeles, who sent it to CNN, who put it up on their iReport, and then it went around the world. Within three days the statement by the Burmese military dictators that it was a "stray bullet" was proven wrong. It only took three days to travel around the world.

I was just so struck by this story because it woke me up to the fact that anywhere there is a cell phone with a camera in it, or anywhere someone has a video camera, we now can get an alternative view of whatever happens. I think that the new media is empowering democracy in ways that not only dictators, but even democracies can't understand—that now it's not what the government tells us happened to Kenji Nagai, or the government tells us what happened in Firdos Square, or the government tells us what happened in Afghanistan: we now have the government's version, and some citizen's version, and a whole set of other versions.

The death of Kenji Nagai
photo courtesy of Google images

> I think this will allow us to witness the world in a new way. The media is now saying to every human being, "You can have a direct relationship to the world." A direct relationship, not mediated by your government or your national intelligence services. You can have your own relationship to the world. You can use your own eyes, your own ears, and listen and see the world.

The technology for recording is becoming ubiquitous, since many people have access to inexpensive devices and can communicate through the Internet. The barrier of the "technology divide" seems to be melting away, eroded by the microphones and cameras built into cell phones and the accessibility of video cameras and editing software. Mark is optimistic about the impacts of these changes. The dark side exists, of course. Terrorist groups can use Google Earth to help target bombs, for example, but then anything can be used for evil purposes. On balance, Mark thinks that maximizing connectivity among people is good.

> My sense is that, on the whole, the democratization of the media is a very positive thing, because it holds people accountable and it democratizes words and images so we can access them without the control of a dominating power. I think that's an overwhelmingly positive force.

> I guess the place I see it most clearly is China. If you said to me, "Are these new media having a positive or negative impact in China," I'd say, "Overwhelmingly positive. They're not being used for terrorism; they're being used by people to get a new view on the world," and China is a quarter of mankind.

> There are a lot of people now who can't be fooled by that old trick of saying we have an enemy, follow me. That's the game

leaders have been playing since tribes were born. I feel that that is ending, and why is that? One media project actually illustrates it. They are putting television sets in Arab villages, and television sets in Israeli villages, and television sets in America, and they're hooking people up one to one to talk to each other, so they can have their own interactions. When you can actually talk with your enemy, say "Hello," have a phone conversation, see each other on the cameras on the computer, governments can no longer mediate that relationship. In the past authorities could convince people that they had an enemy. I think that's much, much harder today, and the media play a key role.

PROFESSOR SHINICHI TAKEMURA IS CONCERNED that we are hiding information about the condition of the planet as a whole from ourselves, and he has set out to produce media to reveal the truth. He talks about his efforts in the next interview.

SHINICHI TAKEMURA

Interviewed June 1, 2008

SHINICHI TAKEMURA

After a career as an anthropologist conducting field research in the Amazon, Tibet, India, and Africa, Shinichi Takemura returned to Japan to teach and work as a curator of museums of cultural anthropology. He became interested in changing the way people understand the world, rather than just observing as a researcher. He looked for new ways to communicate the reality of what's happening to the planet. This led him to embrace new technology and adopt a career as a media producer, harnessing the power of the Internet to develop social information platforms. He founded the Earth Literacy Program, a nonprofit organization that he runs as a base for his activities. He produced the Japanese virtual pavilion Sensorium for the first online Internet World Expo held in 1996, for which he won the 1997 Gold Ars Electronica Nica Award. In 2001 he started developing the Tangible Earth project, a multimedia globe that allows people to understand the condition of our planet using interactive technology, based on information provided by scientists from various fields.

Shinichi Takemura
photos by author

I first met Shinichi Takemura at the Indaba design conference in Cape Town, South Africa, where his presentation captivated everyone in the audience. I immediately asked him if he would like to be interviewed for *Designing Media* and he enthusiastically accepted. When next in Japan, I arranged to meet him at the site of one of his Tangible Earth installations. On the evening before the interview he invited me to his home for dinner, an unusual privilege in Japan.

Shinichi lives in a generous house owned by his extended family, with his parents in a separate apartment and a living space that's richly adorned with sumptuous plants and surrounded by bookshelves and paintings. His retired father Kenichi is a well-known television personality, recognized by many viewers by his habit of smoking his pipe during interviews. As we consumed a delectable dinner of many courses, Kenichi frequently stepped out onto the balcony to light his pipe and take a few puffs. Shinichi's teenage son Taiki joined us for dinner in traditional Japanese dress, moving about the room with the lightness and grace of a young samurai. It was a delightful evening, followed on the next morning by a fascinating demonstration of the project.

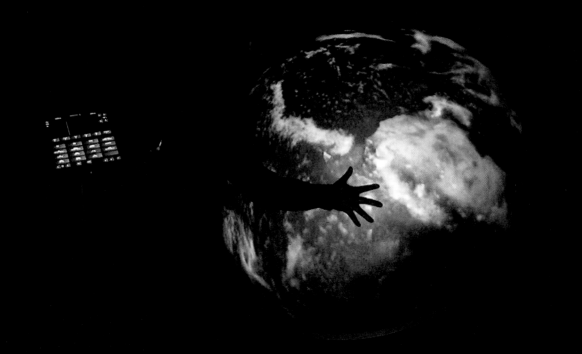

TANGIBLE EARTH

Shinichi Takemura reveals a glowing model of the earth, showing every detail of the continents with the vividness of a satellite photo, but in three dimensions. This is the Tangible Earth installation, a translucent hemisphere containing a high-resolution computer projector with a fish-eye lens located at the center, so that the image of our planet is visible on the frosted inner surface of the sphere. The weather patterns of clouds move slowly over the landmasses, as Shinichi stands ready to demonstrate the full story. He touches the surface with both hands and the world begins to spin under his control.

> Let me introduce our Tangible Earth. It's the world's first interactive digital globe. It's interactive in the sense that you can spin it in any direction. The borderline between the daylight and the shade of the earth is in real time, so you can tell in which area the people are greeting sunrise and on the other side of the planet enjoying the sunset. We can also obtain near real-time data of the cloud movement from the satellite, updated every thirty minutes through the Internet, so you can make the weather forecast.

He interacts with the globe by pushing on the surface. The force is recognized by sensors on the edge of the hemisphere and translated into control of the direction and speed of rotation, giving the uncanny sense that it is moving in spite of the fact that it is really static. The scale is ten million to one, with a diameter of 1.28 meters, making it easier to understand relative sizes intuitively. At this scale the troposphere, the layer of the air surrounding the planet, is only 1 millimeter thick, so all of the cloud movements, thunderstorms, and typhoons are contained in that thin layer, communicating its fragility. At this scale, the moon is the size of a basketball, located 38 meters away.

←···· Tangible Earth demonstration
photo by author

Gulf stream
photo by author

Shinichi continues his demonstration with some animations of dynamic changes in the world, taking data that has been rigorously collected by scientific observation and speeding up the changes to show what is happening. First he shows the ocean currents, with the fast flowing streams illuminated in yellows and reds and serpentine movements indicating the direction of flow. The importance of the Gulf Stream in keeping Northern Europe temperate is dramatically evident, but Shinichi warns that this conveyor of heat is in danger of being deflected by the ice melt caused by global warming. Next he shows the sea surface temperature changing seasonally, expanding and contracting with the strength of the sun, like breathing.

The history of earthquakes and volcanic eruptions is captured in a sequence showing the accumulation of seismological events. The shapes of the tectonic plates become more vivid as the animation builds. The Japanese archipelago is located at the juncture of four plates, showing how vulnerable the islands are to earthquakes, particularly as most of the big cities are located on silt plains.

The tsunami of December 2004 is recreated, showing the waves speeding across the Indian Ocean from the epicenter of the event, which occurred off the coast of Sumatra. Shinichi picks up a pointer that looks like a magnifying glass and uses it to select specific locations on the affected coastlines, which then triggers images of the destruction caused by the disaster to show on a screen behind the globe.

Next he shows the movement of the air pollutants. Sulphur dioxide shows as blue, with nitrogen dioxide and carbon oxide forming a mingled cloud of green and yellow. The greatest concentrations of swirling clouds are emitted from the vehicles and factories of the

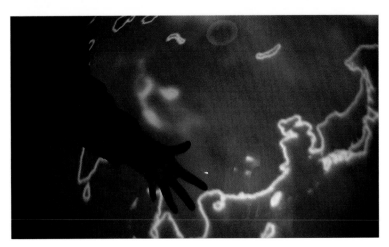

Global warming in 2050
photo by author

Northern Hemisphere, especially from China, Russia, and eastern Europe. The photochemical smog can be seen moving around the whole globe, demonstrating that anything but international regulation is pointless. Shinichi then shows a predictive animation of global warming:

> Now you can see the global warming process in this century. The blue color indicates the average surface temperature in 1900. If the temperature rises three degrees it gets red, and plus six degrees it gets yellow. Let's predict the future of our planet, let's see what happens. I stop around 2050. This is the predicted future if we continue our civilization along current growth paths. The whole globe gets red, especially in the polar regions, Siberia, and the Himalayas in Tibet. These areas are covered with snow and ice and reflect the sunlight, but if the ice melts because of global warming, they lose the ice-albedo effects and the warming process will be accelerated. We see lots of symptoms in these areas even now.

> This is the source of fresh water for more than a billion people in the southern part of the Asian continent. If the glaciers melt in these areas, they will lose the source of the fresh water for the Yangtze River, the Yellow River, the Mekong River, the Ayeyarwady, Ganges, and the Indus. The areas downstream will be affected by flooding, followed by more severe water shortages.

> We may be the first generation to start to understand the mechanism of the spaceship Earth, and how precious this kind of well-tuned planet is in the universe. It's a pity that we seldom think of that, and we never have this kind of global

G8 Summit in Hokkaido
photo by author

media to help us understand the mechanism, the beauty, and the preciousness of our planet.

The Tangible Earth project was chosen for display at the G8 Summit in Hokkaido in 2008. Shinichi and his team from the Earth Literacy Program assembled five units, so that the visiting leaders could experience the interactivity themselves.

New connectivity and data is being included, and the next stage of the project will be able to compile and synthesize knowledge from diverse fields, with the globes connected to one another through the Internet. People will be able to upload and download data from anywhere and link the globes, so that, for example, if one is spun, it will cause another to rotate.

A BOAT FOR THOSE WHO NEED A BOAT

Shinichi is careful and rigorous in using scientific data for his media productions, but he is motivated by a passionate belief that our world is under threat—and he is determined to let people know about the issues. He explains how new technologies can be harnessed to spread the information.

There is a Japanese saying that there should be a boat for those who need a boat. The Internet was a kind of boat for me in that sense.

One of the vital problems for energy consumption is the matter of peak load. An electric power company has to be ready to supply enough electricity for peak load, which occurs only one or two times a year. This leads to the overgeneration of electricity on normal days and overinvestment in conventional and nuclear power plants. So what should we do?

I thought, it's not a matter of politics, it's a matter of the information environment! If we can design a social signal system to let people know that they are operating in peak load, we could save electricity in real time. For example, if you get an urgent email to your cell phone in your pocket, then you can stop wasting electricity and decrease the peak load by voluntary action.

I think that we can do many things by taking advantage of this kind of information. What we need is to design the socially responsible use of the information infrastructure. It is there, but it is not used properly. This is what I call the "social-ware" or "social sense-ware," to make us more conscious and sensitive toward what is going on in the world and how we can affect the environment and society in real time.

When Shinichi came across the writings of Buckminster Fuller and Marshall McLuhan, he recognized many of the ideas that had inspired him to become a media producer. He felt that the Internet could help to "launch the boat" and turn these conceptual thoughts into reality. In 1995 he had the opportunity to design the Japanese theme pavilion for the Internet World Expo. He started a project called Sensorium to create a museum of senses for the Internet age. One of the projects for this was Netsound, listening to network traffic by attaching sounds to each kind of packet.

Another of the projects was called Breathing Earth, which communicated the occurrence of earthquakes, motivated by the 1995 earthquake in Kobe. Shinichi grew up in that area, and some of his friends suffered severe damage. He was shocked both by the disaster of the earthquake itself and also by the lack of people's sensitivity to the likelihood of its occurrence; they seemed to think of the earthquake as an exceptional event that would only occur once in a hundred years.

He decided to compile the seismological data on a computer graphics animation of the planet to try to visualize the fluctuation. The data is updated every day and thus acts as a dynamic communicator of the level of risk in any location. This project proved to him that we are living in an age when even a layman can compile this information using the Internet. The Sensorium project won the Golden Nica award at Ars Electronica, the famous electronic art festival in Linz, Austria. He explains his motivation.

> My interest is to design social infrastructure, a public sensory platform for the global age. I don't feel that I fit to a particular title, like anthropologist, media producer, or artist. I want to enhance our sensitivity, as we are living in a global age. I feel I'm doing my work on behalf of something. It's a strange way of saying, but I'm motivated to do this. In a way, I might be a spiritual person, but again, I don't need those kind of words. Rather, I think if there is a Great Spirit, the Great Spirit needs us to realize these kinds of ideas. We have to work for Great Spirit. We don't need Great Spirit. Great spirit needs us!

FROM SHINICHI'S SENSITIVE COMMUNICATIONS of the holistic truth about our planet, we move on to an interview with Hans Rosling, Ola Rosling, and Anna Rosling Rönnlund, who demonstrate the complex truths about international social changes, making them simple to grasp and engaging with sophisticated computer graphics.

HANS ROSLING WITH OLA ROSLING AND ANNA ROSLING RÖNNLUND

Interviewed October 31, 2008

HANS ROSLING WITH OLA ROSLING AND ANNA ROSLING RÖNNLUND

Hans is a professor of international health in Stockholm, Sweden. He spent two decades studying outbreaks of disease in remote rural areas across Africa. In 2005 he cofounded the Gapminder Foundation with his son and daughter-in-law, who helped him by designing the animated presentations for his lectures. Gapminder is a modern "museum" that helps to make the world understandable using the Internet and animated graphics to communicate statistics and other information about social, economic, and environmental development at local, national, and global levels. Ola and Anna were studying to become artists but were fascinated by the information that Hans was using for his lectures. They taught themselves to design software to convert the statistics into emotionally compelling and enjoyable media presentations. They have won awards by being "humorous, yet deadly serious." Ola and Anna now work at Google, supporting their Trendalyzer software, which Google acquired in 2007.

I invited Hans Rosling to present as the opening plenary speaker at
CONNECTING'07, a meeting of designers from around the world. I served
as congress chair. Our theme for the first day was "People and Places,"
and based on his presentation at TED in 2006, I thought his analysis of
social changes would be an ideal way to start. When I met with him to plan
the details of the presentation, he asked for a ladder and a long pole with
a black painted arrow stuck to the end of it to look like a screen cursor.
When he climbed the ladder he was just able to reach the top of our huge
projection screen with the cursor, demonstrating the animation with a
delightful combination of virtual and physical, explained by a commentary
in his charming Swedish accent.

His command of multiple media made me decide to follow up with an
invitation to be interviewed for this book. He suggested that I could interview
him together with his son Ola and daughter-in-law Anna, as they had helped
him develop the designs for his Trendalyzer software for the animations.
Google had acquired the software and Ola and Anna were working at Google
headquarters, near my home, so I was able to invite all three of them to
be recorded for the video interview together. The result was a very lively
conversation, as you can see from the video segment on the DVD and from
the transcript that follows.

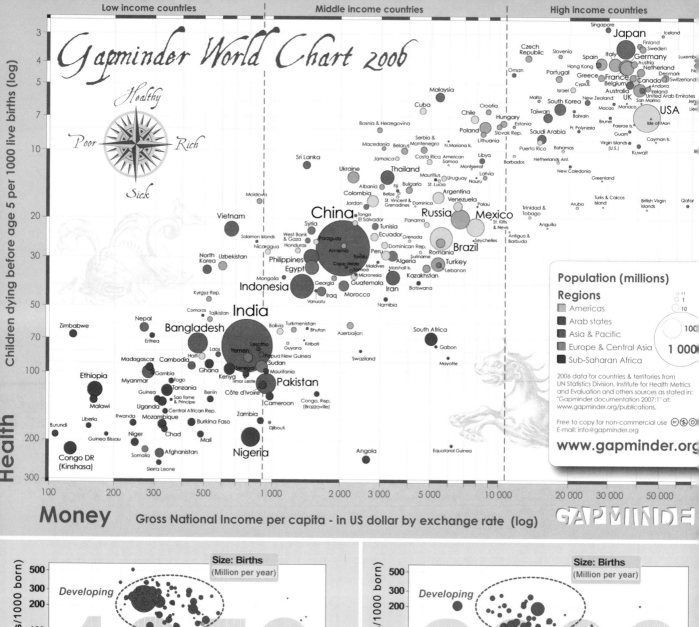

Gapminder World Chart 2006

Health — Children dying before age 5 per 1000 live births (log)

Money — Gross National Income per capita - in US dollar by exchange rate (log)

Low income countries | Middle income countries | High income countries

Healthy — *Poor* — *Rich* — *Sick*

Population (millions)

Regions
- Americas
- Arab states
- Asia & Pacific
- Europe & Central Asia
- Sub-Saharan Africa

2006 data for countries & territories from UN Statistics Division, Institute for Health Metrics and Evaluation and others sources as stated in: "Gapminder documentation 2007:1" at: www.gapminder.org/publications.

Free to copy for non-commercial use
E-mail: info@gapminder.org

www.gapminder.org

GAPMINDER

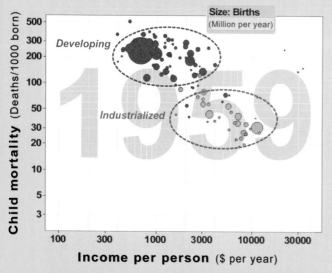

Size: Births (Million per year)

Developing

Industrialized

1959

Child mortality (Deaths/1000 born)

Income per person ($ per year)

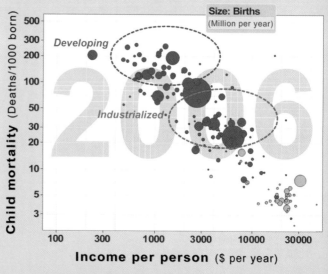

Size: Births (Million per year)

Developing

Industrialized

2006

Child mortality (Deaths/1000 born)

Income per person ($ per year)

BRINGING STATISTICS TO LIFE

After studying statistics and public health, Hans Rosling qualified
as a medical doctor in Sweden. Next he went to work for the
government in Mozambique, with responsibility for the health service
for 360,000 people. In 1981 he found himself facing thirty women
and children with a paralytic disease that was not in the textbooks,
forcing him to become a researcher in real time. He tried to solve the
dilemma by understanding more about health, food, income, and
economic development. The investigations that followed earned him
a doctorate at Uppsala University in 1986, and he spent two decades
studying outbreaks of this disease in remote rural areas across Africa,
eventually discovering that the paralysis was caused by a combination
of malnutrition and toxic exposure to food. He gradually gained a
reputation as a lecturer about these experiences.

> I used to be a professor who was good at lecturing, and once
> in a while I got invited to Copenhagen. In '98 Ola and Anna
> started to develop software technology with which I could
> really explain what I was talking about. Then I got invited all
> the way to California. So really, it was a way of improving the
> way to communicate changes in the world, and that's what
> we've been doing together since '98.

Gapminder statistics
courtesy of Gapminder.org

At first sight Hans seems like a normal academic, with a professorial
air and an engaging conversational manner. The Swedish accent
brings a certain credibility to his English phrases, balanced by a touch
of quaintness. How surprising it was to learn that he performed circus
acts for a living as a young man, and to see the video of his 2007
talk at the TED Conference, when he finished his presentation by
swallowing a bayonet.

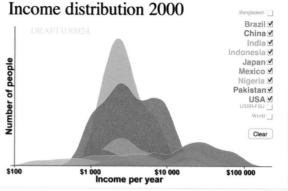

Hans Rosling presenting
courtesy of Gapminder.org

Animated graph of income distribution
courtesy of Gapminder.org

He normally starts by explaining to the audience that he has spent ten years teaching undergraduate students about global development and health at the Karolinska Institute, after spending the previous twenty years studying hunger in Africa. He finds a hook to convince people that there are many misconceptions and preconceived ideas about all sorts of issues of human development, even among the academics of the West. For example, in his first presentation at TED in 2006, he described a test that he had given the elite incoming students in Sweden about their knowledge of the rates of child mortality in different countries. He asked them to identify the higher mortality rates in each of a set of pairs of countries, and then revealed some surprising answers. For example, the mortality rate is twice as high in Turkey as in Sri Lanka, and half as high in Malaysia as in Russia. The students failed the test miserably, and the professors were nearly as bad, so he amused his audience by comparing the students and faculty unfavorably with chimpanzees, who would at least have achieved an average of 50 percent.

The magic of a Hans Rosling presentation starts when he shows the first animated graph, using the software developed by Ola and Anna. He chooses the *x*-axis and *y*-axis to demonstrate a trend, with bubbles representing groups and the animation making the bubbles move over time. In one example the *x*-axis is the fertility rate indicated as the number of children per woman, the *y*-axis is life expectancy in years, and bubbles represent countries, with the diameter of the bubble showing population size. The animation shows the changes from 1962, when good data was first available, up to the present, with large numbers in the background showing the passage of the years. In 1962 the industrialized countries were clustered at the top left corner of the graph, indicating small families and long life expectancy, with the developing countries grouped in the bottom right quadrant, indicating large families and short lives.

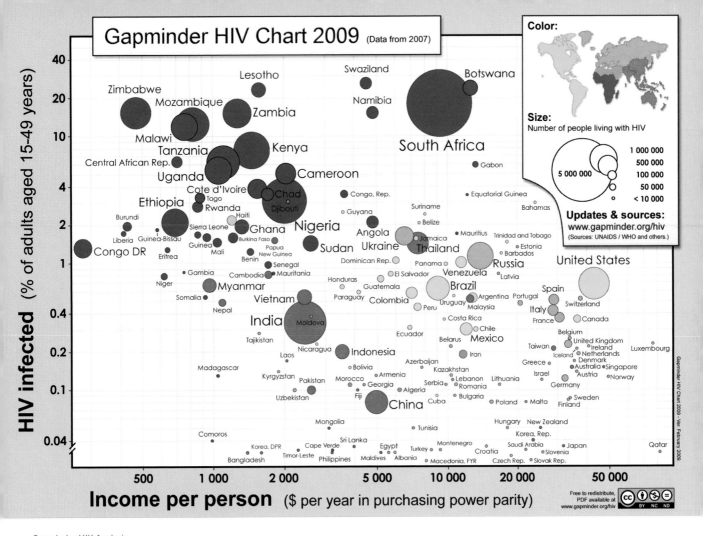

Gapminder HIV Chart 2009 (Data from 2007)

Y-axis: **HIV infected** (% of adults aged 15-49 years) — 40, 20, 10, 4, 2, 1, 0.4, 0.2, 0.1, 0.04

X-axis: **Income per person** ($ per year in purchasing power parity) — 500, 1 000, 2 000, 5 000, 10 000, 20 000, 50 000

Color:

Size:
Number of people living with HIV

1 000 000
500 000
100 000
50 000
< 10 000

5 000 000

Updates & sources:
www.gapminder.org/hiv
(Sources: UNAIDS / WHO and others.)

Gapminder HIV Chart 2009 - Ver. February 2009

Free to redistribute,
PDF available at
www.gapminder.org/hiv

Country labels (partial): Zimbabwe, Lesotho, Swaziland, Botswana, Mozambique, Zambia, Namibia, South Africa, Malawi, Kenya, Tanzania, Central African Rep., Uganda, Cameroon, Gabon, Cote d'Ivoire, Congo, Rep., Equatorial Guinea, Ethiopia, Chad, Djibouti, Suriname, Bahamas, Rwanda, Haiti, Guyana, Belize, Burundi, Ghana, Nigeria, Angola, Mauritius, Trinidad and Tobago, Sierra Leone, Liberia, Guinea-Bissau, Burkina Faso, Estonia, Guinea, Papua New Guinea, Sudan, Ukraine, Thailand, Barbados, Mali, Benin, Jamaica, Eritrea, Dominican Rep., Panama, Russia, United States, Senegal, Gambia, Cambodia, Mauritania, Honduras, El Salvador, Latvia, Niger, Myanmar, Guatemala, Venezuela, Brazil, Spain, Somalia, Vietnam, Paraguay, Colombia, Argentina, Portugal, Nepal, Peru, Uruguay, Malaysia, Italy, Switzerland, India, Moldova, Costa Rica, France, Canada, Tajikistan, Ecuador, Chile, Belgium, United Kingdom, Luxembourg, Laos, Nicaragua, Indonesia, Belarus, Mexico, Taiwan, Ireland, Iceland, Netherlands, Madagascar, Bolivia, Iran, Greece, Denmark, Australia, Singapore, Azerbaijan, Kazakhstan, Israel, Austria, Norway, Kyrgyzstan, Pakistan, Morocco, Armenia, Lebanon, Lithuania, Uzbekistan, Georgia, Serbia, Romania, Germany, Fiji, Algeria, China, Cuba, Bulgaria, Poland, Malta, Sweden, Finland, Mongolia, Tunisia, Hungary, New Zealand, Korea, Rep., Comoros, Sri Lanka, Montenegro, Saudi Arabia, Japan, Qatar, Korea, DPR, Cape Verde, Egypt, Turkey, Croatia, Slovenia, Bangladesh, Timor-Leste, Philippines, Maldives, Albania, Macedonia, FYR, Czech Rep., Slovak Rep.

CC BY NC ND

Gapminder HIV Analysis
courtesy of Gapminder.org

As Hans lets the animation run up to 2003, he gives a verbal description of the changes in an excited voice, like a sportscaster at a crucial moment of a horse race. The nature of the changes is immediately comprehensible. All the countries have converged on the top left quadrant except those in Africa that have been decimated by the AIDS epidemic. He emphasizes the convergence by another version of the animation, in which the United States is compared directly with Vietnam, but this time the bubbles leave a trail as they move. The convergence is dramatic, with Vietnam reaching exactly the same position in 2003 as the United States experienced in 1974 at the end of the war. He changes styles of the graphical representation to illustrate different attributes and show the trends across the world in various aspects of social development and health, but in every case the animations have a magical quality of liquid movement, gentle and insistent in the way they inform the onlooker. Here is the story of how those animations came to be designed.

BUBBLES ON THE MOVE

Hans developed his knowledge of statistics over three decades, collecting information from the data recorded by the United Nations, UNICEF, and national agencies around the world. His research was rigorous, examining the relationships between health, food, income, and economic development in the world. He wrote more than a hundred papers and supervised a dozen PhD students, whose studies helped him analyze the implications of the data. For thirteen years he was teaching preparatory courses for Swedish volunteers in missionary and humanitarian organizations—nurses and medical doctors who were going to work in Africa—providing intense training in how to run health services with very limited resources.

As a teacher he was always interested in how to open his students' consciousness to make them really understand the material, so he developed some tricks to help them learn. He evolved a method that he came to call "evidence-based vulgar simplification," trying to present information with the attention-getting qualities of a tabloid newspaper in front, but also rigorous academic information underneath.

He normally illustrated his lectures using overhead transparencies. He tried using Statview, a program that generated graphs, but he didn't like their appearance, so he printed them on paper, put a transparency on top, and then drew his own version by hand. The most startling truth that emerged from his analysis was the way in which the world was becoming more homogeneous in certain ways. The preconception that the world is starkly divided between rich and poor was no longer accurate. He prepared many graphs to show health plotted against wealth, with the countries distributed in a surprising continuity rather than in distinct groups. He used bar charts, pie charts, and graphs with points representing the countries, but although the information was there, the visualization was not compelling. The breakthrough came in 2006, when he prepared a colored version of the chart, with bubbles representing countries and the diameter of the bubbles indicating population size. He showed the chart to Ola and Anna.

Ola: When you first showed us this bubble chart, Anna said immediately, "This must be the same chart you showed us a year ago, but that one was black and white with just dots, which was very ugly, just a regular chart." But you realized yourself that these black and white boring charts were not attractive enough!

Hans: This graph had an impact because people saw that the bubbles were evenly spread all the way, meaning that there are not two groups of bubbles, poor and rich, but that there are bubbles on all levels. After students had been rejecting my bar charts and my attempts to show this data in other ways, I thought of this one evening in a split second. And then, when students saw it, they asked, "But how did this happen? How did Singapore end up ahead of Sweden? When did that happen? And why is South Korea just like west Europe?" And then gradually the idea came for animation.

Ola: You had actually created this colorful and nice paper chart together with another person at your institute in Uppsala. Suddenly you showed us this beautiful chart with colorful bubbles, which was aesthetically very attractive. So we looked at it, "Wow, this is fun. This looks so nice. This is interesting."

At the same time I was studying economic history, and I was about to write a paper. I hate writing papers, so I saw an opportunity, "Okay, maybe we can make this thing move, and then instead of writing this boring paper for five weeks I can learn Macromedia Director." I saw this win-win situation for myself to animate this thing as a part of the five-week course. I went to my teacher in economic history and I said, "You know what? I wanna make a little software." And this guy, Jan Jörnmark, said, "Yeah, do whatever; nobody will read your paper anyway."

I told you, "In five weeks you're gonna have an animated version of that," because I knew Director had a timeline that could be animated.

Hans: I still remember that second when I saw the first bubble move smoothly and I saw the beauty in the movement. It really moved, and I could see the year pass by. It was like seeing x-ray from your own body. You knew how it was inside there, and more. And suddenly it was there in front of your eyes!

Ola: And then you came to Gothenburg. We were sitting in this publicly funded computer lab where they had a lot of computers that I could use for free. We sat there one evening after your lecture at the university. I was just playing with the mouse-over the timeline in Macromedia Director, and you said, "It's hard to follow this Chinese bubble moving." And I said, "Well, there is a trail feature in Director," so I just turned on "Leave a trail," for the Chinese layer and we could immediately see how China moved. That's how we innovated the trail feature.

Hans: We created the different features step by step, based on the need for understanding the content. We should give a lot of credit to Macromedia and Adobe, who put that technology at hand for easy prototyping. It was very fast. I used the animations for the first time in a big lecture, for all of Scandinavia, and then I really saw the impact. I used to make relatively good lectures, but I had never before had a reaction of that kind. People just got stunned when they saw the movement of the different countries.

You call it mental model or mind-set in English. You say to yourself, "This is how the world is, industrialized separate from developing, and I know things about it," and then we store all the detailed information in this macro mind-set we have. But that mind-set is wrong. It doesn't help to be given detailed information about malaria in Tanzania and traffic accidents in Thailand, and so on, because you have a fixed idea that Africa and Thailand will never be like Europe, so you don't see the catch-up that has happened.

The animations have given us a way of breaking down that mental model of the world using data and beautiful design and showing time as time. Showing time on an *x*-axis never changes a mind-set, but when it is that movement, year, by year, by year, it's almost like hypnosis. Those flipping numbers which you designed: 1950, 1951, 1952, 1953, 1954 ... People get hypnotized!

Ola: We had small numbers in the corner, but then it was hard to follow. Then we moved them into the middle of the screen and made them big, but pale gray to stay in the background. By having Director there in front of us, we could just move things around, and play again and again, and see how it worked as we went along. Anna started to add a lot of design suggestions in the middle of this.

Anna: I think the most important part is that all the time it has been based on the real content. We haven't really thought about design separately in the process at all. Hans has been frustrated about certain content. He brought it to us and we've tried in different ways to make it understandable. We tried a lot of different ideas for different types of data. We've had many, many late nights with heavy arguing.

The setting I remember most often is Ola sitting in the middle with his hands on the keyboard, and Hans and me behind his back complaining constantly. And he actually managed to survive that!

Ola: Yes, you were complaining behind my back. I listened to both of you, and I tried to do the things you were talking about. And then I got a third idea or something, "Maybe like this?" And you were, "What are you doing? What are you doing?" And I'm like, "Wait, wait, wait." And I'd rearrange something and you'd say, "Ah," and then you'd continue.

Hans: This is the process between you two when you were working. It was like Anna was the captain standing behind Ola saying, "No, to the right, to the left. No, a little greener. Oh no, that doesn't work. Ah, that does work!"

Anna: But you were actually bringing the content. We never designed anything generic in the beginning. We were basically trying to communicate certain content. Ola has been super good at coming up with ideas about how things could look, but I think I'm a bit boring.

Ola: But you can pick winners!

Anna: Yes, but I've been a bit boring standing behind, like the angry mad captain, saying, "Nooo," complaining all the time.

Ola: Yes, Anna is a no-sayer. I often get this beautiful advanced idea that would prove that I'm intelligent, but you just don't care because you are not impressed by intelligence, which is very, very good resource!

Anna: When we got feedback from expert people, they always tend to give suggestions about adding more complex features, so they basically want us to create a numeric analysis tool, but I think the important part has been that we never wanted to do that. These tools exist. Experts can use them, but there's nothing out there that normal people understand, so that is what we focused on. Until quite recently we never considered developing software at all. We just wanted to make these lectures understandable.

Ola: Let's help Hans a little bit and make this thing look nicer. And this is an alternative. Wow, this is cool! Let's try to help Hans. At the same time we were in art schools, and we liked that creative environment. We were both studying social science, economic history, art, and theater, but this was more interesting to work on so we spent our time on it.

Anna: I was studying social sciences and photography but started getting interested in this more and more. Suddenly, here was a project where you could actually work with images and design and try to explain something really important to the social sciences.

Ola: Some people at the World Bank had collected household data about income, and there was also data about infant mortality rate per quintile, like 20 percent income groups in a lot of poor countries. We had the success with the animations to answer questions like, How did the countries come to this position? We also knew it was misleading, because even though everybody in Sweden shares similar wealth and health, in Africa and Asia there are some countries with enormous differences.

We started looking for ways to represent the inequalities inside countries and remembered the quintile data. We had the software to plot bubbles so we invented subcountries called "Sweden Poorest 20%," "Sweden Richest 20%," et cetera, so we could put five small Swedish bubbles, the five Indian bubbles, and so on. Anna invented the actual animation, with the idea that you could click the bubble and it could fall apart.

Hans: I can remember a moment when you had done the first split of a bubble, with the different parts flying away and landing. The head of statistics at the United Nations was standing at a conference in Stockholm when you showed him. I was standing fifteen meters away, and I saw when you came to the split, his shoulders went up and back. He really reacted! It was a "Wow" presentation.

DOLLAR STREET

Ola had grown up following his father around the world, so he had a lot of direct experience of different cultures and incomes, but Anna was raised in the heart of Swedish utopia, so she was eager to find a way to communicate the realities of various levels of income. She came up with the idea of Dollar Street, a virtual representation of a street populated by people of various incomes, with the street numbers indicating the daily household spending power, the poorest on the left and the richest on the right. She wanted to show the realities of people's lives and experimented with various recording media, finding that a panoramic photograph worked well, as it showed each room clearly, with more objectivity than video.

Dollar Street
courtesy of Gapminder.org

Anna and Ola built a prototype using a tripod and still camera to record the photographs, and stitching software to create the panoramic views. The first prototype was at the house of Anna's mother. They assembled the views on a representation of a street, so that you could stop at any house and browse the rooms inside. They went to different countries and recorded households on different economic levels within each country.

It was eye-opening to actually visit the bathrooms, kitchens, bedrooms, and so on. If you visited a series of $1-per-day households across different countries and cultures, you could see strong similarities in the living conditions, showing that it is easy to confuse culture with income levels.

Hans: I showed your first prototype in Khartoum, to a large conference of the medical doctors in Sudan. The examples were from the house belonging to Anna's mother and some other houses in the world. I showed the panoramas of her home and came to the kitchen, where her husband was standing doing the washing up. I heard a gasp in the whole room, and then all female MDs of Sudan stood up and clapped. That was strong because it had the feeling of visiting another person's home and seeing the reality.

Anna: The best part of this technology is being able to spin around at your own pace and stop at any point. You feel you can sneak in to the household and spend time on the parts you are interested in.

Ola: We started to think, "So what's the criteria for finding a household that actually can represent all the other households in this quintile? Can we find that?" We looked at the data and tried to find the right criteria. We went to the Dominican Republic and visited people's homes and took photos, but talking to them we realized how hard it is to find one representative household.

Anna: We didn't give up, so we went to Africa as well, to three countries, and tried it further. But after that we got a little bit stuck about how to scale this without funding and without a simple strategy of how to organize it. We had the idea about the street that we believed in, but I think that making the experience more powerful still needs further work.

The word *dollar* had been really sensitive in a lot of settings, either because they are academic or because they are people who hope to save the world and very often they are a little bit leftish. And then *dollar* sounds like something really bad and really mean.

SCALING

The Gapminder Foundation has spread its influence internationally, thanks to the performing genius of Hans Rosling and the design talents of Ola and Anna. The design of the animated presentations helped to spread the ideas, and the presentations at the TED Conference two years in a row triggered notoriety on the Internet. The software grew in sophistication as Ola and Anna built one version after another, ending up with a design that was unique enough to separate it from Macromedia Director. They called it Trendalyzer. In 2007 it was acquired by Google, with Ola and Anna moving from Sweden to Google's headquarters to support development of the design, converting it to a Flash application. So what's next?

Hans: What we need is to scale! The positive response and the kind invitation to talk at TED and work with Google have humbled us, but we haven't scaled yet. This is the challenge now. When I work at Gapminder Foundation, it is to find out how I can bring this into video format, on YouTube and the Internet, and into the TV media. There are a number of amazingly difficult obstacles—small technical details about the software where animation in TV is almost only used for branding.

How do we get this from one, two, three, or five skilled and funny lectures using software, make a breakthrough, and make many people use it and get it on TV?

Ola: There are two possible approaches. One is to deliver one story per day on the actual things that happen today. That requires the data to be well-organized, which it is not, so it's very hard to get all the data to tell the story on a daily basis. The other approach is the one that Al Gore took, to make a very interesting movie and make it perfect. Everything in between is very difficult.

Anna: I get the feeling that this is also a personality thing. I mean, we could settle down and think that we've done the bubbles; they're moving and now everything is set. Or we

could be the types that continue to experiment. I think that
we will continue to be the ones that experiment, and hopefully
others are doing so as well.

We ended up having to develop the software. The best case
would have been that somebody else had already done the
software so we could have just used it. Let's hope that more
people are actually doing this, so it will remove the obstacles.

COMMENTARY

The passion for truth abounds in these interviews, whether in the form of journalistic integrity, political belief, or the desire to make people understand the state of our planet and its people. I like David Fanning's recognition of the dilemma for journalists: "A documentary maker needs to respect the art of storytelling to make a dramatic narrative, but also to resist the temptation to manipulate the truth in favor of the drama." The need to strike that balance makes a valuable design principle that can apply to designing media in general. Mark Gerzon implies something in a more political realm: "The economics of traditional media drive a reinforcement of existing worldviews, and simplistic heroes and villains make good stories—people are always looking for an easily identifiable target."

The Rosling family is more focused on communicating truths that they understand but are not generally recognized. They are helped by the design of their presentations and by the wonderful sense of humor and theatricality that Hans brings to his performances, but they are made credible by the underlying rigor of the data. The information is presented with the attention-getting qualities of a tabloid newspaper in front and rigorous academic information underneath.

Shinichi Takemura changed his role in life from being an academic observer to a media producer in order to communicate information about our situation that he believes to be true. The Tangible Earth project communicates the holistic nature of sustainability for the planet with directness and emotional power.

That direct quality is enhanced by the way the interactions are designed. When you push gently on the surface of the hemisphere with your hands, you ease the world into motion. You can see the border between day and night and follow the weather systems in real time, or change the mode on the control panel to bring up a representation of historical and research data about earthquakes, ocean currents, and so on. You can then use your hands to feel your way around the globe to find out how it really happens, with your sense of touch combining with the animated projections to leave an indelible memory in your mind.

The video timeline that *Frontline* built for "Bush's War" is another example of excellent interaction design. I love the sense of flowing motion that you get when you roll over the segments, with the menu of choices illuminating right there, so that you can watch a segment of the broadcast programming, find related pages, or link to one of the four hundred interviews. You can also take a shortcut by grabbing the little red marker on the miniature timeline. Move it to a date that you're interested in, and then watch the main timeline whoosh across the screen, slow down, and gently arrive at your destination.

There is also magic in motion in the animations of the Gapminder Foundation. Ola and Anna have evolved the design of the behaviors to have a magical quality of liquid movement, gentle and insistent in the way they inform the onlooker. I really felt Hans's enthusiasm. Hans, Ola, and Anna make a great media design team! They work so well together to generate the design ideas through a process of synthesizing the functionality, and they also know how to create beauty, both in appearance and behaviors, while not having "thought about design separately in the process."

The Internet connects people and information, helping documentarians to expose the truth by giving people access to their research. David Fanning opened the door early on with his 1995 Web site about the Branch Davidians in Waco, with the broadcast combined with rich information online. He also realized the potential of harnessing user-generated content.

Mark Gerzon is also excited by the power of the crowd, realizing that the public's ability to generate content is surging forward, making it much easier to see the big picture and harder for the power elite to keep secrets. As he points out, "We are being fed multiple stories, not one story, because there are people there with video cameras to record a second, third and fourth version of an event." The tools to record and distribute information are becoming ubiquitous, so that media empower democracy to reveal a broader interpretation of the truth.

Every day more and more people gain access to the tools for capturing, editing, designing, and disseminating information, so that the truth is harder to hide and told more often. Even people of my age enjoy learning how to make a video or put up a Web site, and the younger generations are growing up with media savvy fluency as the norm. There will be plenty of examples of misuse of media and of bad designs, but I'm optimistic that the democratization of media design and production will turn out to enhance the truth, and on balance be good for us all.

INDEX